C1 571498 60 68

BILLY MITCHELL

BILLY MITCHELL

The Life, Times, and Battles of America's Prophet of Air Power

A BIOGRAPHY

H. Paul Jeffers

Author of *Ace of Aces: The Life of Capt. Eddie Rickenbacker*
and *Theodore Roosevelt, Jr.: The Life of a War Hero*

ZENITH
PRESS

This edition published by Zenith Press, an
imprint of MBI Publishing Company,
Galtier Plaza, Suite 200, 380 Jackson Street,
St. Paul, MN, 55101-3885 USA.

MBI Publishing Company Books are also
available at discounts for in bulk quantities
for industrial or sale-promotional use.
For details write to Special Sales Manager at
MBI Publishing Company, Galtier Plaza,
Suite 200, 380 Jackson Street, St. Paul, MN,
55101-3885 USA

Book Design: Rochelle Brancato

On the front cover: As chief of the
Army Air Service in France, Mitchell flew
in combat as often as his men. *U.S. Army*

On the back cover:

Left: The army's youngest captain and
member of the Army General Staff prior to
World War I, William Mitchell is shown here
in full dress uniform. *Library of Congress*

Middle: Mitchell inspects a new pursuit
plane design, the Thomas-Morse MB3SA,
before taking it up for a test flight in 1923.
U.S. Army

Right: First Lieutenant Mitchell supervising
construction of Alaska's first telegraph line
in 1903. *Library of Congress*

Bottom: Major William Mitchell was the
first U.S. officer to come under fire in
France in 1917 and was awarded France's
highest military medal, the Croix de Guerre.
National Archives

Frontispiece photograph: Brigadier
General Billy Mitchell after World War I.
National Archives

ISBN: 0-7603-2080-2
ISBN-13: 978-0-7603-2080-8

Printed in the United States

TO JACK FRIEND, WITH THANKS
FOR LIVELY TALES ABOUT MY FAVORITE
WORLD WAR II PLANES,
THE MITCHELL B-25, B-17 FLYING FORTRESS,
P-38 LIGHTNING, AND PBY.

Souls of men dreaming of skies to conquer
Gave us wings, ever to soar!

U.S. Air Force song

CONTENTS

MEMORABLE DAY

S aturday, April 18, 1942, in the far western Pacific dawned stormy and the sea rough. In the United States the 167th anniversary of Paul Revere's ride, a day of historical memory, would be celebrated with fresh pride and the satisfaction of payback. In the story of General William L. "Billy" Mitchell it would be a date weighted with ironic vindication.

Sixteen days earlier, U.S. Navy Task Force 18, consisting of the aircraft carrier *Hornet,* the fuel ship *Cimarron,* and cruiser and destroyer escorts, stood off San Francisco in a fog that reduced visibility to about a thousand yards. A northwesterly course was ordered. Poor weather continued for the duration of the voyage. Heavy seas and high winds combined with rain and squalls to reduce their speed and delay a rendezvous with another task force, designated 16, led by the carrier *Enterprise.* Contact was made at dawn on April 13.

For the next seventy-two hours the weather remained dismal and visibility poor. On April 17, fuel ships were detached. The carriers and cruisers continued their westerly advance.

Parked tightly together on the *Hornet*'s deck were sixteen twin-engine, double-fin medium bombers with the designation Mitchell B-25B. They had suffered minor difficulties since the task force's departure from California. Generator failures, spark plug changes, leaky gas tanks, and brake and engine trouble had culminated in the removal of one engine to the *Hornet*'s shops for repairs. The planes were so closely parked that their wings overhung the ship's side. Strong winds caused vibrations in all the control surfaces. Constant surveillance and rigid inspections were required to make certain the planes were properly secured to the flight deck. When they were moved to take-off position, the tail of the last plane stuck far out over the stern. The lead plane would have a scant 467 feet of clear deck for takeoff. The destination was the capital of the Empire of Japan.

At 3:10 a.m. radar contact was made with an unknown object, distance thirty-one hundred yards. At 7:05, the escort *Nashville* opened fire on a suspected Japanese patrol vessel. It was also bombed and strafed by the *Enterprise*'s fighter planes. The boat was still afloat as the *Nashville* tagged behind it to destroy it. Fearing that the Japanese craft had alerted its base of the presence of the American ships, Admiral William "Bull" Halsey decided to launch the attack immediately. The order was flashed at 8:00. Three minutes later, the *Hornet* changed course into the wind and prepared to launch. Removal of lashings from planes consumed several minutes. Flight crews who had expected to fly in the afternoon had to be rounded up for last-minute instructions.

With Lieutenant Colonel James "Jimmy" Doolittle at the controls, the first plane lifted off the deck at 8:25. Winds of more than forty knots and heavy swells caused *Hornet* to pitch violently and occasionally take green seas over the bow, wetting the flight deck. Overall time for launching sixteen bombers was 59 minutes, with an average interval between planes of 3.9 minutes. The last bomber was in the air at 9:20.

The third production version of North American Aviation's medium bomber design, the B-25, had been designed, tested, and re-designed over a period of four years. Delivered to the army in 1941, the plane had been named in posthumous honor of General William Mitchell. For their mission to bomb Tokyo, the air fleet had been stripped of some defensive guns and given extra fuel tanks to extend their range. Two wooden dowels were placed in each plane's plastic tail cone to simulate extra machine guns in the hope that they would persuade enemy fighters to keep their distance. Each B-25 carried four five-hundred-pound bombs. One was decorated with Japanese medals, donated by navy lieutenant Stephen Jurika. He had received them during prewar naval attaché service in Japan and wished "to return them to the government that had awarded them."

At 2:45 p.m. Japanese- and English-language broadcasts from Japan announced that planes of the United States had bombed Tokyo and two other cities. When the news of the attack flashed across the United States, few Americans missed the significance of April 18 in the history of their country. On that date in 1775 Paul Revere made his famous "midnight ride" through "every Middlesex village and farm" in the colony of Massachusetts to spread the alarm that British troops were marching from Boston to capture weapons stashes in the town of Concord. When they reached the village of Lexington, someone fired the first bullet in what would become the War for American Independence.

Although the bombs dropped by Doolittle's B-25s wreaked little damage, the raid sent the morale of the American people soaring. Newspaper headlines and radio broadcasts hailed the daring daylight attack not only as sweet revenge for the Japanese sneak attack on U.S. bases at Pearl Harbor, Hawaii, only four months earlier, but evidence of American determination and ability to carry the war to the Japanese homeland. Asked at a press conference in the White House on April 21 from which base the planes had taken off, President Franklin D. Roosevelt plucked the name of a mysterious place in Tibet from James Hilton's currently best-selling novel *Lost Horizon* and replied, "Shangri-La."

Twelve days later, Roosevelt read a report from the Headquarters of the Army Air Forces that contained a cablegram from Doolittle. Sent from Chunking, China, on April 30, it said:

13 B-25s effectively bombed Tokyo's oil refineries, oil reservoirs, steel and munitions plants, naval docks and other military objectives. One bomber attacked the Mitsubishi airplane factory and other military objectives at Nagoya with incendiary bombs. Two other bombers also attacked Osaka and Kobe with

incendiaries. We all took care to avoid bombing schools, hospitals, churches and other non-military objectives.

Sky over Tokyo was clear. From West Japan to China, however, the mountains were hidden by thick clouds and fog, with the result that we had no way to locate the Chinese airfields at night.

Enemy pursuit took off to attack us and there was intense antiaircraft fire. There were also many barrage balloons. Their fire was ineffective and our planes suffered no loss. At least two enemy planes were shot down. 15 of our planes have been located in East China, with crews totaling 75. 53 of our pilots are safe and are en route to Chunking. 6 are believed to have been taken prisoners. 7 are missing. Sergeant Factor is dead.

With the 15 planes reported located in East China, 1 interned in Siberia, and 1 which the Japanese claim is on exhibition, there is a total of 17 accounted for—which is 1 more than we sent over.

The report was signed by Lieutenant General H. H. Arnold. The commanding general of Army Air Forces, he had known Billy Mitchell since before the First World War. He recalled, "He was a veritable dynamo of energy. Everything he did, he did just as hard as he could." To Arnold, the report on the Doolittle raid was not only a testament to the valor of the men who carried it out and proof of the capabilities of the aircraft, but vindication of the foresight of the aviator for whom the B-25 was named.

An early biographer of Mitchell wrote that as an aviation hero during World War I and leading national spokesman for an independent American air force between the world wars, he had epitomized "the sensationalism and hero worship of the 1920s." This had combined with handsomeness, social charm, a flair for wearing non-regulation uniforms, and unorthodox methods to make him a controversial and dashing figure. He had shared the world stage with most of the major military, political, and heroic personalities of his time, including General John J. "Black Jack" Pershing,

"Ace of Aces" Eddie Rickenbacker, General Douglas MacArthur, Presidents Harding and Coolidge, and a glittering array of Roaring Twenties celebrities vying for headlines. When Mitchell faced a court-martial on charges of insubordination in 1925, Americans became as enthralled by the proceedings as they had been the previous year during the "trial of the century" of Nathan Leopold and Richard Loeb for the thrill killing of fourteen-year-old Bobby Franks in Chicago. Yet, few people in the decade of "Coolidge Prosperity," speakeasies, jazz, and movie comedies paid heed when he predicted in 1925 that Japan would launch a war with the United States "by striking first at Hawaii, some fine Sunday morning."

When he had complained after World War I that brave men were being "sent to their deaths by armchair admirals who don't care about air safety," he had seemed to many Americans to be an amusing crank with a penchant for unwarranted alarmism and theatrics to get his name in the newspapers, perhaps with the intention of enhancing his status by gaining a better job in the War Department. He was described as arrogantly ambitious, conceited, disrespectful of superior officers, and dismissive of army rules and regulations. This was all true. But he was a genuine hero in World War I who had organized and commanded an air armada of a thousand airplanes for an air assault that would not be matched in scope until World War II. In 1930 he predicted that Americans would see aviation "become the greatest means of national defense and transportation all over the world and possibly beyond the world into interstellar space."

To promote air power and warn against the danger of being outstripped by other nations, particularly Japan, Mitchell published books on the subject: *Our Air Force, the Keystone of National Defense* (1921); *Winged Defense* (1925); and *Skyways, a Book of Modern Aeronautics* (1930). Despite these pleas for American readiness based on air power, and regardless of his fame and often sensational methods, he was greeted with apathy from a nation consumed by the fruits of prosperity and revulsion against the United States becoming involved in another war and the continuing hostility of a complacent federal government.

Although Mitchell died in 1936 (some said of a broken heart after having been driven out of the army), he had witnessed a significant step toward creating an independent air force with the creation of General Headquarters of the Air Force in March 1935. Full vindication would come in the Doolittle Raid by Mitchell B-25s, adoption of his ideas by the Army Air Forces in World War II, and in 1946 with a special medal authorized by Congress "in recognition of his outstanding service and foresight in the field of American military aviation."

In a February 2001 article in *Air Force*, the Journal of the Air Force Association, aviation authority Rebecca Grant asked, "Which Billy Mitchell was the real Billy Mitchell?" Was the true Mitchell the firebrand who advocated strategic bombing and predicted in 1925 that in the next war, air forces would routinely strike at the enemy's manufacturing and food centers, railways, bridges, canals and harbors? Was the real Billy Mitchell the World War I air service commander who proved that the airplane was vital to the success of ground forces? Was he at heart an egotist whose unbridled hubris pointed to an inevitable downfall? Or was he a prophet without honor in his time whom history at last judged to be the godfather of an air force that became the mightiest weapon in history? These are questions that this book will examine and attempt to answer.

PART I

NATURALLY A SORT OF SOLDIER

CHAPTER ONE

"STORMY PETREL"

In the early evening hours of February 19, 1936, all that was required of the editor of the *New York Times* to complete the obituary of Brigadier General William "Billy" Mitchell was to write a paragraph or two containing the particulars of his death and the funeral arrangements. He had died in New York City at 5:45 p.m., fifty-two days after celebrating his fifty-sixth birthday at his home in the farmlands of Virginia. Details of his life that had been in the files of the *Times* and periodically updated contained dramatic phrases: "repeated acts of extraordinary heroism" and "bravery beyond that required" as chief of the U.S. Army Air Service in France in the Great War, as well as "flamed into the news consciousness of the American people," "prophetic and vitriolic critic," and "the stormy petrel of American aviation." Charges that he voiced loudly and publicly in the 1920s of "incompetency, criminal negligence and almost treasonable administration of national defense" against the high commands of both the army and navy had provoked the most sensational court-martial in American history.

Rushed to New York's Doctor's Hospital on January 28, 1936, with a failing heart, he saw that he was dying. Contemplating his funeral, he told his wife, "Although I should like to be with the pilots and my comrades at Arlington National Cemetery, I feel that it is better for me to go back to Wisconsin, the home of my family."

With an escort of war veterans from American Legion Aviators Post 743 and a police honor guard, his coffin was carried into Pennsylvania Station to a westbound train. Following the casket were two color-bearers, his widow, two sisters, and friends. Most notable among the mourners was his protégé, comrade, and heroic ace of aces, Captain Eddie Rickenbacker. A stalwart ally in the cause of the independence of military aviation that Mitchell had championed in the years after the war, Rickenbacker would write that in "the dark and cold catacombs of the railway terminal" he heard the "eerie echoes" of the mourners' footsteps and felt "bitter, grief-stricken, and shocked at this ignominious, demeaning ending of Mitchell's brilliant career."

Two days later, Mitchell's flag-draped bier was borne into St. Paul's Protestant Episcopal Church in Milwaukee by three of his nephews, a friend, and two wartime comrades. At Forest Home Cemetery a bugle sounded taps and three volleys were fired by an American Legion guard of honor. While everyone sang "The Battle Hymn of the Republic," the coffin was lowered into a grave next to those of his grandfather and father.

If Milwaukee had a dynasty, wrote a family chronicler, it was "the Mitchell dynasty." Its founder, Alexander Mitchell, was born in Ellon, Aberdeenshire, Scotland, on October 18, 1817. After completing a commercial course in parish schools, he studied law and became a banking-house clerk. Immigrating to the United States in 1839 at age 21, he took a position as a clerk with the recently organized Marine Fire and Insurance Company in Milwaukee. A village on the west shore of Lake Michigan, Milwaukee had a population of about fifteen hundred in a territory with roughly thirty thousand. Adding to those numbers in a burst of immigration in the years following Alexander's arrival were other natives of Scotland. Among them was Arthur MacArthur. Throughout the next eight decades, he and his son Douglas would be significant figures in the life and the military career of Alexander's grandson.

First inhabited in the seventeenth century by the Algonquin (Menominee, Kickapoo, and Miami tribes) and Sioux (Winnebago, Dakota, Fox, Sac, Potawatomi, and Ojibwa tribes), Wisconsin was first explored for France by Jean Nicolet, who landed at Green Bay in 1634 while searching for the Northwest Passage to China." After the French lost possession of its territories east of the Mississippi in the French and Indian War, the British ruled until 1783, when the treaty ending the American Revolution gave control to the United States. The first wave of American settlers in the 1820s was attracted by a boom in mining of lead. A result of this movement of white settlers was a demand that the federal government move the Indian tribes west of the Mississippi. When the Sac people tried to return in 1832, the result was the Black Hawk War, ending in the Bad Axe Massacre with fewer than a thousand Indians surviving. Other Wisconsin tribes either left the area or negotiated reservation lands. With no further opposition from the native population, a second wave of settlers arrived.

After the first commercial cargo vessel called at the struggling village in 1835, settlers and traders were drawn to the site because of the access provided to the farther frontier by the Milwaukee, Menomonee, and Kinnickinnic Rivers. When this blossoming into a trading port brought with it a need for financial institutions, a savvy businessman, George Smith, organized the Marine and Fire Insurance Company. While nominally an insurance business, it functioned as a bank. A century before the liquidity of banks would be guaranteed by the U.S. Treasury in the form of the Federal Deposit Insurance Corporation, and at a time when scant public faith was placed in the value of federal paper money, people transacted business on the basis of bartering or personal promissory notes whose value rested on the integrity of the proffering party, whether an individual signing an IOU or a bank issuing its own paper. Concerning the trustworthiness of the Marine Fire and Insurance Company, noted one historian, nothing whatever stood behind the currency it printed but the reputation for honesty of Alexander Mitchell. Known as "Mitchell Money," it found acceptance from the Allegheny Mountains to Chicago and territories west of the Mississippi. The bank proved so strong that it withstood a financial panic in 1861 resulting from the U.S. government's repudiation of bonds issued by the states that seceded from the Union. "Mr. Mitchell's judicious recommendations," wrote a friend, "resulted in saving many of the western banks from ruin." In that year of panic, citizens of Milwaukee welcomed him as the first commissioner of the Milwaukee Debt Commission. Largely because of his influence, the city's credit was restored.

Having proved his acumen in banking and frontier finance, Alexander looked at the fastest-growing sector of the nation's post–Civil War industrial economy and found that although numerous small railroad systems served Milwaukee, their operations were uncoordinated and inefficient. As railroad fever had spread across the nation after the war, merchants, bankers, manufacturers, and newspaper editors had recognized the commercial opportunities afforded by transportation on trains. As railway historian Marieke van Ophem recorded in *The Iron Horse: The Impact of Railroads on 19th-Century American Society*, "Entrepreneurs could see that the 'iron horse' had taken the place of the waterways in inland transportation and proposed vast projects for covering the nation with railroads."

During the 1850s, the object of most railroad promoters had been to reach the Missouri River, but by the close of the decade, activity had shifted to extension of lines to Iowa. Other railroad magnates turned their attention to reaching the Minnesota Territory. This explosion of railway building was made possible by financial aids from hamlets and towns through which the roads passed, the state in which they ran, and the federal government. From 1850 to 1872 the Congress gave vast tracts of land to railway promoters who promised to lay tracks across barely settled territory of the West covering more than 100 million acres of public domain land. State and local governments provided $280 million in cash or credit. A result of these enticements was a plethora of small railways that served the Milwaukee area, including the Milwaukee & Mississippi; the Milwaukee & Watertown; the Racine, Janesville & Mississippi; the

Milwaukee & Northern; the Wisconsin Union; and the Chicago & Pacific. By consolidating these lines into a single entity called the Chicago, Milwaukee & St. Paul Railroad, Alexander Mitchell, as president of the line, and his corporate associates operated more miles of track than any railroad in the world. He would also be named president of the Chicago & Northwestern, Western Union Railroad Company, and Northwestern National Insurance Company, and a director or trustee of several local institutions. Towns created by the expansion of the railroad were named in his honor. Less than 30 years after leaving Scotland, Alexander Mitchell had become not only a significant figure in the history of American railroads and a respected and revered personality in Milwaukee, but the richest man in the northwestern region of his adopted country.

While nurturing his fledgling bank, Alexander had married Martha Reed. According to a family story related by their granddaughter Ruth, they lived in rooms above the bank in a small building surrounded by a picket fence to which Martha tethered a cow when milking it. Family tradition holds that one day "a blanketed Indian, springing suddenly from the forest, seized the cow, under her vociferous militant protests, and dragged it off, never to be seen again." Able to trace her ancestry to the Pilgrims who reached America on the *Mayflower*, Martha became president of the Colonial Dames and was one of three women who bought and preserved Mount Vernon, the home of George Washington.

Characterized as a "robber baron" by critics of the expansion of railroads, who viewed the men who built them as rapacious, ruthless plunderers, Alexander Mitchell was a stout man with a broad face wreathed by a gray beard who never left his home without a red carnation in his lapel. As a railway executive he earned a reputation for bluntness of demeanor and speech that became steely defiance in the face of what he deemed to be the unwarranted governmental intrusion into the way he chose to run his railroad. When the Wisconsin legislature passed a law to fix and regulate freight rates, he dashed off a letter to the governor declaring that he would "disregard the provisions of the law" until courts decided the validity of the measure. Outraged, Wisconsin's Senator Robert "Fighting Bob" M. La Follette took to the floor of the U.S. Senate and exclaimed, "A more brazen defiance of law could scarcely be conceived."

While president of the Chicago, Milwaukee & St. Paul (1864–1887), Alexander was an unsuccessful candidate for election to Congress in 1868. Trying again in 1870, he won and served two terms from 1871 to 1875. Nominated for governor in 1877, he declined to run and returned to his banking and railroad interests. When grandson William was born two years later, Alexander was president of the American Bankers Association. Milwaukee publisher William G. Bruce wrote, "The name of Alexander Mitchell was blazoned in golden letters. He was the Rothschild of Milwaukee, the owner of a great bank, of stately business blocks, of a railroad, and millions of dollars in money, and the reputation of Milwaukee's great financier and railroad magnate enjoyed among the masses."

The inheritor of Alexander Mitchell's fortune and reputation, John Lendrum Mitchell, was born in Milwaukee on October 19, 1842. He attended public schools and studied at the military academy at Hampton, Connecticut, until his father decided to send him to college in Dresden and Munich, Germany, as well as in Geneva, Switzerland. Returning to the United States in 1860, he enlisted in the army at the beginning of the Civil War. Commissioned first lieutenant and later appointed chief of ordnance, he saw action with Company I, 24th Wisconsin Volunteer Infantry in the battles of Perryville, Murfreesboro, Hoovers Gap, and Chattanooga. Threatened with loss of his eyesight and declared disabled, he resigned his commission and returned to Milwaukee. Making his first venture into politics, he was elected as a Democrat to the state senate for two terms (1873–1877). Elected president of the Milwaukee School Board in 1884, he served two years. His service on the school board, noted a Milwaukee historian, made him "thoroughly acquainted with the educational needs of his native city, especially those of the poor." In 1887 a standing order given to the superintendent of schools stated that schoolbooks "would be furnished by Mr. Mitchell to every child in Milwaukee whose parents were unable to supply them." Wealth also enabled John to establish at the state university a course in agriculture that offered twenty scholarships to poor boys. Through a joint resolution of Congress in 1886, he was appointed a member of the board of managers of the National Home for Disabled Volunteer Soldiers of the Civil War.

Like many sons of wealth who believed that the family fortunes accrued by their fathers should be enjoyed, John spent lavishly to create an estate called Meadowmere. Sprawling across four hundred acres, it had lakes, woods, pastures for cattle, and stables for thoroughbred horses that raced on a private course. His position as a gentleman farmer and horseman garnered for him not only the presidencies of the Wisconsin State Agricultural Society and the Northwestern Trotting Horse Breeders' Association, but the social prominence that enhanced his position as the son of the most powerful figure in Wisconsin's financial affairs.

When marriage to Bianca Cogswell ended in divorce, John wed Harriet Danforth Becker of New York. Escaping the hard winter of Wisconsin with a belated, extended, and combined honeymoon and vacation in Nice on the French Riviera in 1879, they became parents. Born on December 29, William would have six sisters and a brother who survived into adulthood, named Catharine, Florence, Harriet, Janet, Martha, Ruth, and John. Beneficiary of all the trappings that accrued to any scion of wealth and privilege in the era that Mark Twain called the "Gilded Age," William inherited qualities of character that had forged Alexander and John's successes.

Ruth Mitchell recalled that "except for stern honesty," her father was "as different as can be imagined" from her grandfather. If Alexander Mitchell had seen only struggle and shrewd advantage in life, John Lendrum Mitchell saw "the beauty of life, and with a gentle all-pervasive humor." Mitchell family observer William Bruce recalled in his *Memoirs* that John's life was "in many ways a radical departure from that of his father." While Alexander was the "hardheaded banker, who was possessed of a keen vision and remarkable constructive ability," the son was "an idealist who fostered the finer privileges and aspirations of human existence."

This contrast between Alexander and John was enshrined in Mitchell family lore in two stories that may or may not be true, but are nonetheless illuminating of generational differences. When a committee of citizens solicited a contribution from Alexander for a hospital fund, the son of Scotland stroked his beard and pledged a thousand dollars. "But Mr. Mitchell," exclaimed one of the disappointed supplicants, "your son subscribed five thousand."

"Ah, that's it," replied the richest man in all of the Northwest. "You see, my son has a wealthy father."

In the other yarn, Alexander offered his son a cigar. John pulled one of his own from a pocket and said, "Try this one. I think you'll find it better than yours."

The patriarch shook his head and said, "Sorry, my boy. I can't afford your brand."

Pondering both ancestors and her older brother, Ruth Mitchell recalled, "It seems to me that Nature, in order to produce my brother's character, must have taken the very contrasting characters of our Father and Grandfather, put them in a retort, and given them a good shake."

Although John Lendrum Mitchell had certified his first son's American citizenship by immediately informing the U.S. embassy in France of his birth, William did not see his country for three years. Having attained higher education in France, Switzerland, and Germany, John Mitchell had become almost as much a European as an American. Interested in its languages, literature, and culture, and eager to spend as much time in France as possible, he felt no urgency about taking his son to the country of his citizenship. Consequently, when the family returned to Milwaukee in

1882, William spoke French better than English. Returning to the country of his birth twenty-five years later to volunteer his services to France in the world war, he recorded in his diary that the boys of Milwaukee had "so irritated" him by taunting him and calling him "Froggie" that he "would not speak a word of French for years."

The home to which William was taken at the age of three was Meadowmere. A friend who grew up with him in Wisconsin and Washington, D.C., novelist Eleanor Mercein Kelly, recalled the estate as "a wonderful place" for a boy. There were "ponies to ride, cows to milk, a private race course, and a lake large enough to play pirates in a flat-bottomed rowboat." When Eleanor expressed anxiety about what might happen to her and another girl if the leaky boat were to sink, William boasted, "I, myself, shall carry you ashore, two at a time!"

Called Willie, he was remembered as the kind of lad who seemed to have been cut out for the strenuous life. Exploring woods with an air rifle in hand, he climbed trees and discovered an interest in birds and began collecting specimens. Observing this interest in ornithology, his father arranged a meeting with a young but yet unrecognized naturalist named Dr. Carl Akeley for the purpose of teaching William taxidermy. Many years later, Akeley would be one of the country's most famous scientists. His tales of big-game hunting in Africa would inspire another exponent of the strenuous life, Theodore Roosevelt, to go to East Africa at the end of his second term as president in 1909 as the leader of an expedition to collect wildlife specimens for the Smithsonian Institution. It was the largest such expedition ever mounted to that time.

Like Willie Mitchell, the future president of the United States had been born to wealth, exulted in the rigors of outdoor life, and thrived on tales of family history and the exploits of the heroes of American history. Although William Mitchell and Theodore Roosevelt lived half a continent apart as William was growing up in the 1880s and Roosevelt was alternately exploring a career in politics and the rugged terrain of the Dakota Territory, they would eventually find their lives entwined. Within the span of three decades, they would become heroic figures as the United States went to war to free Cuba from Spain, battled rebels in jungles in the Philippines, and fought Germany on land and in the skies of France in 1918. Each would also enter the annals of a fledgling American aviation. Roosevelt would demonstrate intense interest in an experiment in launching an aircraft from the deck of a warship and be the first president to go up in a plane. Mitchell would achieve fame in the air during the "war to end all wars" and "make the world safe for democracy." He would serve with four of Roosevelt's sons in France and have the somber duty of informing Roosevelt that his youngest son, army aviator Quentin, had been shot down and killed by Germany's famous "Flying Circus" on July 14, 1918.

While Theodore Roosevelt always felt disappointed that his father and namesake had not been a combatant during the Civil War, Willie Mitchell passed many evenings in the parlor of the big house at Meadowmere thrilling to his father's stories of raising and leading Company I, 24th Wisconsin Volunteer Infantry, and to those of old campaigners, including a few generals, who visited the farm and reminisced with fading memories about their past glories. Although Willie basked in the tales and enjoyed excursions led by John Mitchell to fields of the famous battles in American and European history, sister Ruth found that their father's "intense interest in military history had a terrible side." She wrote:

We were dragged all over Europe to look at battlefields. Before I was 10 years old we were made to stand and gaze, more despondently than any Anglo-Saxon about to be conquered, at the little bay near Dives in Normandy whence as far back as 1066 A.D. the Norman, William the Conqueror, sailed away to subdue England. "The very last time," we were sternly instructed—and, you bet, remembered, for we were examined and woe, if any detail was forgotten—"for the very last time that an armed enemy ever stood on English soil."

We were marched to that damned "sunken road" at Waterloo which proved Napoleon's undoing. It was a stifling day, I remember. We had gorged on bananas and—it was our undoing too!

We had to go to the most unlikely, un-get-at-able [sic] places in bumbling trains, and if there is anything more dreary than old battlefields, I pray I may never have to see it.

Bill didn't think so. No dreariness could abate his vivid interest. He knew and in his mind's eye could see it all as if it were going on right then. He caught this military-history disease with virulence.

Talk of military matters was inevitable between Willie and his friends, the MacArthur boys. When John Mitchell had been a lieutenant in the 24th Wisconsin, their father, Arthur, was an eighteen-year-old colonel who garnered glory in the battle on the slopes of Missionary Ridge at Chattanooga by sparking a valiant charge against the Confederates with the cry "On Wisconsin." Twenty years later, as his sons spoke earnestly and hopefully of being appointed to the Military Academy at West Point and Naval Academy at Annapolis, former lieutenant John Lendrum Mitchell's son offered his playmates nothing definite regarding his future course.

He certainly was daring enough to be a soldier, as his Scotch governess, Mary Alexander, could attest. When she announced that he was forbidden to climb on the greenhouse, he made it a daily event. The years she spent looking after Willie, she declared, were "the most hectic" of her life. If excellent marksmanship with a rifle were a test of soldierly potential, Mrs. Mitchell could point to holes in the walls of her son's bedroom, put into them by five-year-old Willie as he lay in bed with scarlet fever. Proof of his accuracy with a rifle was a collection of two hundred birds, stuffed with the aid of Dr. Akeley. Were he to choose to be a cavalryman, he was an expert rider who was good enough in the saddle at age thirteen to take up polo. Small, wiry, and fearless, he was always on the go. Recalling her charge's boyhood, Mary Alexander threw up her hands and said wearily, "He absolutely never stopped." Enrolled at age ten in Racine College, an Episcopal preparatory school, he was an able student but chided at least once for "talking before grace in the dining room" and "boisterous conduct at the table and disorder in the dormitory room."

Two years after William entered the school, John Lendrum Mitchell was elected to the Congress and appointed a member of the Democratic National Committee. At the Democratic Presidential Convention in 1892, his Civil War commander, General Edward Bragg, made a speech nominating him for vice president. Declining the honor, he was re-elected to Congress in 1892 in a Democratic sweep that returned Grover Cleveland to the White House after a four-year hiatus in which the president was Republican Benjamin Harrison. However, between Mitchell's re-election to the House of Representatives in 1892 and the convening of the Fifty-Third Congress, the Wisconsin legislature elected him to the U.S. Senate, effective on the day that Cleveland was inaugurated, March 4, 1893.

Aligned with the Progressive movement of the period, Senator John Lendrum Mitchell introduced measures of social security for the laboring class: the eight-hour day and an income tax that were attacked as "ridiculous and wildly visionary." Boasting that he was "a storm bird in politics," he also supported unlimited coinage of silver, by which the U.S. government was required by law to buy all the silver that was mined in the country and issue silver coins. The opponents of the law argued that silver-based money threatened the economic stability of a gold-based currency and invited a raid on the U.S. gold supply by foreign investors that would deplete the $100 million gold reserve that the Treasury Department was legally required to maintain. On April 20, 1893, as a result of foreign and domestic demands for conversion of silver for gold, that grim fear began to unfold. It was the beginning of what became the Great Panic of 1893. In an economic collapse that soon was called the "Cleveland Depression," the stock market crashed, industries closed, and the banks folded, including the one in Milwaukee known as the Mitchell Bank. Vowing that its customers would lose nothing, the son of its founder provided the bank with $1.3 million of his own assets, allowing it to reorganize, reopen, and meet all its obligations with interest. This expenditure depleted the family fortune and left it with only the income that came from breeding horses.

Having been elected to a six-year term in the Senate, John Mitchell moved the family to a spacious house on Capitol Hill and transferred William from Racine College to the Columbian School in Washington, D.C. (an institution that became George Washington University). When he arrived in 1895 at the age of seventeen, he was its youngest student. His classmate, Robert Sterrett, was impressed by William's "munificent" sports equipment, including the latest golf clubs and golfing attire, tennis racquets, fishing tackle, skates, hockey gear, and shotguns. As quarterback for the school's freshmen football squad, his team elected him captain. At the end of his second year, his father was the speaker at the graduation ceremony for the class of 1897.

Always an admirer of Europe, and probably mindful that William had been allowed to spend the preceding summer on an unescorted visit to the continent of his birth, in which he had been greatly impressed by Switzerland, Senator Mitchell chose to hold up that country in his speech as a model nation for all of Europe. Speaking of his "iridescent dream" that nations of Europe that "do not differ more radically in races, religion, speech and local customs than do the Cantons of Switzerland" would strive toward unity, he asked, "Why might not these nations of Europe federate themselves together under a similar system—one which centuries of experience have proved to be more beneficial and more stable than the forms of government under which they live?"

But in the summer of 1897, as the Mitchell family and most of the officials of the U.S. government fled the brutal heat of the nation's capital for cooler climates, the issue crowding the front pages and editorial columns of America's newspapers was not the future of the nations of

Europe, but the stranglehold by one of them—Spain—upon the island of Cuba, and what the United States of America ought to do about it, if anything. Those who demanded action in the form of military intervention were known as "Jingoes." The term derived from an English music hall song. Wildly popular during the Crimean War, it referred to opposing British and Russian designs on the Turkish port of Constantinople and contained this bit of bravado:

We don't want to fight, yet by Jingo!
if we do
We've got the ships, we've got the men,
and got the money too.

American Jingoes in government and newspaper editorial offices envisioned not only liberation of Cuba from Spanish rule, but seizure by the United States of all of Spain's colonies in both the Atlantic and Pacific oceans as part of a grand scheme to create an American empire and hold on to it by deploying a mighty fleet with massive battleships of a two-ocean navy. The leading voice in this militant chorus in Washington, D.C., was Theodore Roosevelt. He had been appointed to the post of assistant secretary of the navy by a reluctant President-elect William McKinley. Hoping that the Cuban issue could be resolved peaceably through negotiations, McKinley feared that Roosevelt would assume command of naval operations with "preconceived plans which he would wish to drive through the moment he got in." Regarding the president's Cuban policy, Roosevelt complained in a letter to his sister, Anna Roosevelt Cowles, "McKinley is bent on peace, I fear."

Although McKinley was a Republican, he found a Democratic ally on the question of a war with Cuba in Senator John Lendrum Mitchell of Wisconsin. As Jingoes called for raising an army, spoke of America's "Manifest Destiny," and called for "mastery of the Pacific," including wrenching the Philippines from Spain and making it a U.S. territory as a fruit of the war, Mitchell told the Senate, "No soldier should be mustered-in for the purpose of shooting our ideas of liberty and justice into an alien people."

While the national debate over Cuba continued and grew louder throughout the summer of 1897 and eighteen-year-old William Mitchell rode horses, fished, hunted, and hiked through the woods of Meadowmere, Assistant Secretary of the Navy Roosevelt was exhibiting enthusiasm over an innovation with military potential that had been brought to his attention by the director of the U.S. Geological Survey during a call at the White House on March 24. As Roosevelt listened with increasing excitement, he described experiments with a "flying machine" by a sixty-three-year-old scientist named Samuel Langley. To test his theories on aerodynamics, he had built two flying machines that he called "aerodromes."

A distinguished astronomer and director of the Smithsonian Institution, Langley was well into his fifties when he was gripped by the lure of flight. He began by making elastic band–propelled models. When a small steam engine that had been designed two decades earlier by John Stringfellow was presented to the Smithsonian in 1896, Langley studied it and realized that better steam engines could be built and that he could do so. In 1891 he built the first of his aerodromes powered by a steam engine, but found that the steel frame was too heavy for the craft to fly. For the next five years he built models and tried to resolve the power-to-weight problem. He succeeded in 1896 with a double monoplane with wings set in tandem that flew for three quarters of a mile and came down only because its fuel ran out.

To illustrate his story about Langley's machine, the Geological Survey director brought photographs. After the meeting, Roosevelt wrote in a memorandum to the Secretary of the Navy, John D. Long, "It seems to me worthwhile for this government to try whether it will work or not on a large scale to be used in the event of war. For this purpose I recommend that you appoint two officers of scientific attainments and practical ability, who in conjunction with two officers appointed by the Secretary of War, shall meet and examine into the flying machine, to inform us whether or not they think it could be duplicated on a large scale, to make recommendations as to its practicability and prepare estimates as to the cost." He concluded the memo with, "I think this is well worth doing."

Roosevelt proposed two "outside experts" as consultants: R. H. Thurston, president of Sibley College at Cornell University, and Octave Chanute, president of the American Society of Civil Engineers at Chicago. With the assent of Secretary Long and Secretary of War R. A. Alger, investigation into the viability of Langley's machine was entrusted to the chief of the U.S. Army Signal Corps, General Adolphus Greely. A famous Arctic explorer and a friend of both Langley and Senator John Lendrum Mitchell, he organized a joint board to explore the possibilities, with Navy Commander C. H. Davis as chairman. After observing Langley's aeroplane, he reported to Navy Secretary Long, "Although its usefulness in its present stage in naval operations would be limited, in military operations its effects would be revolutionary in questions of strategy and offensive warfare."

Because Theodore Roosevelt had left the Navy Department to raise and organize a cavalry regiment to fight in the war to liberate Cuba that was finally declared on April 19, 1898, his interest in developing Langley's aircraft for naval purposes diminished. Remaining enthusiastic about the aeroplane's potential in the U.S. arsenal, General Greely wrote to Secretary of War Alger on May 25, 1898, of "the great importance of such a machine in warfare and the great good that would result to the world at large should the flying machine be made practicable." This plea resulted in congressional approval of $50,000 to fund further experimentation by Langley. The money financed construction of another tandem-wing monoplane with a forty-eight-foot wingspan and a fifty-five-horsepower engine developed by Charles Manly, who was also the pilot. On October 7,

1903, the craft was catapulted from the roof of a houseboat on the Potomac River. Unfortunately, its landing gear ran afoul of an object on the roof. The plane toppled into the water. When another try on December 8 also failed, Langley abandoned the project, leaving it to Orville and Wilbur Wright to prove the viability of manned airplanes nine days later. Discouraged by his failure to reap the glory that was garnered by the Wrights, Langley died in 1906. Many years later in a biography of Greely, Billy Mitchell wrote, "The machine was perfectly capable of flying." Noting that the basis for the heavier-than-air flying machine had been championed by Greely and proved by Langley, he bolstered their place in the history of aviation by quoting Wilbur and Orville Wright's assertion that they had been inspired and assisted in their achievement of the first sustained, manned flight by the work of Langley. "The knowledge that the head of the most prominent scientific institution in America believed in the possibility of human flight," they said, "was one of the influences that led us to undertake the preliminary investigations that preceded our active work. He recommended to us the books that enabled us to form sound ideas at the outset. It was a helping hand at a critical time and we shall always be grateful."

War to drive Spain out of Cuba and the Philippines that the Jingoes had sought and McKinley had resisted had become inevitable after an explosion sank the U.S. battleship *Maine* in the harbor of Havana, Cuba, on the night February 15, 1898, with the loss of 260 sailors. Blaming the blast on the Spanish, Americans rallied to the battle cry "Remember the Maine" and forced McKinley to abandon efforts to achieve a peaceful resolution of the crisis and ask Congress for a declaration of war. He did so in a message that was read to the senators and representatives by clerks on April 11, 1898, which was then referred for consideration to the appropriate committees of both chambers. When the formal war resolution was ready, it contained clauses that recognized the independence of Cuba, demanded withdrawal of Spanish armed forces, disclaimed any intention of the

United States to exercise sovereignty or control over Cuba, and empowered the president to use the army and navy to carry out these demands.

As the resolution was presented, debated, and put to the vote in the Senate on April 20, with Senator John Lendrum Mitchell deciding to vote aye, eighteen-year-old William Mitchell was seated in the packed visitors' gallery and coming to a decision of his own. With the resolution passed and on its way to President McKinley for signing, William arrived at the Mitchell home a few blocks from the Capitol and found the parlor of the house crowded. Breathing hard from the run and with an excited voice, he announced to startled family friends and many of John Lendrum Mitchell's astonished associates, including the Confederacy's famed General Joseph "Fighting Joe" Wheeler, that he would be leaving immediately for Milwaukee to enlist in his father's former regiment.

CHAPTER TWO

ORDERS ARE ORDERS

W hen William Mitchell announced to his flabbergasted parents that he was quitting college and leaving immediately to enlist in the army, Fighting Joe Wheeler protested to William's pacifist father, "John, you're not going to let this little boy go to war, especially as he is your oldest child?"

"He's eighteen," said Senator Mitchell, "and sound mentally and physically."

The youth standing before him was lean, sinewy, hardened by years of hunting, hiking, and shooting at Meadowmere, and as capable with a firearm as he was on horseback.

Eighteen months earlier, Assistant Secretary of the Navy Theodore Roosevelt, who was significantly responsible for setting the stage for the United States to wage the war that Senator Mitchell had opposed, had written in an article in the magazine *The Bookman* to inspire the young men who would have to fight the Spaniards, "No qualities called out by a purely peaceful life stand to a level with those stern and virile virtues which move men of stout heart and strong hand to uphold the honor of their flag in battle." In a speech in the same month at the Naval War College in Rhode Island he had declared, "A nation should never fight unless forced to, but it should always be ready to fight."

Assessing the war fervor that Roosevelt had promoted and that gripped the United States in May 1898, an editorial writer for the *Washington Post* described "a new consciousness of strength—and with it a new appetite, the yearning to show our strength." Animated by this "new sensation," he continued, there was the "taste of Empire" in the mouth of Americans "even as the taste of blood in the jungle."

That the war fever raged in William Mitchell was evidenced by his haste. As a son of a senator, he could have asked his father to exert his influence to obtain an officer's commission and waited for it to be granted. Yet within hours after declaring his intention, he stood with his tearful but proud parents and sisters on a railroad station platform to board a train for Chicago and a connection to Milwaukee via the line that his grandfather had built. Although he didn't record in a diary or letters what he thought as the trains carried him to the city where he'd grown up, he was a member of a generation that could not conceal the joy of adventure of going to war "the way a championship team goes to a tournament," as Mitchell biographer Isaac Don Levine would write.

Riding westward, William Mitchell could not know that his generation would be the last for whom the battlefield was depicted as a place to reap personal glory. He took with him the memory of his father's vivid tales of many long-ago battles fought in places visited on family excursions to Europe and the more recent thrilling yarns about Civil War fights at Perryville and Chattanooga. When he stepped from a Chicago, Milwaukee & St. Paul train at a station that had been built by Alexander Mitchell, he found his hometown bubbling with excitement that the famous "Wisconsin Regiment" of the Civil War was again among the first to respond to the nation's call to arms. One of the best state militias in the country, it had 5,390 volunteers and was divided into regiments numbered in order of their raising. The 1st would be sent to Camp Cuba Libre, at Jacksonville, Florida; the 2nd and 3rd to Camp Thomas, at Chickamauga, Tennessee; and the 4th initially to the state military camp at Camp Douglas and later to Camp Shipp, Alabama. In the influx of volunteers at the muster of the 1st Regiment, the citizens of Milwaukee were surprised to see that the third generation of Mitchells—grandson and son of U.S. Senators and bearer of a distinguished name that adorned city landmarks, from

Alexander Mitchell's mansion to the imposing offices of Martine National Bank, known as the Mitchell Building, and Mitchell Park—was on the roster as a private.

Training would be in the city's outskirts at hastily improvised Camp Harvey. Just how rough and rudely built it was remained a shock years later. Recalling sleeping on the ground with "no screens from the mosquitoes or flies" and that "latrines, garbage receptacles, and trash heaps were alongside of our company kitchen," General Billy Mitchell wrote, "When the flies heard mess call, they came to the kitchens and perched on our food. We had typhoid fever, malaria and every disease possible." He wrote to his mother, "A good many of the boys died and a good many will never get over it, [but] I have not even had a cold and never felt better." Of the nine men in his tent, only three survived the camp diseases.

Just as alarming as the living conditions was the quality of the rifles that the men were issued. While the Spanish troops in Cuba were equipped with state-of-the-gunsmith-art Mauser rifles, the American forces were given Civil War–vintage .45-caliber Springfield rifles that fired bullets loaded with black powder that created a cloud of thick smoke that even an enemy who was a poor shot could target in response. A Springfield's bullet also traveled in a trajectory so high that "a horseman could ride under it at five hundred yards' range."

After three weeks of training, the regiment marched out of Camp Harvey to depart by train for Florida on May 19, 1898. Family friend Mrs. Lucy Mercien wrote to William's mother:

> I have just come back from bidding good-by to your dear brave boy; and my heart is full of sympathy for you. We went to give the young fellow a final handshake and a few trifles for the eighty-hour ride and to chaperone a group of girls [who went to see the boys depart]. It was not a time for levity or foolishness. The speeches, the music and the pitiful parting scenes were sobering enough.

It was the first time we had seen Will in full marching uniform; but I soon recognized him by a certain swing to his walk and the extreme badness of his hat—the very worst hat I ever saw. He gave us a shy little jerk of his hand in response to our frantic wavings. It was a beautiful day, an enormous crowd, and a most thrilling heart-warming scene. The girls sniffled a little, and begged for buttons and offered them their goodies and good-bys all in a breath. Then we left him, gay and debonair, a typical soldier boy, off to the wars.

On route to Florida, William dashed off a note to his mother: "As I write people are cheering, flags waving, and bands playing all along the road, one continuous good-by. We got off the train at Nashville to get some exercise and marched a few miles. Everyone thought us regulars on account of our equipment and fine drilling. Well, we *are* regulars now, having been sworn in to the U.S. Service. I am marching in the front rank in the second set of fours."

Assigned to Company M, 2nd Brigade, 2nd Division of General Fitzhugh Lee's Seventh Army, he traveled with 50 officers and 975 other enlisted men of the 1st Wisconsin Volunteer Infantry to Camp Cuba Libre. Whether he would have a chance to venture from it to visit his grandmother Martha at her nearby orange plantation remained to be seen. Within a few days of his arrival, he struck a bargain to buy a horse for $125. He wrote to his mother, "It's a dandy. As soon as convenient, you might send me the money to pay for it." He also reported, "I have now a great many friends in the regiment."

Having arrived with the expectation that the regiment would receive immediate orders to board another train and shift to the port of Tampa Bay to board a troop ship bound for Cuba, he was disappointed to learn that the strategy of Commanding General William Rufus Shafter's plan for the invasion of Cuba did not call for the Wisconsin Regiment to be part of the initial landings near Santiago at the end of June. It was to be held for a later attack on Havana.

Learning he would not be immediately engaged in combat in Cuba, Private Mitchell felt deeply disappointed and frustrated. In an attempt to console him, an officer of the regiment who had served beside William's father in the Civil War said, "That's always been the army's way, my boy. You get an order to hurry up, and when you get where you were sent, you wait!"

Seven days after he arrived at Camp Cuba Libre, an order that came bearing his name left him shocked and bewildered. Directed to leave immediately for Washington, D.C., he was told to report for duty with the 2nd Volunteer Signal Company. Accompanying the order was a notification that he was "discharged" from the infantry and commissioned a second lieutenant. At age eighteen, he was suddenly the U.S. Army's youngest officer. Whether the order and promotion were the consequence of his father's intervention remains unknown. The general who issued the order, Adolphus Greely, was a friend of Senator Mitchell. Because commissions were (and are) made by the president with the approval of the Congress, Senator Mitchell would have encountered no problem in obtaining one for the son he'd only reluctantly allowed to enlist. Stating later that he had known "little about what this meant" and that he "did not relish" leaving the Wisconsin Regiment, William wrote, "Orders were orders."

After treating his tent mates to a farewell dinner at Pignoli's Restaurant in Jacksonville, the new lieutenant journeyed north to his new post convinced that he had been cheated of an opportunity to strive for glory in combat in a war in which the United States had already achieved astonishing victories. Ten days after President McKinley signed the war declaration, the U.S. Navy's Asiatic Squadron, commanded by Commodore George Dewey, had sailed into Manila harbor in the Philippines and destroyed Spain's Pacific squadron to give the United States its first spoil of victory. This first taste of empire allowed McKinley to exultantly assert, "While we are conducting war and until its conclusion, we must keep what we can get. When the war is over, we must keep what we want."

Now it remained to be seen what ships under the command of Admiral Winfield Scott Schley could do about Spain's Atlantic Fleet in the waters around Cuba. Of the impending clash of navies, war correspondent and famous novelist Stephen Crane of Joseph Pulitzer's *New York World* wrote, "Now is in progress a huge game, with wide and lonely stretches of ocean as the board, and with great steel ships as the counters." At the end of May as Lieutenant Mitchell journeyed to take up his new post in the nation's capital, the Spanish fleet was blockaded within Santiago harbor, and thousands of American soldiers were waiting to board troop ships to invade and free Cuba. On the day Lieutenant Mitchell arrived in Washington– June 1, 1898–the *New York Times* reported, "How many troops are to be moved and where they are bound are questions which the directing spirits of the campaign refuse positively to answer. They have no desire that the Spanish should have an opportunity afforded to gather forces to attack our soldiers as they land." As these naval and land forces were concentrating for the invasion, the youngest officer in an American uniform presented himself at the Washington Barracks.

On the site of the present Fort McNair, the installation had been at the heart of the capital city's defensive units during the Civil War. On June 1, 1898, it was headquarters of the 2nd Volunteer Signal Company, then being organized by General Adolphus Washington Greely. The fifty-four-year-old mutual friend of Senator John Lendrum Mitchell and scientist Samuel Langley, whose flying-machine experiment had captured the fancy of Theodore Roosevelt, was charged with organizing the Army Signal Corps to support operations in Cuba during and after the war.

Born into an old New England family in Newburyport, Massachusetts in 1844, Greely was one of the most famous military figures in the country, not only because he was celebrated as a "soldier-scientist-adventurer" who had embraced modern technology to explore the "last remaining wilderness" of Alaska, but for his service to the nation on battlefields. According to legend, at the beginning of the Civil War, at age seventeen, after being denied enlistment three times, he went home and chalked the numbers one and eight on the soles of his shoes so he that could tell the next recruiter, "I am over eighteen." Fighting in some of the Civil War's fiercest battles, including Antietam and Fredericksburg, as a private with the 19th Massachusetts Volunteer Infantry he was wounded three times. Rising in rank from private to sergeant, he was given a commission and command of the 81st Colored Troops. With the rank of brevet major at war's end, he commanded Federal black troops from 1865 to 1867 in New Orleans, where he faced not only the challenges of occupying a defeated city, but epidemics of yellow fever.

As a second lieutenant in the 36th Infantry, Greely had begun studying telegraphy and electricity under Brigadier General Albert Meyer, founder of the Signal Corps, and worked to establish telegraph lines on the western frontier. Assisting Meyer in the organization of the U.S. Weather Bureau, he became a skilled meteorologist. In 1881, he volunteered to command an expedition to Alaska to establish Arctic weather research stations. Called the Lady Franklin Bay Expedition, it collected significant astronomical, meteorological, and tidal data. Pushing farther north than any prior attempt at exploration, the team found itself stranded at Ellesmere Island. Close to the North Pole, they were marooned for two consecutive summers.

When rescued, Greely and six other survivors returned to the United States amid a swirl of rumors that they had survived through cannibalism of those who perished. With the shocking allegation disproved, and absolved of charges of poor leadership, he published a book in 1894. Titled *Three Years of Arctic Service: An Account of the Lady Franklin Bay Expedition of 1881– 1884 and the Attainment of the Farthest North,* it was dedicated "to its dead who suffered much and to its living who suffered more."

Propelled into a national spotlight by the sensational expedition and rescue, Greely was promoted from captain to brigadier general and appointed chief of the Signal Corps in 1887. For the next eleven years he advanced development of the military use of wireless telegraphy and in 1898 persuaded Congress to appropriate $50,000 for the Signal Corps to explore the possibilities of Langley's flying machine "for war purposes." There is no account of when and where the general, who had a vision of the future use of airplanes in warfare, greeted the second lieutenant, who would fly and lead them in huge fleets to glory and fame twenty years later, and then devote his life to pleading for creation of an American air force separate from the army.

What army archives, newspapers of the day, and Mitchell recorded about his time at the Washington Barracks concerned an episode that had nothing to do with aerial combat. Second Lieutenant William Mitchell's first fight unfolded in the barroom of the American House Hotel. The opposing force was a detachment of about seventy-five soldiers from New York who had deserted their troop train, which had stopped briefly in Washington on route to the camps in Florida. They had invaded the hotel's bar and restaurant and thrown out a handful of city policemen who responded to a call from the frantic hotel manager about a riot in progress. When the police captain saw that his cops were vastly outnumbered by rebellious soldiers, most of them already drunk, and every one equipped with either an army rifle or personal sidearm, he appealed to the War Department for help. "When the riot call reached the barracks," Mitchell recorded, "I asked to be allowed to take the detail to arrest them. As I was the youngest officer, there was some hesitation about it, but finally they let me attempt it."

Leading fourteen enlisted men, including his former college friend, Robert Sterrett, with each man carrying a .45-caliber carbine and ten bullets, Mitchell commandeered a street car and ordered the driver to "go up the track as fast as he could." When the car stopped in front of the hotel, he noted that there were "shouts and sounds of revelry from within," but that none of the riotous soldiers was visible from the street. Warned by the police captain that the soldiers were "very dangerous and that anybody who went in would probably be killed," he "reconnoitered" the building and found that it had only two doors. To guard one, he picked "an enormous private named Bell and another man." Stationed by the second door were Mickey Dugan, "a man of equal proportions," and a companion. They were ordered not to load their guns. Should anyone try to escape, they were to use the weapons with "butt to the front" to knock them down.

Removing his own gun belt and holstered Colt .45 automatic pistol, Mitchell told Sterett to do the same and accompany him. Striding into the barroom, they found several men who had evidently been bartenders as civilians standing behind the long bar and mixing drinks. Most of the men were on chairs at tables. A few who were too drunk to stand lay sprawled on the floor. A large mirror on the wall in back of the bar had been shattered by thrown bottles. The "whole thing was so amusing" that Mitchell had to suppress a laugh in order to call, "Attention!" All but two or three stood up. Ordered to file out of the hotel, they obeyed.

After the detachment's first sergeant called the roll, Mitchell decided to sober them up by marching them the three miles to Washington Barracks. At his request, the police captain recruited several city firemen to go along. They carried water buckets and wrenches for opening hydrants, "not only to furnish the men with drinking water," Mitchell recorded, "but to throw water over those who seemed to need a little bracing up" on a "terribly hot day."

With the by now mostly sobered-up miscreant troops handed over to the officer of the guard at the barracks, Mitchell asked their first sergeant why his men had run amuck. He said that the men were "not particularly well disciplined, especially when officers were not present, and that the officers had gone on in the parlor cars, paying no attention to them. They had had practically nothing to eat for two days. When they saw the hotel across the street from the old Pennsylvania Station, he could not hold them."

After reading Mitchell's report of the action he had taken, General Greely summoned him to commend him for his leadership in defusing a situation that might have had a bloody end. Complimenting him for a report that was "short, concise, to the point and understandable," he offered advice on improving his report-writing in the matter of proper spelling and punctuation. Although Greely's friendship with John Lendrum Mitchell and use of the influence that came with the title of United States Senator had plucked William Mitchell out of the enlisted ranks, made him a lieutenant, and brought him to the Washington Barracks, his seizure of an opportunity to demonstrate leadership by peacefully quelling a riot by disgruntled, dispirited, drunken soldiers who had felt ignored by their officers, his volunteering to lead, and his bravery in acting unarmed had demonstrated that he appreciated the power of an officer's very presence and the effect of a commanding voice. This display of confident authority and leadership had left Greely not only convinced that Lieutenant William Mitchell was worth watching, and that he could have a bright future in the army, but ready and eager to assist him if he were to choose to follow a career in the military.

While the general contemplated a longer future for Mitchell, the second lieutenant who left the office of the chief of the Signal Corps cared only about not being among the thousands of men in the Florida camps who were packing their gear, shouldering rifles, and marching onto troop ships to sail for Cuban shores. Having been suddenly shifted from the infantry to General Greely's Signal Corps, he learned on June 7 that the navy's ships *Marblehead*, *Yankee*, and *St. Louis* had located and severed the telegraph cable linking Cuba with Haiti, cutting off communication with Spain. On Friday, June 10, the 1st Battalion, U.S. Marines, landed at Guantánamo Bay, taking over a parcel of Cuban territory that would still be under U.S. control more than a century later.

Two days after the Marines established Camp McCalla at Guantánamo, named for the naval commander whose ship had put them ashore, the House of Representatives passed a resolution providing for the annexation of the Hawaiian Islands. When the resolution was taken up by the Senate, John Lendrum Mitchell rose to denounce it. "The seizure of Hawaii," he declared, "would remove any doubt as to our all around land grabbing intentions." In a scathing denunciation of terms such as "Manifest Destiny" and "mastery of the Pacific," and President McKinley's policy of taking "what we can" in war and keeping "what we want" after the war, he said, "Since the advent of the white man every leaf in the history of Hawaii is either red with blood or black with intrigue and jobbery." In order to preclude defeat of a treaty of annexation in the Senate, where a two-thirds vote was needed, supporters of annexation maneuvered to effect it by a joint resolution of Congress, which needed only a simple majority. When it passed on July 7, 1899, John Lendrum Mitchell was no longer in the Senate. Disgusted by the war he opposed, he had chosen not to seek re-election in 1898.

In the weeks in which the Hawaii annexation question was debated, the war that Senator Mitchell had resisted proceeded at a pace that left him and the nation astonished, and Lieutenant William Mitchell disappointed. While he remained assigned to the Washington Barracks, more than seventeen thousand regular army troops and volunteers, including a cavalry regiment led by Colonel Leonard Wood and Lieutenant Colonel Theodore Roosevelt, but popularly known as "Teddy's Rough Riders," landed at the small seaside town of Daiquiri and Siboney Bay east of their main objective, Santiago, on June 22. In a daylong battle at El Caney on July 1, U.S. troops captured a Spanish garrison and about six hundred men. In a charge to the flat top of Kettle Hill of the San Juan Heights, overlooking Santiago, Theodore Roosevelt led his dismounted cavalrymen and others to put the Americans in position to place the city and its bay under U.S. guns. Two days later, as the Spanish ships made a desperate escape attempt, they were blown out of the water. On July 17, the twenty-four thousand Spanish troops in Santiago surrendered. With victory in hand, Cuba liberated, and the United States also in possession of Puerto Rico and the Philippines, the American ambassador to Great Britain, John Hay, pronounced the undertaking a "splendid little war." President McKinley would tell his jubilant fellow Americans, "And so it has come to pass that in a few short months we have become a world power."

Disappointed to the point of bitterness at having missed the fighting, Lieutenant Mitchell wrote to his mother, "I really do believe that if we had been up against a first-rate power, they would have whaled the mischief right out of us." Writing from a camp in Florida in August while waiting orders to a post in now-occupied Cuba, he told his mother that "the kids" in his new regiment were complaining that with peace declared, the army had "no use for us now." As for himself, he was "anxiously waiting" to get on a transport for Cuba.

From Camp Cuba Libre in late August he wrote, "I'm going to get there [Cuba] some way or other. I've been waiting all summer to get the chance to do something and have not had it, and I think it would be a shame to go home now. There would be no self satisfaction in going home and would look kind of funny too."

Second in command when he'd arrived at Jacksonville from Washington, he took charge of laying a telegraph line at Pablo Beach. When the job was done in the record time of two days, he found himself in charge of a company and commended for his work "before the other officers" by the commanding officer, "an old regular army man." In another letter he reported, "I like this kind of work very much and find that it is doing me as much good as college would this fall." His former classmate and companion in quelling the American House riot, Robert Sterett, observed that Mitchell was "a crackerjack officer, very alert, energetic, and most interested in the work."

When not on duty, Mitchell practiced using the telegraph, studied physics and trigonometry, and taught himself typewriting. In a letter on September 6, 1898, to his mother, he complained that "the signal office is being run long political lines" and that "political appointments" of officers "have ruined everything." Admitting that he benefitted from his father's influence, he said, "I didn't have any experience to back me up at all." The difference, he noted, was that he had been determined to excel, whereas the son of another U.S. Senator with the rank of major in a South Carolina regiment "ought no more to be in the army than little John [Mitchell's young brother]."

Respite from camp took the form of visits on horseback to his grandmother Martha's estate. A few miles from Jacksonville, it was called Villa Alexandria (named for her husband and Mitchell patriarch) and had a swimming pool. His companion on these excursions, Robert Sterett, recalled Mitchell and himself as "a couple of boys, laughing, joking and racing our horses, ending up at the Villa to spend the day swimming, drinking milk, eating pies, and playing various games."

These occasional idyllic breaks from camp routines ended in November. Four months after the Spanish surrender, an order with Lieutenant William Mitchell's name on it directed him to sail to Cuba with other units to serve in the Army of Occupation. From Camp Columbia near Havana on December 24, he wrote exultantly to his father of "a better Christmas in one way than I expected." Composing the letter on "a high bluff overlooking the sea," he continued, "As I sit here, the company is lined up for retreat, the sky is streaked in red, white and blue in the West, with a few stars showing. It truly looks like our flag."

In signing a peace treaty with the United States on December 10, 1898, in Paris, France, the Spanish had given up all claim and title to Cuba, Puerto Rico, and Guam. For payment by the United States of $20 million, they also ceded a cluster of islands in the western Pacific that had been named the Philippines by sixteenth-century conquistadores for King Philip. Writing to his mother on January 2, 1899, Lieutenant Mitchell described a ceremony in Havana that marked the final act in the cause of Cuba Libre that the Jingoes had sought and McKinley now hailed as the emergence of the United States as a world power. He reported:

Our men were drawn up in a hollow square all around the Court while the Spaniards were lined up in front of the [Governor General's] Palace. At precisely 12:02 by the clock on the Palace the Spanish flag came down and ours went up. As we stood there with bare heads it was . . . undoubtedly the most important in the history of Our Country since the surrender [of the British army at Yorktown in the American Revolution] . . . It marks the beginning of a new policy on the part of the United States, that of territorial expansion and showing itself to the world as one of the greatest of nations.

A few days after exulting in this formal spectacle of the humiliation of the once-great empire of the Old World, Mitchell, whose vision of a new American imperialism had left him so exhilarated and proud, soon confronted a reality of the first territorial conquest by the United States that would be echoed 104 years later in the invasion and liberation of Iraq. For twenty-first-century troops in Baghdad, the symbol of the tyrannical atrocities of decades of rule by Saddam Hussein was Abu Ghraib prison. In Havana in 1899 it was Cabanas fortress. With walls one hundred feet high, it had held thousands of political prisoners. After a visit to Cabanas, he wrote to his father and described "walls of the trenches where prisoners had been executed" that were "encrusted with bullets and machete cuts." In a scene of "bleaching bones, the chains, and the dungeons" he found everything quiet, "except for the multitude of cats, rats and small animals which infest these places." Buzzards sat on the walls of the trenches in long rows and "under them and all around them walk the sentries of the 2nd Artillery." Almost as shocking was the realization that many Cubans were not as welcoming as the Jingoes had confidently predicted. All over the island well-armed insurgents who had fought the Spanish were now shooting at Americans.

This obstinacy became a personal challenge at the end of January when Colonel Halsey H. Dunwoody placed his nineteen-year-old lieutenant, Mitchell, in command of forty men with orders to build telegraph lines between Havana and Santiago de Cuba. "It is the desire of the commanding general of the division," read the order, "that the construction of this line be hastened as rapidly as possible." Sailing from Havana on the steamer *Mortera*, the contingent arrived at the village of Gibara on February 5. In a report to Colonel Dunwoody written on February 11, in which Mitchell begged to be excused for writing it in pencil because "no ink is obtainable," he noted that they had arrived safely in Gibara, unloaded men and equipment, arrived in Holguin, and begun work. Although no mention was made in the report of a tense drama that had unfolded between himself and the Cuban captain of the *Mortera* at Gibara, Mitchell provided details in a letter to his mother. He recorded that when the ship reached Gibara, the captain told him to unload men and equipment using a small boat for landing. Objecting that it appeared unsafe and likely to sink, Mitchell refused and demanded that the captain hire a "big fine flatboat in the harbor." The captain "then called his men to put us off. Telling me he was captain of the ship and so on. He thought as we were such a small detachment he could bluff us and save money as the big boat cost $50 a trip. So I just issued ammunition to my men and ran him and his men to the stern of the ship, then went ashore and ordered the big flatboat to be sent out, which was done."

Informing Dunwoody that work on the telegraph line had begun February 8 and that twelve miles had been completed in two days, he noted that further construction would have to be delayed "a day or two" because "there are three thousand insurgents up the road." Noting that the insurgents were "looking for a little trouble," he assured Dunwoody, "There are six hundred of us here. If they come we will show them something." From the insurgent stronghold of Puerto Padre he wrote to his mother, "This is the home of all this bandit business. I have orders to shoot anyone along the road who acts suspiciously while I am in transit from one point to another."

Written from the interior of Cuba in the summer of 1899, Mitchell's letters to his mother about Cubans could be those of an American army officer sent home from Baghdad in 2004 about Iraqis. "When we first came, they seemed glad to see us," he wrote after a few weeks in the country, but "now they are silent when they know someone understands them." In another letter he noted about the insurgents, "They think themselves very fierce when around Spaniards, but when American privates come along they have nothing to say in an open way. But every day or two they stick a knife into them." He predicted, "This island will not be at peace for years."

Yet, as troublesome as Cuba could be in the spring of 1899, far more exciting events were being reported from America's other prize of the Spanish-American War. Newspaper accounts described an insurgency against the American takeover of the Philippines, led by a nationalist named Emilio Aguinaldo. Denouncing the "army of occupation," "constant outrages and taunts, which have caused misery of the people of Manila," and "premeditated transgression of justice and liberty," he asserted, "I have tried to avoid, as far as it has been possible for me to do so, armed conflict, in my endeavors to assure our independence by pacific means and to avoid more costly sacrifices. But all my efforts have been useless against the measureless pride of the American government."

Proclaiming Philippine independence and naming himself dictator, he rejected Spain's cession under terms of the Paris peace treaty and declared war on the United States. America's response was to send a force of seventy thousand soldiers, commanded by General Arthur MacArthur. With orders to "reduce the Filipinos to submission," they found themselves fighting a guerilla war. Reading accounts of the fighting, still feeling disappointment at having missed the fighting in Cuba, and hungering to see battle in this new war, Mitchell wrote to his influential father on March 21, "You don't know how much I want to go to the Philippines. Can't something to be done to get me assigned there?"

After repeated pleas in a barrage of letters, his mother answered on April 18:

My Dear Boy:

I saw General Greely today and he told me you would remain in Cuba, and would be sent to various places as required. He said you are showing a great deal of ability in your work and they were very much pleased with you, that you seemed to get on well with the men and that you made an excellent officer. You may know how happy it makes me to hear [this]. If you will come back to me the same in heart and character as you went away, I can ask nothing more. . . .

We could not ask to have any assignment for you, as it seems to disgust them at the War Department to have favors asked. And one reason why you stand so well is that you have taken the assignments without question and no relative has been trying to push you.

With 138 miles of telegraph line constructed at the end of May (more than any other Signal Corps unit in Cuba achieved), Mitchell filed a review of the work, which again impressed General Greely with his "ability, energy, and intelligence." The result was appointment to the post of assistant signal officer on the staff of General Fitzhugh Lee and assignment to his headquarters in Havana. As a young officer who enjoyed the approval of two influential generals, and with a record of fine achievement, he confessed to his father that he felt conflicted about a career in the regular army. "As I look at it now," he wrote, "I would not make it my life's work, although after I am in it for a year or so it might look different." After filing an application for transfer to the regular army as an officer, he was informed that law required that commissioned officers be at least twenty-one years of age. Disappointed that he was "below the age limit," he informed his father he had not lost his desire to see service "in the face of the enemy" in the Philippines, even if it were to mean going as a private.

"Here I have been [in Cuba] since the war without any foreign service to speak of and have not been in any engagements as yet," he wrote to his father. "How would you have felt in the Civil War if you had been out of the way somewhere? Just think this over, and perhaps you will think of it favorably."

Although John Lendrum Mitchell vehemently opposed the idea, he intervened on behalf of his son at the War Department. Two weeks later, Lieutenant Mitchell was ordered to leave for the Philippines. "Now I have a good chance to work in the field," he wrote his mother excitedly, "and know I can carry it through in a satisfactory manner."

CHAPTER THREE

"THE WHOLE CROWD IS OUT FOR BUSINESS."

After a journey that took him from Cuba to Puerto Rico, Santo Domingo, and Haiti, Lieutenant Mitchell arrived in Washington, D.C., to find his father packing to join the Mitchell family for a vacation in Europe. Senator Mitchell decided William's army experience had been "the making of him," physically and mentally. He wrote to Mrs. Mitchell, "He stands straight and talks straight, and I may say entertainingly. The impression he has made here on everybody is very favorable."

Stopping briefly in Milwaukee, the handsome young lieutenant had a reunion with his boyhood pal Douglas MacArthur and learned that the elder son of the commander of a division of American troops in the Philippines had been accepted at West Point, and that Douglas had shown a romantic interest in Ruth Mitchell, including writing a poem about her:

Fair Western girl with life awhirl
Of love and fancy free
'Tis thee I love
All things above
Why wilt thou not love me?

MacArthur biographer William Manchester wrote of this 1899 reunion of two young men whose fathers had earned fame and glory in the Civil War and whose own lives would be entwined in the most dramatic events of the next thirty years: "Douglas was not in uniform. The disadvantages of this became painfully clear when young officers, [John Lendrum] Mitchell's son Billy along them, came home to Milwaukee on leave. While girls flocked around the young army officer on his way from one war to another, the wretched civilian in blazer and flannels [MacArthur] skulked in the background . . . fingering his straw boater and vowing that this would be the last war in his lifetime which did not find him serving at the front."

The Mitchell family friend who had described William going off to war in Cuba in the spring of 1898 penned a letter to Mrs. Mitchell. "How handsome fascinating all the girls found him," reported Mrs. Mercien. "He seems the perfect type of the ideal American soldier." Another friend who watched him board a troop ship in San Francisco on October 5, 1899, recorded, "He looked very well and very cheerful and very happy. Your boy seems so very, very young to have charge of men, but he bears himself with great credit."

Mitchell wrote to his father of the troops aboard his ship, "The whole crowd is out for business." On October 31, after a twenty-seven-day crossing of the Pacific Ocean, he wrote to his mother, "We have just arrived in sight of the Island of Luzon." After a description of the geography as a three-transport convoy made their way into Manila Bay, he noted, "The troops have been issued ammunition in case of attack by an armed launch or armed party on the shore. Guards were doubled as we passed among a lot of small islands."

Informed within minutes of going ashore that he had been assigned to General Arthur MacArthur's division, he noted, "There are terrific odds to contend against. There is gong to be a large battle in a few days. This is business right through. We will lick these people this winter."

During the brief meeting with his father in Washington, he had said, "I don't believe much in territorial expansion, but we cannot get out of keeping the Philippines and preserve our dignity." It was a war that no one had planned. When American forces captured the capital of Manila in April 1898, Emilio Aguinaldo's army occupied a trench line surrounding the city. On the evening of February 4, 1899, Private William Grayson of the Nebraska Volunteers fired at a group of Filipinos approaching his position. They returned fire. Shooting soon spread up and down the ten-mile U.S.-Filipino lines, causing hundreds of casualties. Supported by shelling from Admiral George Dewey's fleet, the Americans quickly overwhelmed Filipino positions while inflicting thousands of casualties. Within days, American forces spread outward from the capital, using superior firepower, mobile artillery, and command of the sea. By November the insurgents had been pushed farther into central Luzon. Recognizing that he could not fight with conventional military units, Aguinaldo had ordered his followers to use guerilla tactics

The force that Lieutenant Mitchell joined at the town of Mayalang on his first day consisted of three American columns of about three thousand infantry, four troops of cavalry, and several batteries of artillery under the command of MacArthur and Generals Henry Lawton and Lloyd Wheaton. Armed with Remington and Mauser rifles and Krupp cannons, the rebels were estimated between two and five thousand. Recording his first battle experience, Mitchell noted that the insurgents "had the range of the town exactly and soon it was full of bullets and shells." When the fight ended with the insurgents withdrawing, he wrote, "With all this terrible shooting we did not have more than sixty casualties." He also noted that the building in which he wrote was riddled with bullets "and a shell has dropped right on the other side of it."

During the fighting on MacArthur's front, a coordinated attack with Lawton's division, located about 75 miles away, had been thwarted because enemy snipers made communication by courier impossible. When General MacArthur called in his chief signal officer to ask about establishing telegraphic communication, he was told that sending and receiving devices were available, but there were no batteries, insulators, and wire for construction of a telegraph line. As the general and signal officer contemplated this predicament, Mitchell proposed that he could "improvise" a solution by unwinding wire that was used to make the barrels of captured enemy cannons, rolls of barbed wire, and several old Spanish batteries. Lacking sal ammoniac to power them, he used ordinary table or rock salt. This produced a current, but it proved so weak that Mitchell could detect it only by touching his tongue to a wire and putting his hand in "a muddy place on the earth for a ground." Insulators were made of dried bamboo and pieces of broken bottles. Before setting out on a mission that most of the men at headquarters believed he would not survive, he wrote to his mother, "If anything should happen, you would hear about it immediately, as General MacArthur knows where you are."

Following the route of a railway and working under fire from snipers in the surrounding jungle, he warned inhabitants of villages and farms that if they did not protect the line from being cut, all their houses and cattle within a mile of it would be destroyed. When he and his crew of twelve encountered several terrified Spanish soldiers who had been held captive for months by the natives, he noted in a report on the mission he "could not do much for the poor fellows," so he turned them over to a Philippine priest, with a promise that if "any harm befell them," on his return he would "kill him and burn everything he had."

Reaching Lawton's Division at two o'clock in the morning, all the men of his crew had lacerations of arms and legs, torn uniforms, and ruined boots. When he reported to Lawton in a headquarters set up in a convent that a telegraph line to MacArthur's headquarters had been built and was operating, the general was not only astonished by the feat, but by the fact that none of Mitchell's men had been killed and their only wounds were the result of work that ruined their uniforms.

A fifty-six-year-old veteran of the Civil War, Henry Ware Lawton had joined the Indiana Volunteers as a private in August 1861 and by May of the following year had been promoted to captain. He'd led men in the battles of Corinth, Stones River, and Chickamauga and displayed conspicuous bravery at Atlanta by leading a charge of skirmishers, described by a witness as "a splendid dash," toward a line of Confederate rifle pits. Credited with successfully capturing them and their Confederate riflemen, he was appointed commander of the 30th Indiana and continued serving in Texas until November 1865 as part of an occupation force. Entering the regular army as a second lieutenant of a unit of "colored troops," he advanced through the ranks, serving in various branches until 1888 when he was made a major in the Inspector General's Office. By the time of the war with Spain he was a colonel who first saw duty as a Fifth Army division commander in Cuba and then was sent to the Philippines to command the defenses of Manila.

Informed by Lawton that he was unable to provide any replacements for the tattered uniforms, Mitchell located a supply of Spanish army gear and told his men to wear them inside out so that they could not be mistaken as Spaniards by either insurgents or Americans as they went back to MacArthur's lines.

In the first war in which the telegraph replaced couriers and messengers as the means by which field commanders were kept fully and instantly informed of the status of the battlefield, noted an editorial in the *New York Times*, the "signal men and officers covered themselves with glory." The Signal Corps "is one of the departments of the army in which a fighting man who wants to fight need not be ashamed to go; if it is a fight that he is looking for he can be accommodated in this corps about as well as in the line of the army. It requires even more to lay telegraph lines under fire, for a lineman's first business is not to fight but to work. To be under fire and not able to reply is a situation trying even to veteran soldiers."

Clearly enjoying being in the thick of the fighting, Mitchell found time to write about his adventures in a steady stream of letters, primarily to his father in Europe. The next "scrap" after running the telegraph line to Lawton's headquarters was at Mabalang, "where I got out line into the rebel trenches ahead of the [American] troops." Reporting the "*insurrectos* ran, blowing up a big railroad bridge," he noted, "As they retreated along the railroad track they were not more than three hundred yards away from us in columns of fours; but there was not a single company of our troops within sight of them. I thought I could bring somebody down with my pistol, they looked so near, but had to use my carbine."

On December 10 he exultantly wrote, "Am now acting Chief Signal Officer of this division [MacArthur's]. Have got the work pretty well organized in this short time and only hope I'll be left alone for awhile." Describing conditions under which he and his men had to work, he wrote, "We have come through rice fields with water up to one's waist, through woods, thickets of bamboo, across rivers with currents like a mill race, where men drown instantly if they are washed off rafts or lose their hold on ropes we stretch across—and all of this right in the face of these *insurrectos*, who are well armed, apparently well officered and with plenty of ammunition, but pitifully incompetent in marksmanship."

Learning that General Lawton had been killed walking along the firing line wearing a white helmet and yellow raincoat when a sharpshooter's bullet struck him in the chest, Mitchell wrote, "We will make them pay dearly for it." After a "sharp exchange" with rebels in which they lined up five U.S. infantrymen against a fence, shot them, and "cut them up as we were entering the town" of Arryat, he wrote, "We took no prisoners after that. Don't think they will capture me alive at this stage of the game if I am armed."

But atrocities were also committed by Americans. A reporter for the *Philadelphia Ledger* who witnessed them wrote, "The present war is no bloodless, fake, opera bouffé engagement. Our men have been relentless; have killed to exterminate men, women, children, prisoners and captives, active insurgents and suspected people, from lads of ten and up, an idea prevailing that the Filipino, as such, was little better than a dog, a noisome reptile in some instances, whose best disposition was to the rubbish heap. Our soldiers have pumped salt water into men to 'make them talk,' have taken prisoner people who held up their hands and peacefully surrendered, and an hour later, without an atom of evidence to show they were even *insurrectos*, stood them up on a bridge and shot them down one by one, to drop them into the water below and float down as an example to those who found their bullet-riddled corpses."

Much of this was rooted in racism. President McKinley called the Filipinos "little brown brothers." The soldiers, including Mitchell, called them "Gugus," "goo-goos," and "niggers." In popular American imagination, noted a historical review of the war in the *Manila Post* more than a century later, "the natives were a bewildering blend of savagery, childishness, racial inferiority, Asian decadence and animality. American soldiers spoke of the Filipinos they shot down with their Krag rifles as little more than small game or water fowl." A volunteer from Washington state wrote home, "Our fighting blood was up, and we wanted to kill niggers." Shooting human beings was a "hot game" that "beats hunting all to pieces," he continued. "We charged them and such a slaughter you never saw. We killed them like rabbits; hundreds, yes, thousands of them. Every-one was crazy." Another soldier wrote that the killing was "fast and furious," with dead "goo-goos piling up thicker than buffalo chips." Another trooper described "picking off niggers in the water" and found it "more fun than a turkey shoot." One soldier proclaimed, "I'm in my glory when I can sight my gun on some brown skin and pull the trigger."

Although some Americans understood that the Filipinos were not closely related to the people of Africa, Senator John McLaurin of South Carolina declared them a "mongrel and semi-barbarous population" who were "inferior but akin to the Negro" morally and intellectually.

"No cruelty is too severe for these brainless monkeys," said another U.S. soldier, "who can appreciate no honor, kindness, or justice. With an enemy like this to fight, it is not surprising that the boys should adapt 'no quarter' as a motto and fill the blacks with lead."

Lieutenant William Mitchell opined in a letter to his father, "The U.S.

is trying to do a thing here in two years with one hundred thousand men that another [country] would do with three hundred thousand in twenty." He had been in the field for three months, "drinking out of every pool, sometimes little or nothing to eat and sleeping anywhere in wet clothes on or dry clothes on, as the occasion demanded it, and I am all right." In a letter Mitchell wrote while seated on "an old gun carriage" and a sentry was "walking his post," he provided a picture of a twenty-year-old army officer at war in a strange and dangerous place half-way around the world from the placid pastures of Meadowmere and majestic buildings of Washington, D.C. "I have to be very vigilant," he wrote, "[that] I always inspect every guard myself, four times in all, every night. When vigilance is relaxed in the least, there are always more or less consequences and of course I always avoid a scrap if possible and still obtain what we are after."

In a new kind of warfare in which there were no massed armies in uniforms facing each other on a limited field of battle, gathering information on the enemy by specialists that in future wars would be called "military intelligence" was a function of the Signal Corps. During the Civil War and in the fighting in Cuba, this had taken the form of signalmen in balloons scanning with binoculars. Except for scouts to carry out land reconnaissance, and the capture and questioning of enemy combatants and some civilians at the time of an engagement, the army in the Philippines had no system for gathering information on an enemy who operated as guerillas and wore the same clothing as a native population. Having observed that the *insurrectos* generally terrorized and exploited the civilians in villages and towns as cruelly as had the despised Spaniards, Mitchell proposed to General MacArthur that he be permitted to recruit allies among the natives for the purpose of gathering information on rebel hideouts and arms caches. Authorized to set up such a network, Mitchell quickly assembled a group of enthusiastic Filipinos who provided the location of sixty members of a revolutionary society known as the Katipunan. Capturing them during a raid on May 7, 1900, he reported that those who could write signed an oath with their own blood and that those who were not able to write were "branded on with the bottom of a bottle," so that "it is not a hard matter to find them."

With his encampment taking fire from snipers a week later, Mitchell ordered all the men in a nearby village detained for questioning. Eager to cooperate, they gave him the location of an enemy camp that the villagers identified as headquarters of a Captain Mendoza, known to the Americans as second in command to General Aguinaldo. Locating the camp after three night reconnaissance ventures into the jungle with three of his men, he requested a party of fifteen enlisted men and an officer and accompanied them on a raid that he described in a letter home:

> Started about 11 p.m., deployed at 12:30 around them and charged up to their camp across an open field. Their sentry was asleep and very little fighting occurred. Mendoza surrendered to me personally, and his whole outfit with their arms. Captain Mendoza is adjutant general of what is left of Aguinaldo's army and the capture is a very important one. I do not care to have it known all over the world that I worked it up, as it is not exactly my business. But [I] understand that I am to be mentioned in orders about it.

On May 13, the commander of the 48th Infantry sent a message of congratulations to those who "captured Mendoza and his people." Mitchell's reward was a rise in rank to First Lieutenant. The intelligence provided by Mendoza's capture in 1900 compares in importance to the capture of significant figures in Osama bin Laden's al Qaeda terrorist organization during the wars in Afghanistan and Iraq. Documents confiscated during the raid provided information about Aguinaldo's military organization and gave impetus to an intensive campaign to locate and capture Aguinaldo himself.

A man who proved as elusive in June of 1900 as bin Laden in 2004,

Aguinaldo was to First Lieutenant William Mitchell "this little rascal, with the power of assassination over a good many natives." While the U.S. Army looked for the rebel leader in dense tropical forests of northern Luzon, Mitchell and his Signal Corpsmen were stringing telegraph lines and fighting not only enemy snipers, scorpions, and leeches, but tribes of head-hunting natives who swooped out of the jungle with flailing arms and slashing machetes. In the process of the Signal Corps' building twelve thousand miles of telegraph lines, he wrote proudly to his father that he and his men had captured "more then seventy insurgent flags." He wrote to his mother, "It's funny how a man gets after being in the field a long time. Nothing seems impossible for him to do."

Expressing confidence that the U.S. army would suppress the insurrection and capture "Aggie," as he called Aguinaldo, his letters also provided insight into the emerging character of a young officer who would become famous for criticism of the military hierarchy. In the 1920s and 1930s he would be a general who earned notoriety and provoked enmity and retribution of superior generals and admirals, but in the summer of 1900 he was a first lieutenant griping about himself and his soldiers being told "to go and do, with our hands tied behind our backs, our feet in a quagmire, and our mouths sealed when one word will release them and no one will be the worse for it." At the time he was voicing these complaints, he met a colonel whose commission, like his own, was not in the regular army, but the volunteers. Thirty-five years old, Frederick Funston would prove to be, in the words of Mitchell biographer Isaac Don Levine, "the greatest single influence upon Lieutenant Mitchell during the campaign in the Philippines."

Born on November 9, 1865, in New Carlisle, Ohio, Funston lived in a period of rapid expansion and exploration in the United States. The Civil War was over and, like Mitchell, he grew up with his father's stories of the conflict. During his boyhood, Alaska was purchased, the Wyoming Territory was organized, Nebraska and Colorado were admitted to the union, and railroads were expanding across the continent. In 1868, the Funston family moved to Allen County, Kansas. After high school, he tried to get into West Point and begin a military career, but his grades and admission test score were not good enough. Not even the intervention of his father, a congressman, could gain him acceptance. Disappointed, he entered the state university at Lawrence, Kansas, in 1886, only to withdraw after two semesters for financial reasons. For a brief period, he reported for a newspaper in Fort Smith, Arkansas. In 1890, he joined the Department of Agriculture and took part in an expedition to the Dakota badlands and in the following year served as a botanist on a similar expedition to Death Valley, California, where he worked for eight months collecting different flora and fauna and helping the expedition discover 150 new species of plant life. While opening a new trail in the Yosemite Valley and living with the Panamint Indians, he fell in love with California.

Returning home in the fall of 1891, he again found work on a newspaper in Kansas City, Missouri. In 1892 he was again off to Alaska to study the flora of the territory, and in 1893–1894 he wintered alone on the banks of the Klondike. In the spring he built a boat and paddled some fifteen hundred miles down the Yukon River to the open sea, where he boarded a ship and was transported to California. Two years later, he tried to establish a coffee plantation in Central America. When it failed he moved to New York, where he became a deputy comptroller for the Atchison, Topeka & Santa Fe Railroad. In New York City in 1896 he became interested in the cause of Cuban freedom, led by a group of revolutionists who were fighting for independence from Spain. After listening to a speech by Civil War general Daniel E. Sickles, he was stirred to enlist in the cause. A captain of artillery with the Cuban freedom fighters even though he had never fired a cannon, he was able to get his hands on a twelve-pound Hotchkiss cannon and with an instruction manual spent weeks training himself in gunnery. A 5-foot-4-inch, 120-pound redhead, he had fought in twenty-two individual battles and had seventeen horses shot out from under him. He rose in rank to lieutenant colonel and was shot through both lungs and an arm, and finally, in a cavalry charge, had large shards of wood thrust into his hip from the roots of an upturned tree when his horse rolled over. After he led a charge through a barrage of withering rifle fire, his men named him "Fearless Freddie." Twenty-three months later, he weighed only 80 pounds and was coughing up blood. Extremely ill, he was forced to return home with a nearly fatal case of malaria.

Barely recovered when the Spanish-American War commenced, Funston was appointed by the governor of Kansas to the rank of colonel of the 20th Kansas Regiment on May 13, 1898. While the 20th was waiting to get into the war, Spain signed the peace treaty with the United States, giving it possession of the Philippines. Eager to join the fight against the *insurrectos*, he bought a book on military tactics that he read on the way west to join his command at San Francisco. When his father asked him what he knew about military tactics, Funston answered, "Not much, but I am halfway through this book and by the time I reach San Francisco, I will."

Finding his men poorly trained, he started drilling them in maneuvers and rifle practice. He also did his best to improve their living conditions. After five months of intensive training in San Francisco, the 20th Kansas Regiment left for the Philippines and became one of the first units committed to battle. In their first attack the Kansans went far beyond their assigned objective, an occurrence that they were to repeat several times before the war was over. For several weeks Colonel Funston and his 20th Kansas were engaged in the drive to take Caloocan and the rebel capital at Malolos, where Funston was shot in the left hand. After the fall of Malolos, the press reported, "Colonel Funston, always at the front, was the first man in Malolos, followed by a group of dashing Kansans." On his way to Manila to recuperate, he received a telegram informing him of his promotion to brigadier general of volunteers. Late in April 1899, with the American advance brought to a standstill by the partial destruction of the bridge spanning the Río Grande de la Pampanga at Calumpit, according to Funston the "position was by all means the strongest that we had yet been brought against, the river being about four hundred feet wide, deep, and swift, while to opposite bank was defended by fully four thousand men occupying elaborate trenches." After several attempts of crossing the river had failed, a small raft was discovered that Funston undertook to use as a ferry. Two Kansas privates, William B. Trembley and Edward White, volunteered to swim the river and attach a towrope on the opposite shore. Under the protective fire of their own comrades they accomplished their mission, and the raft made its first trip carrying Funston and seven others. When enough men had been ferried to the little beachhead on the other side of the river, they drove the Filipinos from their trenches. The damaged portion of the bridge was then repaired, and infantry troops began making the crossing.

For their heroism in action, Funston, White, and Trembley were awarded the Medal of Honor. A week later, at the age of thirty-five, Funston was promoted to the rank of brigadier general of volunteers and given command of a brigade composed of the 1st Montana and the 20th Kansas. These troops were soon replaced by fresh units, and the veterans were ordered home for discharge. Praise for his valor came in a letter from Vice President Theodore Roosevelt, who, when he learned that Funston was thinking of quitting the army, pleaded with him in another letter to remain in uniform. Instructed to report to San Francisco for mustering out, Funston accompanied his regiment even as Major General MacArthur recommended him for major general of volunteers for gallant and meritorious services throughout the campaign against Filipino insurgents from February 4 to July 1, 1899. Arriving at San Francisco on October 10, 1899, he found orders sending him back to service in the islands. By this time the fighting was guerilla warfare.

Fascinated by the veteran fighter and eager to learn from him, Mitchell listened to Funston's ideas and opinions of what a modern army ought to be. In captivating soliloquies delivered as they sat around campfires, Funston railed against "stand-patters," "mossbacks," "short-sighted" generals in the War Department, and the corrosive effects of political influence. But sprinkled among these diatribes were riveting tales of Funston's "adventures" in the vast Arctic regions of Alaska. The young lieutenant was especially fascinated by Funston's colorful description of a baseball game played on the ice with the thermometer registering forty degrees below zero. "If the ball got rolling," said Funston, "it would not stop for a mile or so."

Mitchell would recall that these hours spent with Funston stirred him to examine his own army experiences and question whether he should remain in the service. "I have found that I have accomplished more in these nearly two years," he wrote to his father, "than in all the rest put together. It has been to my liking and mixed with plenty of outdoor exercise, with horses and guns which I think I shall always have to have in some form or other." Noting that in a two-month period of stringing telegraph lines he had "taken more than seventy insurgent flags and seven official seals, besides a great quantity of insurgent orders, receipts, rolls" and other documents, he felt that the back of the rebellion had been broken. Although Aguinaldo remained at large, he believed that the insurrection was "finished." While in the Philippines, he had acquired knowledge of every branch of the military, learned battlefield tactics, mastered the rudiments of electricity, completed the longest stretch of telegraph wires in the Philippines, and contracted malaria.

Describing himself as "a doddering old man," and with accumulated leave-time, he wrote to his parents, then on an extended trip to Europe, "I had better resign." The itinerary he outlined in the letter would take him first to Tokyo; westward through China, where the Boxer Rebellion was in full bloom; India in the hope of hunting tigers; Suez; Turkey; and Morocco, including a reunion with his father in Egypt; and on to France to ring in the twentieth century in Paris and celebrate his twenty-first birthday.

CHAPTER FOUR

"LAST FRONTIER"

Determined to present his resignation from the army personally to the chief of the Signal Corps, General Adolphus Greely, and return to Milwaukee to enter the family banking business, Lieutenant William Mitchell had written to his mother from the Philippines that he yearned to "have a home, some settled aim, business and association and try to earn one's self-respect and of one's neighbors." While in Europe he had learned of the dramatic capture of the elusive rebel leader Aguinaldo by his friend and favorite campfire story-spinner, Frederick Funston. Gaunt, with his skin tinted pale yellow from recurrent bouts of malaria, he climbed the steps of the War Department in an imposing and ornate building adjacent to the White House, where President William McKinley savored the ending of the Philippine Insurrection, and found his way to the office of the man who had done so much to foster his army service.

Awaiting the arrival of his protégé, and eager to listen to Mitchell's first-hand account of his achievements in the Philippines, General Greely was a commander facing a quandary. Thirty-five years after Secretary of State William Seward had negotiated a treaty with Russia for the sale of Alaska to the United States, and five years after the discovery of gold on Bonanza Creek in the Yukon region had unleashed what newspapers colorfully termed a gold rush that surpassed that of the gold strike in California in 1849, attempts by the Signal Corps to link the sprawling new northern territory's interior regions to the United States had failed. While the Signal Corps had been successful in laying an underwater telegraph cable between Seattle, Washington, and the Alaskan seaport of Valdez, the closest inland telegraph line, built by the Canadians, was located at Dawson City, approximately one hundred miles from the eastern Alaskan border. Two of Greely's officers who had been sent to survey the challenge had returned to report their opinion that because of daunting terrain and climate, stringing even a single wire across a vast interior that was frozen solid in winter and soggy in the summer was an impossibility.

Despite this verdict, Greely had set out for Alaska in 1900, at the age of fifty-six, to assess the situation. Having endured hardships of living in the Arctic during an exploration that had made him both famous and controversial, he returned to write an optimistic report. His survey, he noted, afforded him "invaluable knowledge" as to "topographical features of line construction" that confirmed his belief "that such a line could be built and operated, despite the predictions of many persons of Alaskan experience that such work was impossible of execution."

With only thirty-five officers in the Signal Corps, including himself, Greely desperately needed a man who possessed not only the experience of running telegraph line under hard conditions in difficult terrain, but qualities that the army could not command by issuing an order—youth and enthusiasm. Deciding that just the man he needed was Lieutenant William Mitchell, he wasted no time in broaching the subject of a new assignment. Having gone to Greely's office to resign from the army, the young officer was astonished to hear, "Billy, I think I may have something for you. Something you're going to like. Something that will suit you right down to the ground, and give you a splendid opportunity. How would you like to go to Alaska?"

As Greely described a task that would involve studying the challenge of establishing a telegraph line to Alaska's interior and reporting difficulties and possibilities, while serving as second in command of the Signal Corps in a territory that was half the size of the United States, Mitchell recalled Frederick Funston's campfire yarns of his experiences in Alaska, remembered the thrills and satisfactions of having strung wires in the jungles of the Philippines, weighed his decision to become a banker in Milwaukee against the prospect of an adventure that would test his mettle like none he had ever undertaken, and cast aside his plan to quit the army. "General," he said, "whatever you order me to do, I'll do it to the best of my ability, and be honored."

Beaming with delight, Greely promised Mitchell he would have orders in two days that would outline his duties. Receiving them on July 31, 1901, Mitchell wrote to his mother:

I have just been ordered to Alaska. The order came so unexpectedly that I hardly have time to pack. I have a great [assignment]. I don't understand why they gave me such a detail. But General Greely said to me that there is no one in the American Army who has had the amount of service in the same number of years that I have. It seems strange to me even. I am to be second in rank. If the [commander] should leave, that would make me Chief [Signal] Officer.

It will entail a great deal of travel and I shall see the whole interior as well. I am to have my own command at all times. It is certain I could not get the same from any line of business at my age. But afterwards, if there is nothing in sight but a long term of peace, I will quit the army.

Given a small detachment of enlisted men from Fort Myer, Virginia, he arrived a few days later in Seattle, Washington. The great outfitting point for the Alaskan gold fields, with a population of thirty thousand, the seaport was a wide-open town. Crowded with adventurers with eyes gleaming in anticipation of striking it rich, and hosting some who had done so and were heading for home to live on the proceeds, it bristled with saloons, dance halls, and gambling dens. One account noted, "Night was hideous with strident music, yells, brawls, and wild laughter under the flaring torches or the new electric lights, then just being installed. All sorts and conditions of men, bitten by fierce gold hunger, thronged the streets; lumberjacks shouldered with bankers, backsliding clergymen, escaped criminals, college professors, farmers, section hands, and absconding clerks spending their ex-employers' funds. Most traveled under assumed names."

On the evening of Mitchell's arrival, as he dined in the restaurant of the Rainier Grand Hotel, a prospector who had "hit it big" plunked a bag of gold dust on a table and roared to a waiter, "Bring me two-thousand dollars worth of ham and eggs."

Such flaunted new-found wealth and tales of men scooping handfuls of gold nuggets from the ground caused Mitchell to worry that men of his detail who earned fifteen dollars a month from the army might desert, but when his sergeant called the roll at dockside, all the men who had crossed the country from Fort Myer were accounted for as they boarded an old wooden steamer, *Cottage Queen*, bound for Alaska via the Inland Passage. He wrote to his mother:

Shall start for Skagway day after tomorrow. Have been collecting what information I can. The greatest trouble, it seems to me, with the building of a line in Alaska will be the labor problem. Laborers are scarce and get from $1 to $3 per hour. As the ground is frozen it takes at least one day to dig a hole and $8 or more is pretty expensive per hole. I shall probably recommend that Chinese coolies be employed to do this work and request that they let me go to China, say around Jaku, North China, or Manchuria to get the coolies and take them direct to Alaska. This would also give me a good trip.

From Skagway I shall go over the White Pass to the headwaters of the Yukon (in Canada), down the Yukon to Dawson and the White Horse rapids, and down to St. Michael, in all about 2,500 miles, the greatest trip one could take in Alaska.

I have my men with our arctic clothing all ready to start. If I can get through before the place freezes up I may be back in a few months. If not I will have to stay a year or possibly two years.

Good-by, dear, dear Mother, with love to all.

As the *Cottage Queen* chugged northward through the Inland Passage, he wrote home of "mountains which rise sheer from the water covered with enormous cedar trees, six or seven feet in diameter," narrow and extremely precipitous fiords running inland for miles, and "numbers of white-tailed deer and black and brown bears." Determined to miss none of it, he stood for hours on the bow of the wooden boat with the Scandinavian captain observing their progress toward Skagway. Called "the gateway to Alaska," it teemed with gold-seekers and those who knew that the easiest way to riches was to remain in Skagway as merchants and purveyors of everything that the prospectors needed and wanted.

Of this sojourn into the north Mitchell would later write, "Alaska attracted and interested me not only because it was our last frontier, but also because it represented a stepping-stone to Asia." As a veteran of the Philippines, and having visited Japan and China on his way home, he had come to believe, as did Theodore Roosevelt and other men with the desire to make the United States a world power, that the nation must not concede the Pacific. While thousands of men flocked into Skagway with dreams of riches, he was an army officer envisioning Alaska as a future bastion of army and naval bases linked to the War Department by telegraph lines stretched across the hardest terrain in the world. As a young man who enjoyed the outdoor life, he entertained the prospect of spending time "in the heart of one of the best hunting" regions in the world.

Departing Skagway after a few days, he and his small contingent boarded the first railway in Alaska, recently completed, for a 121-mile ride to White Horse. In Canada, it was the head of navigation on the Yukon River. Transferring to a small stern-wheel steamboat named the *White Horse*, the expedition traveled to Dawson City, Canada. In winter it was one of the coldest inhabited places in the world. With men and equipment shifted to a flatboat (forty feet long, fourteen feet wide), the next portion of the journey was via the Yukon to Eagle City and a U.S. army garrison under the command of Lieutenant Benjamin Tillman, a nephew of a colorful U.S. Senator, Ben "Pitchfork" Tillman of South Carolina.

Having arrived in August, Mitchell found himself swatting mosquitoes as vigorously as he had in the Philippines and discovered that the Alaskan earth in summer was as soft as swamps in the tropics and that pack horses could carry no more than two hundred pounds without sinking in the mud to their knees. Noting these conditions, he wrote, "It was evident to me that very little would be accomplished by attempting to transport material through this area in the summer, but in the winter these same animals could pull from a thousand to two thousand pounds over the frozen snow." Learning from both the locals and soldiers that the policy in winter was to "hole up" and attempt no outside work, he decided that if the telegraph lines were ever to be constructed, "the thing to do was to work clear through the winter, getting the material out—the wire, insulators, poles, food for the men and forage for the animals; then to actually construct the lines in the summer, when we could get into the ground and set the post holes."

Returning to the United States to recommend this strategy to General Greely, he offered his "services" in carrying out the plan. Endorsing the idea and accepting his offer, Greely drew up an order sending him back. When he reached White Pass, on the approach to Dawson, he found snow forty to fifty feet deep and the temperature at thirty-five degrees below zero. Traversing the pass by sledge with relays of horses, his destination was a small army garrison at Fort Egbert, with the goal of driving a line south to the coast at Prince William Sound. At the other end of the line at Valdez another work party, led by Lieutenant George Gibbs, was to push north. Both teams set out in the first week of January 1902, transporting all that would be needed to sink poles and string wires with the advent of the thawing spring.

With about one hundred miles left to be built in order to connect with the Gibbs team, the last stretch ran through the valley of the Tanana River. The lumberjacks working in crews of twenty, Mitchell recorded, were "great bearded men in blue denim clothing, high horsehide boots, slouch hats with remnants of mosquito netting around the edges." Without such men, he wrote, "the lines in the North could never have been completed."

On June 27, 1903, he made the last connection of the Alaska system himself. The first telegraph message to Washington, D.C., from the interior of Alaska, addressed to General A. W. Greely, read: "LINE THROUGH ALASKA COMPLETED. SIGNED WILLIAM MITCHELL."

"Alaska was open to civilization," the proud sender wrote in a later account of what he and his men had achieved. "No longer was it the land of the unknown, sealed tight by the god of everlasting snow and frost. We had broken the portal with which he shut out the white man from the North. We had worked straight through his coldest winters, over his highest mountains, down his broadest rivers, both in winter and summer. His mosquitoes had failed to stop us, and we not only had surmounted all the difficulties, but had grown intensely fond of this wonderful country. America's last frontier had been roped and hog-tied."

Often snowed-in, Mitchell had read with increasing fascination and excitement reports in engineering periodicals about aeronautical experiments by Otto Lillienthal, using gliders, and powered aircraft by Samuel P. Langley. But as the completion of his work neared, Mitchell once again pondered his future. In a letter to his father from Fort Egbert he wrote:

You know I always try to look ahead as far as possible and make my plans accordingly. . . . It seems best at this time to write to you about what my future work will be. After this is finished do you want me to come home and help you with business matters, or do you think it better for me to remain in the Army? You know I am fairly well adapted to army service and if I ever get a chance in the field I think I can do some-thing. But I think I could do fairly well in business too, if necessary.

The ambivalent letter continued:

In the last few years I hope I have shown you that I have some administrative ability, am fairly steady, and can be relied on to get through where other people have been unable to. As far as making money is concerned I am confident I could do pretty well, if I wanted to. It is evident that one can never get to the top of the ladder and be in command of an army in the Signal Corps. If I am going to stay in the Army that is the end I am going to work for. I should therefore have to transfer to another branch . . . I like the service, I like to have my command. I like service in the field and don't like to live in crowded cities. I am never so happy as when I lay out plans for construction of the lines, survey the routes, push the work, and, in between, hunt over these snow-covered mountains. But I want to do whatever you think is best for all the family.

For his accomplishment in Alaska, the U.S. Army rewarded him with promotion in rank, making him, at the age of twenty-three, its youngest captain.

CHAPTER FIVE

"AMBITIOUS AND WILLING"

S everal pounds heavier and with no trace of malaria, but having injured a knee that would plague him for much of his life, Captain William Mitchell returned from the adventures of connecting the "last frontier" to a country that since the Spanish-American War had expanded its territory deep into the Pacific to become a become a world power with a two-ocean navy and an army expanded to one hundred thousand men. When he left for Alaska, the commander-in-chief was William McKinley. As the result of his assassination in 1901, the president was now Theodore Roosevelt. With Cuba having been given independence, but with restrictions that left it a U.S. protectorate, and the Philippines having been largely pacified, the American people were rapidly reverting to an aversion to foreign entanglements that dated back to President Washington. Making it clear that he saw a necessary, rightful place for the nation on the world stage, Roosevelt warned the Congress in his first annual message, "Whether we desire it or not, we must henceforth recognize that we have international duties no less than international rights." If the United States were to preserve stability in the Western Hemisphere and retain its gains in the Pacific, he believed, the only means to do so was with naval power. "The American people must either build and maintain an adequate Navy," he said, "or else make their minds definitely to accept a secondary position in international affairs." Having declared in 1900 his "wish to see the United States the dominant power on the shores of the Pacific," he let it be known quickly as president that he intended to link the Atlantic and Pacific with a canal across the Isthmus of Panama. Rejecting the nation's historic embrace of isolationism and promoting the projection of American might across the oceans, he declared, "More and more, the increasing interdependence and complexity of international and political and economic relations render it incumbent on all civilized and orderly powers on the proper policing of the world."

On the day Roosevelt took the oath of office as president, the United States ranked fifth in naval power, with few battleships. By 1907, the U.S. Navy had twenty and stood behind only the British in fleet strength. Throughout the next thirty years the battleship would be the cornerstone of the navies of all world powers and the pride of admirals of the U.S. Navy who looked warily across the seven seas at potential future challenges from the Royal Navy, Germany, and Japan.

For the first large-scale training maneuvers by the U.S. Army since the months leading up to the war for the liberation of Cuba, William Mitchell traveled to Kentucky in the fall of 1903 amid rumors sweeping through the South that the "Yankees" were planning to renew the Civil War. But for the army's youngest captain, the only planning that mattered involved matrimony. Immediately before leaving for Alaska he had become engaged to childhood friend Caroline Stoddard. Telling his mother in a letter that "Caroline will probably be Mrs. William Mitchell some day," he cautioned that "there is no use saying anything about it to anyone yet." According to a Mitchell family story, neither his mother nor Mrs. Stoddard was surprised. Having lived in the same boarding school as girls, they had imagined that when they married, if one of them had a boy and the other a girl, their children would marry each other.

With wedding vows exchanged on December 2, 1903, the couple honeymooned in Cuba and Mexico. Finding that the excursion was often "a mission of investigation," the bride told her mother-in-law that on a tour of the Mexican countryside William studied the terrain and decided where the vantage position for an artillery battery would be "or how skillfully men could be deployed on the slopes, or if it is a historic spot, explain where the armies were stationed and tell us the entire story of the place."

There is no indication that the honeymooners heard of an historic event fifteen days after their wedding that would ultimately shape Mitchell's military career. On December 17, 1903, at Kitty Hawk, North Carolina, brothers Wilbur and Orville Wright, who had been in the bicycle business in Ohio, had demonstrated the practicability of motor-powered aircraft with a flight that went 852 feet and lasted 59 seconds. A first attempt three days earlier from Kill Devil Hill, with Wilbur Wright at the controls, had gone 105 feet in 3.5 seconds, but had ended in a crash. Nor is it noted whether Mitchell was aware that Samuel P. Langley's second and last trial of launching a gasoline-powered airplane from the rooftop of a houseboat on December 8 had failed when the craft crashed into the Potomac River.

Posted to Colorado in early 1904, Mitchell vowed not to become one of the officers that he described as "house rats" who did only what was required of them and spent their off-duty hours socializing. Continuing the reading of technical publications that had filled long, cold Alaska nights, he absorbed everything available on radio, motorized equipment, experiments in signal rockets, and the use of reconnaissance balloons. Reporting to his father, he wrote, "I have made a few drawings of new instruments and appliances which I shall forward to the Signal Office during the coming week. This and some investigations in balloon work have been my week's work. I have also been working on a new military signal rocket, which, if it works, will be a great thing,"

Invited by the *Denver Times* to tell about his Alaska experience, he made his first venture into public print on June 10, 1904. This would be followed by a more detailed account in an article entitled "How Uncle Sam Built the Alaska Telegraph" that was published in the September edition of the *National Geographic Magazine*."

Seven weeks after the *Denver Times* article appeared, he was informed by telegram from Milwaukee of the death of his father on June 29, 1904, at age sixty-two. Senator Mitchell's death came five years after retiring from the U.S. Senate and two years after returning to the United States from France, where he had studied at Grenoble University. With Milwaukee's public buildings draped in mourning bunting, he was buried near Mitchell family patriarch Alexander in Forest Home Cemetery.

Within weeks after returning to Colorado from the funeral, Captain Mitchell received an order to take part in extensive war games at Manassas, Virginia. Vividly recalling Mitchell's ingenuity years later, an early army comrade, and the future commander of U.S. Army Air Forces in World War II, General Henry H. "Hap" Arnold, wrote, "One of the first things Mitchell did, unbeknownst to anyone else, was to select the highest hill in that part of the country and put up a two hundred foot tower. The day the maneuvers started, Mitchell climbed to the top of the tower and with the aid of high-powered field glasses was able to pick up the enemy while they were concentrating for deployment on the field of battle. He identified the different units so positively that as soon as his army commander secured the information, the war was over and they had to start a new war and rule out Mitchell and his high tower."

During these maneuvers, Mitchell also claimed the distinction of using the army's first automobile. With the war games ended he found himself again posted to Fort Myer with orders to organize and equip the first field company of the Signal Corps, then proceed with it from the nation's capital to Fort Leavenworth, Kansas. Stopping in St. Louis, he and his men visited the city's World's Fair, officially named The Lewis and Clark Centennial Exposition, forever to be remembered for the popular song "Meet Me in St. Louis." Of considerably more interest to him than the fair's extensive use of electric lights was an aeronautical attraction in the form of a small dirigible, the *California Arrow*, powered by a Glenn Curtiss engine.

While stationed at Fort Leavenworth, Mitchell organized the first field radio station and conducted experiments with kites to carry telegraph wires, resulting in a world record for distance in radio communication using army equipment. A wire lifted ten thousand feet in the air by kite picked up a transmission from the steamer *Navarik* as it was sailing into the harbor of San Juan, Puerto Rico, a distance of nineteen hundred miles. Mitchell repeated the achievement the next night by catching a transmission from the steamer *Concho* as it left Key West, Florida.

"The signals were slow and heavy and at a rather low key," he recalled. "The radiogram was addressed to 'Miss Mamie Fisher, 408 San Joaquin Street, Houston, Texas.' As her name was pronounced, a lieutenant standing beside me, named Olney Place, exclaimed, 'Why, I have known that young lady for many years.'"

Having impressed his superiors, he was appointed an instructor of radio communications at the Infantry and Cavalry School of the Army Staff College at Fort Leavenworth. His lectures were so authoritative that they were published as textbooks for other military schools. Joining the Field Artillery Board at Fort Riley, Kansas, in 1905, he sponsored the army's adoption of the use of telephonic communications in controlling the firing of artillery, pioneered in photography from kites, and wrote an article for *Cavalry Journal* in which he predicted that wars would be waged "in the air, on the surface of the earth and water, and under the earth and water."

A few weeks after this article was published, an urgent order was flashed from the War Department directing Mitchell and his Signal Corps field unit from Fort Leavenworth to the site of a calamity half a continent away. In a titanic shifting of the earth at 4:15 a.m. on April 18, 1906, the city of San Francisco had been almost entirely reduced to rubble in a matter of seconds. Outbreaks of fire threatened to consume what was left. Delayed in obtaining a special train, he and his men reached the stricken City by the Bay on the third day following the most devastating earthquake in American history.

Upon his arrival Mitchell learned that the U.S. Army, based at the

Presidio, was under the command of General Adolphus Greely, but that Greely had been absent from the city at the time of the quake to attend the wedding of a daughter. His second in command was Frederick Funston, now a general. Keenly aware that fate in the form of nature had reunited him with the two men who had done so much to shape his own army career, Mitchell located Funston and was told that all lines of transportation and communication were destroyed or disrupted. What was urgently required, said Funston, was to establish telegraphic contact with Oakland, across the bay. As they conferred, the city shook with the force of explosions as dynamite was set off across the city to create firebreaks and prevent the inferno from enveloping everything. As ranking army officer, Funston had ordered fourteen hundred troops into the streets and summoned sailors from the nearby Mare Island Naval Shipyard, California Naval Militia, and National Guardsmen to duty in what became in effect a declaration of martial law. "There was no legal authority whatever for doing this," Mitchell correctly recalled, "but the law of necessity and humanity dictated the action."

Describing his own efforts to bring order out of chaos, he wrote, "We went to work right away [to establish] communication all over the city and with the outside world." This required ingenuity. To open a line to a Western Union office in Oakland, he opened a post at San Francisco's relatively undamaged, towering Ferry Building. Using wire cut from electric lines that had been felled by the quake and pieces of snapped streetcar cables, Mitchell's Signal Corpsmen rigged a connection to a line that ran on the bottom of the bay to the Oakland side. With communication to the rest of the country re-established, General Funston assigned Mitchell to the command of the largest of six districts established to organize the fire fighting, ensure law and order, and provide relief to thousands of the homeless and dispossessed. When General Greely sent his first report to the War Department in Washington, he noted that in the week after the earthquake and fire the army had issued a million rations to feed two hundred and fifty thousand people, more than half the city's population.

"It was a revelation to me," wrote Mitchell of his San Francisco experience, "to see men who were masters of business and captains of industry utterly at a loss and incapable of any initiative in such a terrible emergency; and it was equally interesting to see how officers of the military service, from second lieutenant up, who were trained to act definitely and quickly in emergencies, did exactly the right thing under the most trying and difficult circumstances."

Six months after rushing to the West Coast, he found himself under orders to respond to a crisis on the island whose suffering under Spanish rule in 1898 had stirred him to join the army. Struggling to adapt to the freedom and self-government that American intervention had given them, Cubans in the fall of 1906 were again on the verge of civil war. Feeling pressured to send soldiers to settle the matter, President Theodore Roosevelt exclaimed to a friend in September, "Just at the moment I am so angry with the infernal little Cuban republic that I would like to wipe its people off the face of the earth. All we have wanted from them is that they would behave themselves and be prosperous and happy so that we would not have to intervene. And now, lo and behold, they have started an utterly unjustifiable and pointless revolution and may get things into such a snarl that we have no alternative save to intervene—which will at once convince the suspicious idiots in South America that we do wish to intervene after all, and perhaps have some land hunger."

The consequence of the return of the American military to Cuba for Captain Mitchell was an order to proceed to the island as chief signal officer to reorganize and rebuild the telegraph system. Having supervised construction of the first high-powered wireless station in Cuba, and with the fledgling republic reasonably stabilized, he returned to Fort Leavenworth and began a period of studies at the Army School of the Line and the Army Staff College, graduating "with distinction." An evaluation report that was typical of the assessments of his ability provided by his superior officers noted, "Captain Mitchell is an earnest, zealous, efficient young officer, intensely interested in his professional work [and] an enthusiast in whatever he undertakes. One of the most indefatigable workers I have ever known. Presentable and agreeable personality; courageous and subordinate, cheerful and sanguine, [an officer who] will undertake to accomplish anything; ambitious and willing."

Although he was posted to Fort Myer, Virginia, in August 1908, there is no evidence that he was present on the day that the Signal Corps took delivery of the first "flying machine" ordered by the army from the Wright brothers. He did meet Orville Wright, along with the U.S. Army's first aviators, Lieutenants Frank Lahm and Frederic Humphreys, but was not on hand to witness the official test flight on September 17 that ended in a crash, the death of Lieutenant Thomas Selfridge (aviation's first fatality), and serious injury to Orville Wright.

Directed to return to the Philippines in 1909 as chief signal officer for the Department of Luzon, he devoted the next two years to studying the territory's defenses and contemplating the military and political realities of the western Pacific. Acting on suspicions that the Japanese had been building wireless stations on small islands near the Philippines, he engaged in espionage by donning civilian clothing and posing as a tourist aboard the ship *Mindanao* headed for Japanese waters. Secretly mapping the island of Botel Tobago, the southern coast of Formosa, and other islands north of Luzon, he braved three typhoons on the return voyage to Manila by way of Pratas Reef. Following the eruption of Luzon's Taal volcano in 1910, he acted on his own initiative and took his signal company to the scene and installed a communication system that facilitated the relief of the population.

Still intrigued by what the Japanese might be up to, he requested an overdue leave and went to Japan for the purpose of observing Japan's army in maneuvers and studying the structure of its order of battle. After noting that the Japanese had a fleet of twelve airplanes, he inspected troop dispositions in Korea, traveling on horseback, and moved north into Manchuria to visit the battlefields of the recent Russo-Japanese War, including explorations of Port Arthur, Mukden, and Harbin. Crossing the border to China, he spent time in Changchung witnessing a revolution against the Manchu dynasty. As the guest of honor of a republican warlord, Chang Tso-lin, he watched a victory parade of twenty thousand well-trained troops. Powerfully impressed, he later wrote, "If the uncounted millions of Chinese could be organized, equipped, and led properly, and if they were imbued with a national spirit, there is nothing they could not accomplish."

But it was the potential power of Japan that most concerned him. "That increasing friction between Japan and the United States will take place in the future there can be little doubt," he wrote in 1910, "and that this will lead to war sooner or later seems quite certain."

Joined by his family at Yokohoma, Japan (he was now father of two daughters, Harriet and Elizabeth), he returned to the United States for a posting at Fort Russell, Wyoming, but was soon dispatched to El Paso, Texas, to build telegraph lines in support of the army's operations along the southern border at a time of revolution and unrest in Mexico. Compared to the jungles of Cuba and the Philippines and the winters of Alaska, the task of erecting poles and stringing of wires across Texas was almost effortless. With plenty of time off, he indulged his lifelong love of riding with a horse named Peanuts and hunting by pursuing black-tailed deer and jaguar in the Sacramento Mountains. While tracking an especially elusive jaguar that had escaped into a cave near El Paso, and planning to force it out of its den with smoke grenades "consisting of woolen yarn dipped in turpentine, then rolled in red pepper and gunpowder" that would be set afire and flung into the cave, he received orders to report to the War Department to join the general staff.

At thirty-two, he was the youngest officer in the history of the army to be elevated to its highest echelon. "It is the most sought-after position which a military man can aspire to," he wrote to his mother. It will be the greatest thing in my career so far. I may be a general before many years have passed."

PART II

THE GREAT ADVENTURE

CHAPTER SIX

EXPERT WITNESS

S ettling with wife and daughters in a large house on Q Street, William Mitchell had not resided in the nation's capital since he joined the army in 1898. In those fourteen years he had fought *insurrectos* in Cuba and the Philippines, strung telegraph wires to connect Alaska to the world and earthquake-ruined San Francisco with the rest of the country, and risen from private of Wisconsin Volunteers to the rank of captain in the regular army and intelligence officer in the War Department. "I am practically committed to the Army as a career," he told his mother in a letter from the house on Q Street, "and am already probably too old to change, although I do not feel so myself."

A handsome young couple with the added attraction of coming from two wealthy families, Captain and Mrs. Mitchell were immediately welcomed into the whirl of capital city society that was buzzing with talk of a presidential election in which Theodore Roosevelt had announced that his hat was in the ring and he was "fit as a bull moose." Ready for a political comeback and a third term in the White House after four disappointing presidential years of his hand-picked heir, William Howard Taft, "Teddy" was running as the Progressive "Bull Moose" Party's candidate against Taft and Democrat Woodrow Wilson. Accepting the Progressive nomination, he rallied convention delegates with a "Confession of Faith" speech. "Our cause," he declared, "is based on the eternal principles of righteousness; and even though we who now lead may for the time fail, in the end the cause itself shall triumph. We stand at Armageddon, and we battle for the Lord!"

The grandson and son of Democrats who served in both branches of Congress, Mitchell had chosen an army career over politics, but now found himself working at a desk in a building adjacent to the White House and attending dinner parties and other social galas where politics seemed to be the only topic. He was also acutely aware that his elevation to the general staff had in part been the result of War Department politics. "All the general officers I have served with are good friends," he admitted to his mother. "My trip to Manchuria and my report had considerable to do with it, I imagine. This combined with the fact that there is not a spot on my record [and my] knowledge of horses and shooting have done it."

Arriving in Washington with a reputation as one of the army's most skillful equestrians, he found himself invited to shows and hunts, not only in the Virginia horse country, but estates in Long Island, New York, where polo was the rage. Within his circle of acquaintances and friends, civilian and military, he gained admiration for his natural skills at riding, swinging at a ball with a mallet from the back of a polo pony, fishing, and tennis. At the dinner table he charmed everyone with tales of his adventures from the tropics to the frozen North, in China and Japan, and amid the rubble-strewn streets of San Francisco. Hostesses and their guests also listened patiently to him talk of his "certainty" that the United States and Germany would eventually be at war with each other, but that the U.S. military was woefully unready.

In his seven years between marriage and appointment to the U.S. Army General Staff in 1910, the first step toward proving that wars of the future would necessarily involve the use of airplanes in a decisive manner was taken by President Theodore Roosevelt. At the urging of Cortlandt F. Bishop, president of the Aero Club of New York, which was founded in November 1905, Roosevelt authorized the army to enter into a contract with the Wright brothers for development of a military airplane. This resulted in creation of an aeronautical division in August 1907. Based on the assumption that aircraft would be simply an extension of the Signal

Corps' responsibility since the Civil War for gathering of battlefield intelligence, the unit was placed in the Office of the Chief Signal Officer, General James Allen (Greely had retired). Comprising two enlisted men and an officer, Captain Charles Chandler, the new division was directed to "study the flying machine and the possibility of adapting it to military purposes."

Following the allocation of $25,000 for "procurement of an airship" by the Army Board of Ordnance and Fortification three months later, Wilbur Wright offered the government an airplane for exactly that amount. The board recommended that the Signal Corps submit specifications. On December 23, 1907, the Chief Signal Officer called for bids for a lighter-than-air craft (dirigible) and a "flying machine" (airplane). The Board awarded a contract for both to J. F. Scott and A. M. Herring and a contract for an airplane to the Wrights, signed on February 10, 1908, by Captain Charles S. Wallace on behalf of the Signal Corps. When Scott and Herring failed to produce either a dirigible or an airplane, the lighter-than-air project was awarded to Thomas S. Baldwin, leaving the Wright brothers unchallenged in plane development. Although tests of balloons were conducted under the supervision of Lieutenant Frank P. Lahm in the summer of 1908, resulting in the acquisition in August of Army Dirigible No. 1, the Wrights did not conduct their test flight until September 3, at Fort Myer, Virginia, with Orville Wright at the controls. Six days later, Lahm became the first passenger on a Wright Flyer.

Undaunted by the death of Lieutenant Thomas Selfridge in the crash of a Wright Flyer on September 17, 1908, the army continued the trials, culminating in the purchase in August 1909 of a Wright plane for $30,000. The first army officer to fly it solo was Lieutenant Frank E. Humphreys, on October 26, at College Park, Maryland. With an appropriation by Congress of $125,000 for "air operations" on March 3, 1911, the army established its first permanent flying school at College Park, with a request that four hangars be built. A second school would be opened at Augusta, Georgia, and another in the Philippines.

Although Captain William Mitchell's duties as a staff officer gave him no responsibility for aircraft development, he retained the interest in aviation that had occupied his spare time in the Alaskan wilderness and at various posts following his return. Placed in charge of watching all military developments occurring in Europe at a time when wars were being fought in the Balkans (1912–1914), he noted that twenty-six nations had spent more than $100 million—almost $4 million each—on the development of aircraft while the United States had committed less than $2 million total. Of more than two thousand pilots in the world, the United States had fewer than fifty. Whereas France had built an air service with fourteen hundred planes, the combined air fleet of the United States Army and Navy was seven. Mitchell also noted that in a siege of Adrianople in the First Balkan War (1912–1913), Bulgarian aviators had dropped small bombs that caused little damage but created widespread panic. In the Dardanelles airplanes flown by Greeks had attempted to bomb warships, the first such attack in history.

In the year before receiving the order to join the general staff in Washington, Mitchell had noted that at the San Francisco Air Meet (held at Tanforan Racetrack on January 15, 1911) Lieutenant Myron S. Crissy, flying with P. O. Parmalee, had dropped a bomb and hit a target from a Wright Flyer. The next day, Infantry Lieutenant G. E. M. Kelly, in a Wright airplane piloted by Walter Brookins at an altitude of two thousand feet, carried out an experiment in aerial photographic reconnaissance in the San Bruno Hills. This was followed by a landing and takeoff of a Curtiss Pusher airplane on the afterdeck of the anchored battleship *Pennsylvania* by exhibition pilot Eugene Ely. A month later, Glenn H. Curtiss flew one of his Seaplanes to the *Pennsylvania* in San Diego harbor, demonstrating the practical use of amphibian aircraft. This so impressed the navy that it ordered one of the planes in May, designating it U.S. Navy A-1. In August the navy acquired a Wright Flyer, delivered by Orville

Wright at Annapolis, Maryland.

Mitchell also noted that on January 21, 1911, Lieutenant Paul W. Beck made the army's first radio-telegraphic transmission from an airplane from an altitude of 100 feet to a station at Selfridge Field, Michigan, a mile and a half away. Pilots were setting speed and distance records. On January 30, in the longest over-water flight to date, J. A. D. McCurdy took a Curtiss Hydroplane from Key West, Florida, to a spot ten miles outside Havana, Cuba, where he was picked up by a U.S. Navy torpedo boat. Flying from North Island, San Diego, on February 7, 1911, Harry S. Harkness carried a military message twenty-one miles to a U.S. troop encampment at Tijuana, Mexico, in twenty-five minutes. In August, Lincoln Beachey won the Gimbel Prize of $5,000 by flying from New York to Philadelphia in an elapsed time of one hour, fifty minutes, and eight seconds with one stop for fuel. On August 20, he set a new American altitude record of 10,837 feet at an air meet in Chicago. Five months later, an Army altitude record—4,674 feet—was set at the Army Aviation School at Augusta, Georgia, in a flight that lasted fifty minutes.

The pilot, Lieutenant H. H. Arnold, was born in the Philadelphia suburb of Gladwyne, Pennsylvania, on June 25, 1886. Named Henry Harley after a great, great grandfather who had been a private in the state's militia in the Revolutionary War, he had another relative who had served with General George Washington. During the Civil War, Henry's grandfather, Thomas G. Arnold, fought at the Battle of Gettysburg. His father, Herbert, was a physician in the Spanish-American War, serving in Puerto Rico in 1898. When his bother Thomas declined to accept an appointment to the U.S. Military Academy at West Point, it fell to Henry to carry on the family's military tradition. Graduated in 1908 with a commission in the infantry, he served two years in the Philippines, followed by two at Governors Island in New York City. Transferred to the Signal Corps Aeronautical Division in April 1911, he earned his pilot's certificate in June after receiving instruction from Orville Wright, and then served as an instructor at the army's new aviation school, inaugurated on April 11, 1911, at College Park, Maryland. In September he flew the first U.S. airmail and on the last day of that month performed as stunt man for the leading actor in the first motion picture about flying, titled *The Military Air Scout* and filmed at Nassau Boulevard, New York, following an air meet by the Aero Club of America. On June 1, 1912, he received the first Charles H. Mackay Trophy, given by the War Department for the most meritorious flight of the year. Because of his genial personality, happy disposition, and almost constant smile while at West Point, he had been given the nickname "Hap."

Although the date of his first meeting at the flying school in College Park with the Signal Corps captain and member of the U.S. Army General Staff known to his comrades as "Billy" is not recorded, Arnold remembered "a sharp faced eager young captain" who was "full of talk of Alaska and the air forces of Japan, and intent upon learning." Recalling that Mitchell's questions "about the air were intelligent and to the point," he noted that it was Mitchell "who did most of the talking, asking questions only to get concrete facts." Impressed by his earnestness, Arnold introduced him to other aviators, including Lahm, Humphreys, and Benjamin Foulois.

Like Mitchell, Foulois had enlisted as a volunteer in the Spanish-American War and joined the infantry as a private. Commissioned lieutenant in 1901, he served in the infantry until 1908. Graduated from Signal School in 1908, he was assigned to the Office of Chief Signal Officer, Washington, D.C., and operated the first dirigible purchased by the U.S. government. One of the first three officers in the army to operate the first military airplane purchased from the Wright brothers in 1909, he accompanied Orville Wright on the final trial flight from Fort Myer. Transferred to Fort Sam Houston, San Antonio, Texas, he became the army's officially designated "aviator." An instructor, observer, and commander in the heavier-than-air division from November 1909 to April

1911, he made numerous mechanical improvements on the Wright airplane, including replacing landing skids with wheels. Using written instructions from the Wright brothers, he taught himself to fly. From May to July 1911 he was with the Maneuver Division at San Antonio. While there, he designed and used the first radio receiving set in a military airplane. He also broke a world cross-country record with a passenger, and carried out the first aerial reconnaissance flights. Because of a deepening conviction that the airplane was essential in the structure of the nation's defenses, Mitchell expressed himself on the subject at dinner parties, during horseback rides, and at social functions attended by members of Congress. Consequently, when a bill to create an aviation branch separate from the Signal Corps was introduced in August 1913 and referred to the Military Affairs Committee of the House of Representatives, he was called to testify as an expert witness, along with Arnold and Foulois. The position of the Signal Corps was that "time for creation of a separate, experimental force has not yet arrived."

Adhering to this policy when he appeared for the first time before a committee of the Congress, Mitchell described the proposal as "a mistake." Seeing "all sorts of complications," he forcefully argued for keeping aviation within the Signal Corps and urged the Congress to provide "inducements" in the way of recruitment of aviators and "rapid promotion" of officers who took up flying. While the airplane had a future in warfare, he said, much more experimentation was required into its use as a weapon. Noting that aviation was a branch of the reconnaissance arm of the military which had proved its value, while its offensive power was still in the experimental stage, he ventured that some day, instead of airplanes being an adjunct to "lines of information, the lines of information may grow to be an adjunct to the airplanes, and very probably will."

When the hearing concluded, the committee agreed to leave military aviation within the Signal Corps, then invited Mitchell to draft the legislation. Suddenly recognized on Capitol Hill as not only an expert on aviation, but a source of information because of his role in gathering and analysis of foreign intelligence, he frequently briefed members of the House and Senate on events in a Europe teetering on the brink of war. When it commenced in August 1914 with Germany's forces smashing into the Low Countries and France, he wrote to his mother, "People who have not studied the German organization in every line do not appreciate what a wonderful and coordinated empire it is, both for war and in peace. We may run up against it before many years are over, or against an almost equally well organized one, Japan."

Assigned to keep up-to-date war maps in the War Department, the White House, and on Capitol Hill, he began contemplating the role of the United States in the new world order that he anticipated arising from the European conflict. But as these events unfolded, he was stricken with inflammatory rheumatism that resulted from the leg injury he suffered in Alaska. Recalling this in a biography of her brother, Ruth Mitchell wrote, "The doctor warned him that it had affected his heart and if he wished to live he must give up forever all strenuous exercise. He must never again take any risks, must never again play polo or even tennis. He must, in fact, resign from the army. Bill laughed. He had entirely different plans and was not going to allow any foolishness of his internal pump to interfere with them. He therefore gritted his teeth and lay for three months on his back, absolutely supine without moving a muscle, to give his heart a chance to think it over and get back on the job."

Although bedridden, Mitchell was able to write. Adopting a pen name because of army regulations against an officer publishing articles, he began a military affairs column for the *Chicago Tribune* and wrote an anonymous article on the European war for the magazine *World's Work*. He recovered sufficiently in 1915 to give a lecture to a group of engineers. Noting that it took the United States three years to field an effective army in the Civil War, he speculated that it might take as long "for this war."

One of the engineers asked, "Have we got a Navy?"

Mitchell answered, "Well, I'm an Army man and supposed to know very little about the Navy, but I hear we have several pretty good ships."

These remarks were reported by a Washington newspaper with the headline:

SAYS FOE CAN TAKE U.S.
ERE ARMY IS RAISED
Capt. Mitchell, U.S. Army General
Staff, Gives Startling Military Facts
NOT SURE WE HAVE A NAVY

Called to account by the War Department, Mitchell explained that the newspaper had misquoted him, and provided the text of his lecture. Exonerating him, the army in the person of Major General Hugh L. "Three Fingers" Scott, issued an order forbidding any officer to express an opinion on any subject publicly. This edict did not apply to a paper that Mitchell delivered to the Army War College in July 1915 that he titled "Our Faulty Military Policy."

Noting that Americans "for many years have looked upon our isolated geographical position as so good a defense against aggression that even consideration of questions of military policy was wholly unnecessary," and that the policy of the United States government "is and has been to prepare for war *after such war has actually broken out* [Mitchell's emphasis], and to have practically no machinery in time of peace with which an army could be created with rapidity," he warned that without "preparation in time of peace, no nation today has the remotest chance of defending itself against a world power." Calling for the implementation of a compulsory selective service system, he urged creation of a Council of National Defense in which the War Department (the army) and Navy Department would be merged "under one roof and the duties of the two services could be correlated."

Soon after making these controversial recommendations, perhaps by coincidence, he was described in an efficiency report as "better suited to active service with troops than on General Staff duty." The assessment saw him especially suited to serve as "an efficient aide-de-camp to a general in the field." Along with the judgment by a superior officer that he was very capable and alert, demonstrating "resourcefulness and initiative in an emergency," came promotion to a rank suitable for an aide to a general. Pinning the bronze oak leaves of major on his uniform, he was thirty-six years old, with a strengthened heart, but complaining that "the rheumatism stays a little in my hands and shoulders and does not seem to want to leave." He pondered his future and saw himself leaving the general staff and returning to field duty as an officer in the Aviation Section that he had persuaded Congress to leave within the Signal Corps, then climbing into the seat of an airplane and learning how to fly. "The only time I could get away [from General Staff duties] was on Sunday," he noted in his diary. Taking a boat down the Potomac River from Washington to Newport News on Saturday night, he would fly all day Sunday and be back in the office at the War Department on Monday.

When he met his instructor, Jimmy Johnson, he said, "Let's get this straight. You forget I'm an Army major, and treat me like anyone else who's here to learn."

Although Johnson found him "quick and self-confident," he was reluctant to permit him to solo as quickly as Mitchell desired. The opportunity came on a day when Johnson was ill and replaced by Walter Lees. Discovering that when Mitchell "really wanted anything, he could be 'pretty persuasive,'" the substitute instructor was "fast-talked into letting him solo" twice that day.

During a third solo flight the next Sunday in a Jenny airplane, with Johnson anxiously observing, Mitchell leveled off too high for landing on the rough grass field and flipped the Jenny onto its back. Rushing to Mitchell, Johnson asked, "Are you all right?"

Dangling upside down in the cockpit, Mitchell asked, "What did I do wrong?"

Of the crash he said, "It taught me more than anything that ever happened to me in the air."

By mid-January 1917, after five months of training, fifteen hours of instruction, and thirty-six flights, at a cost of $1,470, of which the army paid only $500, he was a certified army aviator. Transferred to the Aviation Section, an organization that his testimony before the House Military Affairs Committee helped to ensure remained part of the Signal Corps, he served under an old friend from Fort Leavenworth, Colonel George O. Squier, who commanded 35 pilots, 4,987 enlisted men, and 55 training airplanes.

Assessing the war in Europe that had been raging since August of 1914, Mitchell was "firmly convinced" that the Allied Powers, led by England and France, could not defeat Germany and its allies "without entrance of the United States into the conflict." With ground action on the Western Front a "practical stalemate as early as 1916," he would later write, and the "Russian menace" removed from the German rear lines by the destruction of the Russian army, "the war had settled down to a gruesome competition to see who could kill the greatest number of men on the other side." The art of war had departed, he noted in his *Memoirs of World War I.* "Attrition, or the gradual killing off of the enemy, was all the ground armies were capable of. The high command of neither army could bring about a decision, and the alarming conviction was beginning to dawn on the world that it must stand by and witness European civilization being destroyed and ruined for many years, if not for all time."

At the start of the war, cables reaching his desk from London reported that the French possessed about 1,500 military aircraft. Germany claimed 1,000. Britain's Royal Flying Corps (RFC), under command of Brigadier General Sir David Henderson, had only 179 planes and 2,073 men, but on August 23, 1914, a British plane carrying out one of the first reconnaissance patrols in France detected a German corps moving toward the British front. Two days later, three planes of No. 2 Squadron, RFC, with their pilots and observers armed with rifles and pistols, forced down a German plane. In the first air combat of the war in January 1915, a German airman was killed by rifle fire from an Allied aircraft. A month later, French pilot Lieutenant Roland Geros was the first to shoot down a German plane with a wing-mounted machine gun, a few weeks before the German aircraft builder Anthony H. G. Fokker perfected synchronizing gear to allow a machine gun to fire through a rotating propellor.

Mitchell also observed that on March 15, 1916, the first U.S. tactical air unit in the field, designated 1st Aero Squadron, commanded by Captain Benjamin Foulois, began operations with General John J. Pershing's expedition into Mexico in pursuit of rebel leader Pancho Villa. Six days later in France, the French air department authorized creation of a volunteer American air unit, the Escadrille Americaine, later to become known as the Lafayette Escadrille. On March 20, 1916, the French medaille militaire was presented to the first American aviator, Sergeant Major Elliott Cowdin. On June 18, H. Clyde Balsley of the Lafayette Escadrille was the first American to be shot down, crashing near Verdun. During the Battle of the Somme (July to November), the Royal Flying Corps established air superiority over the German line and some thirty miles behind it. In contrast to ground activities, Mitchell observed, air services were "increasing in importance and effectiveness, and it was quite apparent to me that if the war lasted until 1919 or 1920, air power would be the deciding element."

Still, American public opinion was against the country's entering the war, and Woodrow Wilson had pledged in his successful campaigns for the presidency in 1912 and 1916 that he would not take the country to war. Such thinking was impeding those in government, like Major Mitchell, who believed that U.S. involvement was inevitable. They were also frustrated by what Mitchell saw as the "almost impossible" task of awakening "the slow working minds of our regular army officers to any action." While a few showed "a passing interest," he noted, "there was practically no effort made to revise the old military system we had been using since the Civil War. In spite of the fact that foreigners were ordering a great number of aircraft in this country and taking many of our best young men into their services, we still sat by and did practically nothing."

As a private in the Spanish-American War in 1898, he had longed to fight in Cuba. When the rebellion began in the Philippines, he had begged for battle. Now a major in the air service, he yearned to test his freshly acquired skills as a pilot in a war that he believed would ultimately be settled by air power. Envisioning a significant and possibly decisive role for the air service, he decided to "seek service in Europe and learn as much as possible," and hoped that the United States would either recognize its duty to save the world for democracy, or be drawn into the conflict by events beyond American control. Learning that the army planned to send a five-man party of observers to France, he launched a campaign among his superiors to be included that in the view of one observer amounted to "badgering." This effort culminated in an order on March 3, 1917, directing him to report to the U.S. ambassador in Paris "for the specific purpose of observing the manufacture and development of aircraft, and to report on French methods of combat, training, and organization of airmen."

Hap Arnold thought that Mitchell had "inadvertently" achieved his goal because the high command saw his departure as a way to stifle his criticisms of them. Having gotten "permission to go to Europe as a military observer for aviation," in Mitchell's phrasing in his World War I memoirs, he left Washington on St. Patrick's Day for Havana, Cuba, where he would board the Spanish ship *Alfonso XIII*, bound for Corunna, Spain. During the crossing, he wondered if Spain were capable of playing a decisive role in the war by choosing to side with Germany to avenge Spain's brutal treatment by the French under Napoleon. When he arrived, he found Spain "in rather a nervous state" and "flooded with spies from all countries." Newspapers were "filled with propaganda put out by the agents of every belligerent country in Europe in an effort to influence the people's minds." The English were afraid the Germans might induce the Spanish government to attack France. King Alfonso was, after all, related to the Austrian emperor. Germany feared that the English would prevail upon Spain's Queen Victoria, a British princess and namesake of Britain's late queen, to use her influence to enter the war on the Allied side. All were suspicious of the American army's Major Mitchell. "Where ever I went," he noted, "I was watched by one side or the other, or both of them together."

Assessing the potential value of Spanish intervention on either side, Mitchell decided that Spain had too many internal problems, the country's industries were incapable of "rapidly turning out great quantities of munitions," and the troops themselves were poorly armed and trained. His only positive comment on Spain's military capacity concerned "the wonderful new Hispano-Suiza airplane engine that had been invented there."

Although he had expected the United States to enter the war "for some time," Mitchell was "startled" by the actual declaration of war, voted by Congress at Wilson's request, on April 6, 1917. Setting out immediately for the town of Santander, he crossed the French border, hurried to Paris, arrived on April 10, and began preparing for a kind of warfare that was new to him and to the nation that had sent him.

CHAPTER SEVEN

"FOOLISH KIND OF WAR"

A lthough Mitchell had learned French before English, he had stopped speaking it as a boy growing up in Milwaukee because schoolmates had teased him and called him "Froggie." But as he traveled by train from Spain toward Paris on April 8, he remembered enough of the language to understand the conversation of passengers. Their subject was an imminent "great attack" and a "spring offensive" with French and British armies simultaneously assailing the Hindenburg Line of the Germans at Arras, Vimy Ridge, and along the river Aisne. This bold initiative, he learned, was the consequence of the dismissal by the Chamber of Deputies of General Joseph Joffre. The man who had "saved France" at the Battle of the Marne in 1914 had refused to launch an attack that he believed would be vastly out of proportion to results obtained. His replacement, General Robert Nivelle, was "committed" to an offensive.

Arriving in Paris on April 10, Mitchell found front pages of newspapers full of accounts of success. The previous day, Easter Monday, British and Canadian forces had overrun almost the entire German frontline trenches in less than two hours, capturing nearly ten thousand enemy. The victory was attributed in large measure to a new artillery tactic. Called a "creeping barrage," it involved the firing of guns advancing steadily, with infantry following closely behind. Of more interest to Mitchell was that for five days prior to the ground attack, British pilots fought to clear the skies of German planes to allow British aerial reconnaissance of the battlefield. In the ensuing combat, the Royal Flying Corps suffered eighteen pilots killed and seventy-five aircraft shot down.

Recalling this ground assault in his *Memoirs of World War I*, Mitchell noted that it ultimately failed because the Germans anticipated it. As they "retired from the front," destroying everything in a region of thirty miles, they "left the British army high and dry" for at least two months, unable to cross the area with their heavy guns, ammunition, and supplies in time to attack the Germans before the spring was over. "What a foolish kind of war this seemed," he wrote, "where an army could not advance twenty or thirty miles for months, even with nobody opposing them! How could such an army ever possibly win a war, except by indirect pressure? It seemed to me that the utility of ground armies was rapidly falling to about zero, due to the great defensive power of modern firearms."

Wearing civilian clothing, he hurried from the train station to the U.S. embassy to report to ambassador William Graves Sharp, and then to the office of the military attaché, where he met Majors James A. Logan and Marlborough Churchill, an American with two names that were famous in the military history of England. He was a graduate of Harvard University and had served in the U.S. Army infantry and artillery until assigned to serve as the American military observer in France in January 1916. Writing in his memoir that Logan and Churchill "merit more than passing notice, as few officers in our history have rendered as valuable a service to their country and received so little credit," Mitchell recorded:

> Long before our declaration of war, they had laid out in remarkable detail plans which included the designation of ports at which American troops should be debarked, the railroads they should use, the areas to which they should be assigned for training, what their organization should consist of, their points of supply, locations for hospitals, military schools, parks for motor vehicles, horses and mules. They thoroughly realized that our regular army, bound by red tape and obsolete traditions, would be unequal to the task of organizing, training and handling the vast hordes we were about to

throw into the contest, [but that] French and British officers of experience had to direct that.

Recognizing that they had little knowledge of what would be needed to organize an air service, and content to turn such matters over to an aviator, Logan and Churchill assisted Mitchell in finding a location for his office. At 49 Boulevard Hausemann, the space was donated by the American Radiator Company because Mitchell had no funds to rent space, and no authorization from Washington to do so. Coordinating his activities with the French, he was assigned a pair of officers of the French Amy, Captains Raulin and Benedict, and an adjutant named Boyreven, a volunteer who had been badly wounded early in the war. Also joining the staff was Lieutenant Laurence Miller, U.S. Army. Consulting with the French aeronautic headquarters on "a scheme of organization" for the prospective arrival in France of American aviators, Mitchell and his aides began planning by making lists of equipment; types of planes; varieties of engines, instruments, armament, and radio equipment; and estimates of the time required to assemble an American air presence. Sending the list and a menu of other requirements to the War Department only ten days after setting foot in Paris, Mitchell asked for $50,000 in operating funds. General Squier replied by cable that it was "not customary" to send so much money to a junior officer. When Mitchell read the message to Miller, the lieutenant shook his head in disbelief. "It's also not customary," he said, "to have world war."

On the day he sent the request for funds, Mitchell boarded a train at Gare de l'Est in Paris with four French officers for the town of Châlons to meet with two officers of the aeronautical headquarters, Captains Olivier Raulin and de la Colombe, for a tour of the French airdromes. When he stepped from the train, he heard the dull thuds of distant artillery. After a lunch and a champagne toast to the United States and France, they proceeded by automobile for the front. As they rolled along, artillery fire grew louder and louder until it was a continuous roar. Along the way Mitchell studied tethered observation balloons, known to the troops as "sausages," each with two baskets slung beneath them that carried two observers armed with automatic rifles. In case of attack by German planes, the balloons could be quickly lowered by men on the ground pulling on the ropes. Farther on, Mitchell arrived at the airdrome of the French Fourth Army Corps. In his first look at an airfield in wartime, he found squadrons of fifteen pilots, each with his own plane, and total ground crew of sixty to eighty men. The aircraft were a mixture of older, French-manufactured Nieuports and newer Spads. Built by Société pour Aviation et ses Dérivés and made originally for racing, the Spad was a single-seat fighter with a 140-horsepower Hispano-Suiza liquid-cooled engine and armed with a single machine gun.

By late afternoon Mitchell had inspected fifty planes and seen the photo reconnaissance section. "The photos were very good," he noted, "and were carefully pieced together to give the most detailed information of the ground." While inspecting the darkroom, he heard the roar of a plane overhead. Stepping outside the "little board house" where the pictures were developed, he looked up as a Spad began a dive from ten thousand feet and followed it down to about five hundred feet, where it did two vertical banks, looped, and glided slowly to the ground. Bounding from it was the commander of all French pursuit squadrons: Captain Victor Menard.

Menard had been a prisoner in Germany and had escaped by scaling walls, swimming rivers, and eluding German troops to get to Holland and back to France through Belgium. Introducing himself to Mitchell, he said that he had heard about "an American visitor" at the airdrome and had decided "to pay a call." Mitchell questioned the French air hero on the subject of training pilots for combat, who replied that at least a year was required and that no men should take to the skies who were not "alert specimens with good training in athletics and sports." He also stated that he encouraged all his pilots to do as much acrobatic flying as possible just to "keep their hand in." Mitchell agreed, noting that in "what little flying" he had done, he had seen many returning pilots make some maneuver to break their speed as they approached the ground because they had been ordered not to engage in acrobatics because they were "dangerous." This instilled fear, and "when they got into a dangerous place and had to maneuver, they were incapable of doing so, and disaster ensued."

Captain Menard departed by zooming his Spad almost straight up to seven thousand feet, then made a spinning dive that was "absolutely vertical and the rhythm perfect." Straightening out into a nosedive, he came out of it to make a couple of steep climbs and descents, then sped off. As Mitchell watched in awe and admiration, he recognized his own deficiencies as a pilot and made up his mind to improve his skills by taking lessons from France's best instructor in flying pursuit planes, Victor Fumat. After a month in the cockpits of French aircraft, Mitchell learned the superiority of European warplanes "firsthand." Recalling this awakening, he wrote, "I had been able to flounder around the animated kites that we called airplanes in the United States. But when I laid my hand on the greyhounds of the air they had in Europe, which went twice as fast as ours, it was an entirely different matter."

With his lessons from Fumat completed, he was tested to qualify for the title junior military aviator, the highest ranking open to him. With two judges appointed to assess his performance, he flew an eighty-horsepower Nieuport in simple maneuvers that included climbing, gliding, landing within a one-hundred-foot circle, spiraling left and right, and flying figures of eight. The penultimate test was a round-trip flight–Paris to Châteauroux–a distance of more than three hundred miles, in under six hours, using map and compass. The last flight, in rough weather, thick clouds, and fog, was a triangular course from Le Bourget, near Paris, to other towns over a range of sixty-four miles in fifty minutes. Citing him for handling "his machine with ease and very good control," the two-man evaluation board found that "his technical and theoretical knowledge and flying ability are well above that of the average applicant."

Certified as a junior military aviator, Mitchell became friendly with France's top men in aviation, including the minister of aviation, Daniel Vincent. These associations, and France's desire to see American ground forces and airmen arriving as soon as possible, would become important tools in Mitchell's efforts to prove to the generals and politicians in Washington, D.C., the urgency of American intervention in a tangible way. The French were also eager for Mitchell to observe their pilots and soldiers in action. For Mitchell, this meant not only inspecting the airdromes, but going to the front. Captain Raulin did not share this eagerness. To Mitchell's request to be taken to the scene of an attack, Raulin expressed his opinion that an American officer killed "at this stage of the game" might have "a bad effect on sentiment in America toward the war."

Mitchell responded that Americans were at war and France's ally, but that "no Americans had ever actually been with their men at such a time, so it was necessary to go in order to find out about things first hand."

Heading for the front on Sunday, April 22, 1917, Mitchell, Raulin, and de la Colombe stopped near the town of Suippes to investigate a German plane that had been shot down. It was a six-cylinder, 170-horsepower, Albatros pursuit plane. Not as speedy as a Spad, but much faster than a Nieuport, it could dive better than any plane in the war. With the name *Vera* painted on the fuselage, the plane slammed into a tree when its wounded pilot was forced to land. Because the Albatros had been found in a "splendid condition" and repairable, Mitchell suggested that it be sent to the United States for inspection by the public as "a trophy of the war."

Mitchell and his aides next visited a military hospital for the funeral of two pilots who had been killed two days earlier. He remembered the service not only for the solemn honors for the aviators, but seeing for the first time a mother of a dead pilot. A "fine picture of a French matron," she stood erect with tears streaking her face. Eight months before, she mourned her husband, killed in action in one of the countless trenches that laced France and which, to a pilot flying above them, resembled a gigantic spider web.

Carrying a helmet, gas mask, and field glasses, Mitchell resumed the journey to the front and the headquarters of division commander General de Gallais. In a deep dugout that contained offices for a staff of ten, a mess room, and bunks, he was a handsome man about fifty-five years old and seemed to his young American visitor "very much worn and a little nervous" from the strain and tension of battle. The general explained that the day's action would be carried out by artillery "to obtain the ascendency over the enemy's heavy artillery, because unless they are put out, almost nothing of lasting nature can be accomplished." Before infantry could advance from their trenches, the enemy's defensive works had to be "demolished." An attempt to photograph a German redoubt by airplanes the previous day had been thwarted by thick woods.

Accompanied by a captain of engineers, Mitchell left the general's position for brigade headquarters in a much smaller bunker that the French called an *abri*. In surrounding trenches men stood guard at roughly forty-yard intervals to the booming of heavy artillery. "To get forward now," Mitchell wrote of his venture to the front line, "was an operation requiring a good deal of exertion, because one had to run across the places where trenches had been knocked down, or almost certainly would be knocked down. I had seen a good deal of artillery fire before, but never anything that equaled this."

The colonel of the 227th Regiment was a man of about forty, "not very tall but well knit and energetic, and strong," although he looked as if "he had been pulled through a knot hole." Exclaiming that he had "no idea that any foreign officer would come of his own free will" to see his regiment, he turned to an aide and sent him to tell his men, "An American officer is here."

"The word spread quickly," Mitchell recorded in his diary, "and smiling faces appeared wherever we went, looking out of their gopher holes. I say smiling faces, but one could hardly discern the look on the men's faces, so heavily were they covered with the grime of the trenches."

For most of the afternoon the hill that was the objective of the French had been under an intense, continuous artillery barrage while the German defenders laid down fire on all approaches with heavy field guns loaded with shrapnel charges. At 5:30 p.m. the troops surged out of their trenches under the cover of artillery hitting the German line four hundred yards ahead. Mitchell described his actions in the company of a French colonel:

The left flank of the French attack was about three hundred yards from my position. The Colonel and I got up where we could see over the parapet and saw the men jump out. They were covered in a cloud of dust. Within an instant a great number of white calcium fore signals were sent up, one ball at a time. These rose about fifty feet in the air. There was a short wait, possibly a minute, and then all the French 75's [artillery] behind us began the barrage fire, about one hundred and fifty of these guns firing against an enemy front of about four hundred yards. . . . We went forward to the battalion where we saw [its] major, who was all caked up with clay. In fact, none of the officers could be distinguished from the men without looking twice. All carried automatic pistols or revolvers.

The fire of the big guns suddenly shifted directly to our position and we jumped into the Major's abri. The ground shook to where we were, thirty feet below the surface; several tons of metal landed within a radius of fifty yards while we were there. Within about ten minutes [the firing] slackened a little and we ran forward to the first line trench, the Major with us. He impressed me as a splendid example of all a battalion commander should be, strong, agile, cool and educated.

After some two hundred yards of trench, we reached the first fire trench. The men had been in it two days and were attempting to deepen it. Very little could be done during the day, on account of the enemy fire, and the men were lying in excavations under the parapet. . . . A few dead bodies of Frenchmen were scattered around and a good many dead Germans lay in front of the trench, the result of the counterattack just delivered.

At this time the French barrage was moving forward slowly. The attacking French line was armed solely with machine guns, pistols, and grenades. With a direct view of the side of the hill under attack, Mitchell observed "a fantastic and very uncomfortable inferno" as the French flashed signal lights to ask for more artillery. When German artillery fire grew more intense, he and the battalion commander scrambled for the nearest cover in a former German listening post.

In one day on the front line Mitchell had been "most forcibly" struck by the helplessness of the infantry when attacking over open ground against modern machine guns and cannon. No side had developed a system that would protect the individual foot soldier, so that for him it was simply a case of sacrificing men for an infinitesimal gain. "Truly this war was being waged under the ground and over the ground," he wrote. "The men on the surface did the least actual work. Life could not exist in the presence of the dreadful weapons of modern war, and men were forced to burrow in the ground like gophers." Yet, above them in the air, where pilots could penetrate deep into the enemy's country, Mitchell envisioned "the immemorial battleground" being displaced and rendered obsolete. He had been the first American army officer to venture into the trenches. For this act that was seen as so astonishing and potentially helpful in hastening the arrival of many thousands of Americans, the French gave him the croix de guerre.

CHAPTER EIGHT

"GO IN AND CLEAN UP THE AIR"

The day after his historic visit to the trenches, Mitchell headed to the town of Villeneuve. It had been the site of one of France's largest aviation schools and was now a base for bombing squadrons. One-man planes that carried out raids at night had twin engines, large wingspans, flew at slow speeds, and generally went up alone. Their cocky pilots expressed confidence that if they were given enough planes and explosives, "there would be nothing left of Germany in a short while." Just as enthusiastic, "day-bombarding" airmen who flew both single and double seaters reported with pride that a couple of days before Mitchell's visit they had dropped "a thousand kilos" on a German town, forcing its evacuation and destroying ammunition factories.

Moving from Villeneuve in the afternoon to a school for balloon observers at Vardeny, within range of German artillery, Mitchell was given a tour by Major Jacques Saconey, the head of France's balloon organization. As he explained the training of observers and the deployment of the "sausages" on a perfect day, a battle for the summit of Cornouilet Hill could be plainly seen. Despite assertions by balloonists that very few of the craft had been destroyed by airplanes, Mitchell left the school with a belief that "planes would shoot a good many down in the future."

On the road to a base for French aerial reconnaissance planes at La Cheppe the following day, Tuesday, April 24, 1917, where he was invited to fly as an observer over the front, he and his aides stopped to examine forty-eight new French tanks hidden in a little wood. Fascinated by this other new development in warfare that, like the plane, was being put to the test in France, he was interested in its mechanics, armament, and "a little wireless outfit for communication" with a transmission wire "thrown out to the rear." He later wrote that the enthusiastic tank officers believed "that in their arm of the service they have a branch that will revolutionize land warfare." He learned that they were also "strong believers in aircraft" used "in conjunction with tanks," with planes striking at the enemy's rear areas, while their tanks made the direct attack on the front.

Having entered the annals of the war as the first American army officer under fire in the trenches, Major William Mitchell was about to become the first to fly over the German lines. The purpose of the mission was "the spotting of fire" for the heaviest long-range French artillery. The planes were three-seaters powered by two 140-horsepower engines. Seated in front with a Lewis machine gun, compass, map, "speaking tube" for communication with the pilot, and a radio, he would be the observer. A gunner with twin Lewis weapons occupied the rear seat. The pilot, Lieutenant François Lafont, sat in the middle.

Taking off "in fine style" at about 5:30 p.m., Mitchell remembered in *Memoirs of World War I*, Lafont "jumped her up pretty well, then straightened out to get speed and climbed up in long spirals, with the two Hispanos buzzing regularly. The fuselage was so constructed that most of the wind was blown up over one's head. The pilot and gunner wore no glasses, I took some as I was used to wearing them, but soon pulled them off. There was very little vibration and I found I could see very easily with field glasses. These were eight-power instruments with large rubber eye pieces that fit closely and so let no wind in."

Starting for the lines at six thousand feet, passing a row of observation balloons, he was impressed by how plainly he saw the flash of German antiaircraft guns firing at them at long range. With shells bursting three to four hundred yards away, Lafont turned the plane to the right and flew parallel to the lines below. As French guns fired at two German pursuit planes about a thousand yards off, Mitchell saw a patrol of five Spads approaching and the German airplanes scurrying away. On the ground, French artillery pounded Germans on Mt. Cornouilet, but he saw no troops. Looking down the Marne River, he could see the city of Reims plainly, ten miles away. He also observed a "compact formation" of several units of French pursuit planes, "passing very close to me, both under and over," apparently for his "benefit."

With Lafont starting back to base at seven o'clock, Mitchell asked him how the plane handled when he "threw her around a little." Lafont replied that he could not demonstrate the craft's maneuverability because the gunner was not strapped in, but he made several banks, nose dives, and extremely tight spirals that left Mitchell impressed with how "beautifully" the plane handled, with little vibration. It also landed superbly. Bringing it down to earth at a "very low speed," Lafont used the motor until within three hundred feet of the ground and "gave her a kick" just before touching down, and rolled to stop in no more than a hundred feet.

Persuaded that Lafont was the best pilot "in the organization," Mitchell dined with the squadron officers in a mess hall decorated with pieces of German planes that had been shot down. They also discussed the tactical use of airplanes.

"One flight over the lines," he wrote later, "gave me a much clearer impression of how the armies were laid out than any amount of traveling around on the ground. A very significant thing to me was that we could cross the lines of these contending armies in a few minutes in our airplane, whereas the armies had been locked in the struggle, immovable, powerless to advance in three years. It looked as though the war would keep up indefinitely until either the airplanes brought an end to the war or the contending nations dropped from sheer exhaustion."

Two days after his flight over the lines, he went to French army group headquarters to meet with the aeronautical officer, Major Paul Armenguad, and other members of the staff. All wanted to know how soon they would be receiving America's help in men and equipment and expressed the fear that German production of equipment and personnel might surpass the French. Evidently to underscore this urgency, the chief of staff invited their American guest to dine with the French commander in chief, General Henri Philippe Pétain. When Mitchell arrived at the general's residence in Châlons in the company of the most prominent American civilian in Paris at the time, James H. Hyde, they found the American flag flying above the front door.

Presenting Mitchell a copy of a study of France's needs and how the United States could "cooperate," Pétain cited an urgent desire for men, and a need for artillery and aircraft. While he spoke, Mitchell gained the impression that Pétain was "largely his own chief of staff," and that as a soldier Pétain felt that he was being required to push an attack that was being made more for political reasons than military. Mitchell confided to his diary, "I do not believe he ever had the idea that it would succeed, or even be of advantage to the French—on the contrary, [he] is terribly afraid that the losses in men, munitions and morale will encourage the Germans to counter-attack and enable them to smash the French front."

Continuing his explorations of French military units, Mitchell observed them coordinating with aviation, visited an infantry school, observed an attack at Moronvilliers in which he estimated the French casualties at 50 percent, and experienced his first air raid. On his return to his hotel in Châlons on a "beautiful moonlit night," he sat at his desk to compose a report on his small Corona typewriter, only to be interrupted by "the hum of a strange airplane." A moment later, all the windows and doors shook. Rushing outside, he saw searchlights probing the sky. Machine guns rattled. Bombs fell. A sliver of shrapnel struck his leg.

When the raid was over, he returned to his room and wrote in his diary, "No one can ever tell me that there is nothing in airplane bombing. It will have a great effect on all the operations, if efficiently carried out." The bombing of Châlons, with its demoralizing effect on the people, was evidence of "a menace from an entirely new quarter." It was "in the interests of the United States to defeat the Germans." If not, he wrote, "With the present means of electric communication which can encircle the world in an instant, with aircraft and submarines and automotive transportation, they can forge a world empire and hold it indefinitely under their heel."

In a report to the War Department, he advised quick American help, but independent of the French. He wrote:

French aviation is now on the defensive, in both tactics and strategy. The men have been at this too long and have lost their nerve, with very few exceptions. If we feed in our own organizations by driblets, our men will have the nerve taken out of them also. We must keep our whole organization separate, under our own command, and go in and clean up the air. The formation of pursuit squadrons is to take and maintain the offensive, to seek the enemy and attack him wherever found, and to destroy him.

Having been taught the importance of understanding history by his father, especially that of Europe, and of France in particular, Mitchell quickly discerned a fact about the French that would come to frustrate and infuriate Americans who rushed to France's rescue in two world wars, only to be frequently opposed by them throughout the Cold War and following the demise of the Soviet Union in which the United States emerged as the world's only superpower. In Paris in May 1917, Mitchell saw that "within themselves" the French "feel they are the superiors of any people on earth and it wounded their sensibilities that their country had come to such a turn." He also saw that both the French and English were "attempting in every way to obtain the greatest influence with the United States, because after the war when the [diplomats] would sit around the table determining what should be done, whichever side had America behind it would unquestionably carry its point." Consequently, "there was the greatest amount of pulling and hauling, propaganda and inside work going on both in the United States and with our emissaries in Europe, to get the inside track with us."

As one of a handful of American military officers in Paris, Major Mitchell suddenly found himself courted militarily, politically, and socially. He was introduced to diplomats, leaders in the arts, bankers, and *grandes dames*. After one lavish dinner, U.S. General James G. Harbord noted in his diary, "Since last night I realize the meaning of decolette. . . . It was the lowest-necked party I ever attended." Although Mitchell felt that the Army General Staff in Washington gave scant attention to his reports, and even his friend Hap Arnold thought him "prone to exaggeration" in his fervor for a powerful American air force, the French regarded him as an "authority" with such unbounded influence that he was invited to lecture the French senate on the subject. When the Socialist leader in the Chamber of Deputies, Henry Franklin-Bouillon, was about to leave for a visit to the United States, he asked Mitchell for advice on whom to meet in Washington, and how to treat them. As a member of the Allied Board that had been established to provide airplanes for the American ying squadrons that would presently be coming to France, Mitchell was often the guest of honor at luncheons and dinners given by the Marquess de Brantes, heiress of an arms-manufacturing empire. The subject of discussion at these and other meetings was the French desire to have the Americans integrated into the French air force under French command.

Mitchell disagreed. "I felt that we were over here fighting in our right," he wrote. "We were over here as Americans and not as French or English. We had to insist upon having our own army as I was sure the American people would never stand to have their sons killed on foreign soil under foreign leaders. . . . Consequently, we had to make an American army because when this particular squabble ended, another might start soon after. We need to keep our powder dry, keep it in our own possession, and get weapons that we can use with it."

Aware of his influence among the French, Mitchell decided to take advantage of it in a way that he was certain would gain the attention of policy makers in Washington that his reports had failed to attract. He persuaded the French premier, Alexandre F. Ribot, to send a cable to the War Department that demanded the United States provide forty-five hundred planes, five thousand pilots, and fifty thousand mechanics with the necessary personnel and material to "enable the Allies to win supremacy in the air." The cable reached President Woodrow Wilson's desk on May 24, 1917. In the opinion of the official historian of the American Expeditionary Force (AEF), Colonel Edgar S. Correll, the message was the beginning of "America's world war aeronautical program."

Forwarded to the War Department, the cable had, in Hap Arnold's eyes, the hand of Billy Mitchell all over it. "We were told to prepare a bill for Congress," Arnold recalled. "Our under-staffed Airplane Division in the War Department received the news with great interest. It was our first program." Noting that the United States ranked fourteenth among the nations of the world in aviation, he continued, "In the raw, the country's manpower, industrial strength, and the national know-how in general assured the building of any kind of military force we wanted—*if* there was a realistic organization of energy and material, and *if* there was time,"

Placed in charge of the effort was Major Benjamin Foulois, the senior flying officer then in Washington. Conscious of a "supreme opportunity" and working under extreme pressure, he and his staff drafted a measure in a few days that asked Congress for funds to build 22,265 planes, including 12,000 of the latest models; create a training establishment equipped to graduate 6,210 pilots; and provide money for approximately forty-five thousand aircraft engines and spare parts. Secretary of War Newton Baker approved the plan in June and informed Congress, "The aircraft program seems by all means the most effective way in which to exert America's force at once in telling fashion." Two months after the Ribot cable, Congress passed the largest appropriation for a single purpose to that time. In August the Aviation Section of the Signal Corps was authorized to raise 345 combat squadrons, 81 supply squadrons, 11 repair units, 45 construction companies, and 26 balloon companies. The plan called for deployment of 263 combat squadrons to Europe by the last day of June 1918.

Promoted to lieutenant colonel, Mitchell turned his attention from learning all he could about the French air force to finding out how the English air force operated. After several days of waiting for a reply to his request to inspect the status of the Royal Flying Corps, and to meet its commander, General Hugh Trenchard, he traveled to the British base near Abbeville near the English Channel. Situated in a "nice country house, off by itself," Trenchard's headquarters was about twenty miles from the front. Mitchell found a man in his forties, about six feet tall, erect in carriage, decided in manner, and very direct in speech. Regarded as the father of British fighting aviation, Trenchard was a pilot and "thoroughly convinced of the enormous value of this great arm of the service." Because of him the Royal Flying Corps had grown from a few second-class planes to a mighty force of more than two thousand planes on the line. Not a man to waste time, he asked Mitchell what he wanted.

Mitchell replied that he desired to learn about the RFC's organization, equipment, system of supply, and operations then underway against the Germans. Trenchard asked how much time Mitchell had to give him. Mitchell replied that he thought "the first part of it could be gone over that afternoon and evening and the next part might be started the following day."

Trenchard asked, "Do you think I have no other duty except to show you around?"

Mitchell responded that Trenchard had "such an excellent organization that it should not need his leadership for the space of a day or two, no matter how serious the condition might be."

Trenchard laughed and invited Mitchell to sit down. In an office with large maps of the entire British front spread over the walls, Trenchard explained the current situation and outlined the policies that air forces had pursued from the start of the war. What few planes there were at the beginning, he said, were used for observation, "like moveable platforms which could see and report the movement of the enemy to the ground troops."

When the airplanes began to attack each other and drop bombs, Trenchard continued in his history lecture, the troops "yelled for protection" and brought the air forces to task for not keeping all enemy planes out of the air near them. This use of air power strictly for defense, he proposed, was wrong. The best employment of the airplane was on the offensive. Aviation, he said, "should be carried just as far into the enemy country as possible and destroy all its means of supply, subsistence and replacement." After four "instructive" days with the British and "a man with whom it was a greater pleasure to talk and associate," Mitchell returned to Paris with Trenchard's promise of "every assistance in future" and an invitation to "come back whenever I wanted to talk matters over with him, or see more of the British air operations."

Since the U.S. declaration of war, Mitchell had found speculation "rife" in Paris as to who would be in command of American forces when they arrived. He was astonished by talk among Parisians that favored Theodore Roosevelt. This idea ended when a story went around that the former president and hero of the Spanish-American War had volunteered to lead a regiment, but had been refused by his arch political foe, President Wilson. Others said that the obvious choice was General Leonard Wood. A few speculated that the right man ought to be General Frederick Funston, but the hero of the Philippines Insurrection and "savior" of San Francisco in 1906 had died of a heart attack on February 19, 1917. All this speculation ended with the word from Washington that Wilson had chosen General John J. "Black Jack" Pershing. On May 28, 1917, news flashed to France that Pershing and a staff of about 180 had sailed for France from New York on the S.S. *Baltic*. Some Frenchmen made a play on his name by joking, "Now we will have two *peres* running the war, Pere Joffre and Pere Shing."

Needing larger office space, Mitchell moved his planning operations into "a fine new six-story structure" that had been taken over by the ministry of aviation at 45 Avenue Montaigne and began compiling lists of raw materials necessary for making airplane engines, including Clerget, Renault, Lorraine, and Hispano-Suiza, along with amounts of gasoline and oil. With his staff settled in their new space, he obtained permission for another visit to the British front and went first to Dunkerque to see how operations were being conducted against the German submarine base at Zeebrugge and along channel ports. That afternoon he saw two Handley-Page heavy bombers capable of carrying more than two thousand pounds of ordnance and enough fuel to last eight hours. Finding the war-ravaged countryside of Flanders flat and pockmarked with shell holes, he noted that towns near the lines were heaps of stones and the city of Ypres destroyed. On the day he prepared to return to Paris he heard of a raid of thirty-five German Gotha bombers on London in daylight, flying in V formation at thirty-five hundred feet, without losing any planes, because British antiaircraft guns were ineffective, pursuit planes of the Royal Flying Corps had to turn back at the edge of the English Channel, and no navy planes were available to pick up the chase. This might not have happened had the British created a unified army-navy air force, he wrote of the episode, but "all the old mossbacks" in Britain's army and navy, "jealous of their privileges and authority," had been able to block the merger.

On June 13, 1917, Mitchell and Marlborough Churchill went to Paris's Gare du Nord to attend the welcome ceremony prepared by the French for General Pershing. They wore uniforms they had had specially tailored that broke with the army's "Mother Hubbard" style of blouses, which stopped "a little bit below the waist belt." They were popularly known as "Seymours," because "you could see more of the seat of a person's trousers than anything else." They also donned the diagonal Sam Browne belt that all European officers wore because without them "one was always mistaken for an enlisted man."

For the reception of the hero of the American-Mexican frontier "who had now arrived in Europe to settle the dispute between the French and Germans," Mitchell recorded, the city of Paris had made elaborate preparations and taken precautions "to prevent anyone," presumably a German agent "from taking a shot at him." Mitchell's description of the grand debut in the City of Lights of the commander of the American Expeditionary Force continued:

The train rolled in and there was great cheering as General Pershing, Lieutenant-Colonel James G. Harbord and the rest of his staff dismounted and came into the waiting room of the station, looking a little bewildered. It certainly was good to see them. They were escorted to their automobiles through the tremendous jam by Colonel de Chambrun, the great-grandson of Lafayette and a brother-in-law of [Congressman Nicholas] Longworth, and by General Pelletier, a one-armed veteran of the French Army. I rode in automobile No. 8 with a couple of the staff.

As the train of automobiles proceeded toward the Hotel Crillon, flowers were thrown on them and in their path, and cheer after cheer greeted them. A great program had been arranged for General Pershing and his staff, which had to be gone through before they could do anything else.

Pershing had brought his aviator officer, Major Townsend F. Dodd. Described by Mitchell as "an excellent man and one of our oldest flyers," he had been with Pershing in Mexico "and had great confidence in his chief." Informing Mitchell "what was going on in the United States," Dodd expressed confidence that "the great effort being put forth" would result in "our getting partially trained aviators within a few months." Dodd was "dubious about an efficient airplane coming for over a year." This was in very great measure because the office of Chief Signal Officer was "a madhouse" of disorganization and confusion, and the army itself was "perfectly hopeless to cope with the aviation problem."

Having been promoted to lieutenant colonel in May and as the highest-ranking aviation officer in Europe, Mitchell requested a conference with Pershing and was invited, with Major Dodd, to dinner in Pershing's palatial suite. When Dodd proposed that Mitchell be named the AEF's chief of the air service, Mitchell explained that he was there "to fight the Germans, and would just as soon be a pilot in one of the squadrons." Dodd and Mitchell recommended that aviation be detached from the Signal Corps and made an independent fighting force. They also proposed creation of a board of officers to review data on the status of the war and make recommendations as to the future of the American organization. Pershing gave his approval to both ideas, thereby designating for the first time in American military history that aviation be regarded as an independent combatant arm. The decision was formalized in a cable from Pershing to the War Department: "I strongly urge the importance of having all aviation matters in Europe handled only through these Headquarters, both the matters that originate in Europe either in the American service or in the European governments and those matters that originate in the United States and that are handled in Europe either by the American air service or by the European governments."

While this was "more or less carried out," Mitchell noted, for quite a long time "different aviation offices existed in England, France and Italy, and the navy as well as the army had an organization at each place, neither coordinated with the other." This resulted in tremendous waste that "kept up till the end of the war."

Because Mitchell was a lieutenant colonel and had been in Europe since before the U.S. declaration of war, Pershing brushed aside his plea to be a combat pilot and named him air chief of a force that consisted of one borrowed French Nieuport.

CHAPTER NINE

"EVERY TOM, DICK AND HARRY"

Two events in the United States prior to General Pershing's arrival in France had caught Lieutenant Colonel William Mitchell's attention. On June 2, 1917, there was an official change of the name of the Aviation Section of the Signal Corps to the Airplane Division, with Major Benjamin Foulois officer-in-charge. On the same day, Mitchell heard of the departure from New York of the first group of aviation personnel, consisting of ninety-three civilian mechanics, to study British and French airplanes and manufacturing methods. Two days later, the Aircraft Production Board and the Joint Technical Board on Aviation gave their approval to the construction of five prototype models of eight- and twelve-cylinder engines. Designated Liberty engines, they would, if they passed acceptability tests, become the standard engines for all American-built warplanes. When Mitchell learned his recommendation of a French design for an observation plane had been ignored and that the plane would be a copy of Britain's two seat de Havilland, an aircraft he had found "not suited for observation work," he suspected that British manufacturers had "done a lot of inside work" in Washington "to put this thing over." These developments were accompanied by a boast from a member of the Aircraft Production Board in Washington that within a year ten thousand American pilots would be in the skies of France in American planes. When an exuberant King George V met with Pershing on June 7 at Buckingham Palace and mentioned "rumors" that the United States would soon have fifty thousand airplanes in action, Pershing advised the monarch that "such reports were extremely exaggerated and that we should not be sending over any planes for some time."

Although feeling impatient because Pershing "moved slowly about aviation," Mitchell understood that the general was keenly aware that the new aspect of warfare was "assuming great political importance on account of the tremendous sums that were being appropriated." (Funds for an expansion of the air service in the amount of $640 million, approved by Congress on July 24, authorized an expansion of personnel to 9,989 officers and 87,083 enlisted men.) "He [Pershing] knew that there would be attempts to make a political football of [aviation]," continued Mitchell, "and that sooner or later, the interests that control the manufacture and supply of the equipment might try to put their own men in charge of the whole thing, both in America and Europe."

Confirmation that Mitchell's anxiety was justified occurred less than a month after Pershing's arrival. Called "an air mission" by Secretary of War Baker, a delegation of about one hundred men sent to "study British and French aviation," train about ninety mechanics, and return to Washington with "a proposed organization" arrived in France, headed by Major Reynald C. Bolling. Described by Mitchell as "an able negotiator" as a lawyer for U.S. Steel, he was a son-in-law of a powerful Senator from Wyoming and an experienced pilot. A result of the "Bolling Mission," as it was called, was the decision to adopt the de Havilland model, powered by the Liberty motor, that Mitchell found unacceptable. When members of the mission departed for the United States to present their recommendations, Bolling remained in Paris with a promotion to the rank of lieutenant colonel and was assigned the task of setting up a complex system of bases, supply centers, and flying schools for the training of U.S. aviators in combat tactics.

Increasingly frustrated by Pershing's slow pace in acting to get an air force organized, Mitchell complained that the AEF commander viewed aviation as "full" of political "dynamite" and "pussyfooted just when we needed the most action." Mitchell believed that the solution was a single

American air commander in Europe, "and not have every Tom, Dick and Harry" in the United States, who were neither pilots nor had ever seen an armed German, "prescribe what should be done against the enemy." Finding the general staff "interfering in air matters," he griped that it was "terrible to have to fight with an organization of this kind, instead of devoting all our attention to the powerful enemy in our front."

To remain informed of developments on the battlefield around Verdun, and to escape the combat within the Paris headquarters, Mitchell took Marlborough Churchill on an excursion to the French air base at Souilly. Flying a borrowed British Sopwith plane with a French Clerget engine, he found the lines in the same position as in July, but observed "more aviation in the sky." He watched two aerial combats, both at a short distance, in which a French plane went down in flames, "shooting to the earth with a long trail of very black smoke, caused by the ignition of the gasoline." Because Allied airplanes were not equipped with parachutes, the pilot burned to death.

During this trip to the front, Mitchell sent Major Churchill to find either a chateau or large house suitable for use as quarters for Mitchell and his staff. The result of the search was the Château-de-Chamarandes. Within a mile of Chaumont, it had been built by King Louis XV as a hunting lodge and stood on an island in the Marne River. Soon after making the choice, Mitchell was back in Paris and learning of several decisions rendered by Pershing. The general's staff had been reorganized along British lines into five parts, each designated by the letter *G*. Administration and personnel was G-1; intelligence and espionage, G-2; war plans, G-3; supply and transport was G-4; and G-5 handled training. Pershing had also acted to end internal squabbling with the naming of a chief of air service. He chose General William L. Kenly. Although Kenly was not a pilot, he had attended the school of aviation at San Diego, California, and had done all he could to learn about the air service since arriving in France. Mitchell found him eager and willing "to do anything in his power to improve this very important branch."

Designated chief of the Air Service Line of Communication was Lieutenant Colonel Bolling. The director of Air Service Instruction would be Major Thomas DeWitt Milling. Mitchell was named commander of the air service in the Zone of Advance (the front lines). Delighted with his post, he felt "free to go ahead and prepare everything for fighting the Germans."

Assembling an "excellent body of officers," he settled into "a most interesting place" for their headquarters and encouraged his staff members to study French and converse in it as much as possible. In his spare moments he "took every opportunity" to get to know his neighbors in the country of the upper Marne by going hunting with them, especially for wild boar that had become over-populated and a nuisance to farmers. Many of the hunters were quite elderly and a few had served in the Franco-Prussian War (1870–1871). Taking their stand along trails in the woods, they waited for the quarry to wander by. "There was a bounty of fifty francs on each boar," Mitchell recorded, "so whenever I killed one I used the bounty to entertain the old men at luncheon on the days of the hunts."

Sojourns to the woods for hunting and visits to towns and French airdromes at Nancy and Toul were made in a captured German automobile. A Mercedes, it was the car that had won the last pre-war road race at Lyons in 1914. It satisfied Mitchell's zest for speedy cars by reaching ninety miles an hour on a clear road. During one of these excursions, the engine of the Mercedes failed, stranding him at the side of a lonely country road. Prepared to walk to his chateau in search of help, he heard the approaching roar of another fast car and was delighted to see that the driver and passenger were in American uniforms. When the auto stopped, Dodd bounded out to inform Mitchell that if anyone could get the Mercedes running, it was his chauffeur. "Billy," he said, "I'm pleased to introduce you to the best racing car driver in the States before the war, and now sergeant in the U.S. Army, Eddie Rickenbacker."

One of the most famous figures in America, hailed by racing-car enthusiasts and writers of headlines in newspaper sports pages as "Fast

Eddy," Rickenbacker had set and held speed records and done more to promote auto racing than anyone in the country. Born in Columbus, Ohio, in 1890, of German parents, he had been in England when the United States entered the war and had rushed home with the intention of organizing the Aero Reserves of America, made up of pilots who were auto mechanics, only to have the proposal dismissed out of hand by a Signal Corps officer. "We don't believe," the officer explained, "that it would be wise for a pilot to have any knowledge of engines and mechanics. Airplane engines are always breaking down, and a man who knew a great deal about engines would know if his engine wasn't functioning correctly and be hesitant about going into combat."

A few weeks later, while preparing for the Memorial Day five-hundred-mile race at Cincinnati, Ohio, Rickenbacker received a phone call from an Army friend, Major Burgess Lewis. "Eddie," he said, "we're organizing a secret sailing [of U.S. Army officers to France to prepare for the American Expeditionary Force] and we need staff drivers. Would you like to go?" After thinking about it overnight, Rickenbacker agreed, but with the intention of becoming a combat pilot.

Recalling his roadside meeting with Mitchell and his stalled Mercedes, Rickenbacker wrote, "I concluded that the strainer in the carburetor was not letting gas through. I took it out and, sure enough, it was clogged with dirt. After I had cleaned it, the engine ran perfectly."

Impressed, and liking the idea of being driven around by a well-known racing driver, Mitchell frequently requested Rickenbacker's services at the steering wheel of the Mercedes or a "big flashy Packard," and occasionally a Hudson that was always burning out its connecting-rod bearings. Still yearning to fly, Rickenbacker was not above using an influential friend to help put him into a cockpit. That friend was a New York banker, James Miller, who had volunteered to join Mitchell's staff. Unexpectedly meeting Miller on a Paris street, Rickenbacker learned that Miller was slated to command the Issoudun flying school. Just as surprised to see Rickenbacker, Miller said, "You're just the man I'm looking for. I need an engineering officer."

"I'll be glad to do the best I can to help you," Rickenbacker replied. "But I think that an engineering officer for a flying school ought to know how to fly himself."

Miller said, "I'll see what I can do."

When Miller made a formal request to Mitchell that Rickenbacker be transferred to the flying school, Mitchell was reluctant to lose his famous driver. Calling Rickenbacker into his office, he asked, a little incredulously, "Do you really want to fly?"

"Anybody can drive your car," Rickenbacker replied.

Mitchell said he would consent, but only after Rickenbacker passed a medical examination. The problem was Rickenbacker's age. He was twenty-seven, two years past the maximum age for a pilot. The physician who examined him was not only a Rickenbacker friend, but a racing enthusiast. Falsifying Rickenbacker's birth date, he recorded his age as twenty-five and approved him for training at a French flight school in Tours. But this did not relieve him of his duty as Miller's engineering officer. He arrived at the base at Issoudun in September 1917.

The U.S. 1st Aero Squadron had arrived in France on August 13, commanded by Major Ralph Royce. Among the arrivals was twenty-year-old Quentin Roosevelt, the youngest of four sons of former President Theodore Roosevelt. Quentin surveyed the muddy training base at Issoudun and wrote to his father that it was a "hell of a place."

Another arrival at the base was William Mitchell's brother, John Lendrum Mitchell, Jr. At the age of thirteen on a visit to Fort Leavenworth, William had had John fitted by his tailor for an army private's uniform so that the boy could march with William's company to Fort Riley for five days of maneuvers, much to the consternation of their mother. Thirteen years younger than William, John was a graduate of the University of Wisconsin with a degree in engineering and had been inspired by his brother's career to take up flying. The difference in rank and age between the brothers and the fact that Colonel Mitchell was commander of combat aviation did not dissuade the twenty-two-year-old second lieutenant from pulling a prank. When he found his brother's Mercedes parked outside the headquarters building at Issoudun, he cracked to a few fellow pilots that his brother "disliked the Germans but liked their automobiles." He told William's driver that Colonel Mitchell had given him permission to use the car for a jaunt by him and his friends into Paris. Colonel Mitchell saw neither brother nor Mercedes for thirty-six hours.

As a cold and damp autumn settled upon France, antics of a playful brother were the least of Mitchell's problems. With the "constant work in the office and the flying and traveling I had done," he recorded, "I had become rather tired and the bad weather brought on a severe cold." Ordered into a hospital in Chaumont by his doctor, he was visited daily by General Kenly. They discussed the status and problems of establishing special schools for pursuit, observation, and bombardment; further training of pilots; lack of aircraft; and continuing rivalries among the top echelons of the air service. When Mitchell left the hospital, these issues had become so troublesome that the high command in Washington intervened, informing Pershing that Brigadier General Benjamin Foulois was on the way to France, along with more than one hundred aviation officers, and that Foulois was to be in charge of aviation in Europe. Before leaving, Foulois informed the press that he would command not only the American air services, but in a short time he would be in charge "of all the Allies as well."

"The orders to General Pershing left him no discretion," Mitchell noted, "so he had to relieve General Kenly and put Foulois in full charge." Those who came with him, he continued, "almost none of whom had been in an airplane," were the most "incompetent air warriors" ever to set foot in France. "As rapidly as possible, the competent men, who had learned their duties in the face of the enemy, were displaced and their positions taken by these carpetbaggers. Colonel Bolling was relieved of his command in Paris and the contacts he had made with the French for aeronautical material were canceled. This was serious as it occasioned another long delay in our getting suitable planes."

It was decided that Mitchell should remain as air commander, Zone of the Advance, until that position was gradually abolished. Because none of the ranking officers who had come with Foulois could fly, Mitchell was given command of the air service of the I Corps as soon as it was formed. Meanwhile, the first American air squadron was sent to Amanty to receive battle instructions prior to forming s nucleus of training for future observation squadrons, under command of Major Ralph Royce. On November 4, 1917, Mitchell wrote the first order given to an American squadron. It required Royce to supervise construction of an air base at Amanty, organize instruction, and establish discipline among men who in the great majority "will be without previous military experience."

Because there were no airplanes to provide to these students, Mitchell proposed to Pershing that half the pilots be sent to the French air service "to perfect them for duty on the front, with the idea of bringing them back to us as soon as their training was finished." This agreement, he said, in no way meant that Americans should be considered replacements for the French and British. They were to become flight commanders and squadron and group commanders "as soon as our men became sufficiently trained" and were provided with airplanes to fly in American units.

As 1917 drew toward a close, Mitchell was ensconced at Château de Chamarandes for the holidays, "working hard on projects and visiting the fronts when opportunity offered," and contemplating how different the air service was from what he had experienced in Cuba and Philippines, marching constantly through torrential rains, over mountains and through valleys. He wrote:

Here we had the best food that the world produces, we had permanent habitations, excellent medical attendance, and everything that a grateful republic could give its men. Sometimes I think we were pampered and petted too much, particularly the private soldiers [in the air service]. They sometimes seemed to expect more than we could give them. On the other hand, this was not an interesting war for the troops on the ground. There was no marching and maneuvering, no songs, no flying colors and no bands playing while going into action. It was just groveling in dirty mud holes and being killed or maimed by giant projectiles, or permanently incapacitated by gas.

The only interest in this war for him, he believed, was in the men who took to the air. He was right. Aviators "mount their saddles in the morning, after a cigarette or two," wrote a reporter for a London newspaper, "as though they were just taking a taxi-cab to Piccadilly Circus instead of mounting on frail wings into a wind-driven sky." A writer in the *New York Times* opined, "If such fighters cry out, their shrieks are only a whisper in the limitless space until now a solitude. If those who come back alive from such experiences feel henceforth that they are a little apart and resplendent, touched with the radiance of that thinner upper air, who will care to deny them?" An American who was among the first to soar above the trenches of France said, "The mere conception of two opposing flyers, each controlling, through the medium of a viciously high-speed engine, a little, flimsy spiderwork of wood and linen, and fighting with machine guns two or three miles above the earth, is enough to flog the laziest imagination."

At the end of 1917, Mitchell felt that "we had done everything possible" to create an American air service "worthy of the name and representative of our country."

CHAPTER TEN

"STALWART SONS OF AMERICA"

W ith the coldest December in memory blanketing battle lines that had been static from almost the outset of the war in 1914, the first American troops to go to the front were in positions in an area of the Verdun region known as the Toul sector. They had relieved French units that were holding that line on October 21. In addition to coping with the problems of keeping his men warm on the ground, Mitchell had to contend with sub-zero temperatures at high altitudes that could freeze noses and faces "to such a degree that they turned black." He had requested the War Department in June to supply winter aviation suits made of waterproof gabardine and lined with Belgian hare and collared with Australian opossum that could have been obtained in France. What arrived was a supply of coats made in the United States of heavy duck material lined with dog skin, "scarcely cured, that smelled to heaven," and "a billy-goat hair collar stuck into your neck and made it so sore you could not turn your head." Thousands of dollars spent to purchase the "worthless" clothing confirmed his belief that military decisions were influenced by greedy manufacturers who had the right political connections in the War Department among officials who had no understanding or appreciation of aviation.

This feeling extended to the acquisition of aircraft. In a conference in Paris with Colonel Bolling, who had been relieved of practically all duties by General Foulois, Mitchell listened glumly to Bolling voice doubts that "we could expect any definite number of airplanes from the French, British or Italians" because Bolling's arrangements had been ordered stopped.

Along with this dismaying report, the "kaleidoscopic changes" in the air service took another upsetting turn. As Mitchell put it in his wartime memoir, "General Foulois came to Chaumont with his staff of non-flyers." It was bad enough having "this crowd in Paris," he wrote, "but to bring them up near the line was worse." It reminded him of a story he had heard in the Philippines of a cavalry major explaining his unit's inaction to his commanding general. The major said that he had two hundred men who had never seen a horse, two hundred horses that had never seen a man, and twenty-five officers who had never seen either. The situation facing Mitchell in France in December 1917 was similar. He had aviators but no planes. Commanding officers were plentiful, but most had never sat in a cockpit and few had any concept of the use of air power.

Assessing the situation on the ground, Mitchell discerned signs that Germany would soon concentrate all its forces on delivering "a knockout blow" against the Allies before the Americans could arrive in force and swing into action. Although it would mean thousands of lost lives and catastrophic losses in national resources and treasure for the Europeans, he surmised, "the United States might reap the great benefit from this contest, because we would probably have to use up comparatively little of our national power, and with our resources, manufactories and manpower intact at the end of the war, we could step in and get the world's markets."

Now assigned to command of the U.S. Air Service of the I Corps, Mitchell set up his headquarters in Neufchâteau at No. 10 Rue de le Comedie, an address that he found apt because of "the state of our air organization at the front." He was pleased with the corps commander, General Hunter Liggett, whom Mitchell considered "one of the ablest soldiers," with "an appreciation of terrain and the military features of ground to be used that was superior to that of any other man I had known." Another human asset was "the indefatigable" Lieutenant W. L. Miller, who "prepared everything at Neufchateau" for the arrival of Mitchell and his staff. Making his residence in the house of Madame

Garcin, whose father had been France's consul general in New York during the Civil War, Mitchell was pleased to note that "the whole face" of France was now covered with "the stalwart sons of America, a people that the makers of history here [in France] had never heard or even dreamed of."

The doughboys were streaming across the Atlantic Ocean in converted ocean liners to keep the promise of a George M. Cohan song that vowed the Americans would not go back till it was "over, over there." When war was declared by Congress, the U.S. Army had about two hundred thousand men. By the end of the war, nearly five million would be in uniform, with more than two million serving in France. As the flow of Americans increased, Prime Minister Lloyd George of Britain worried that the Germans were planning a massive attack to win the war before the Americans could make a difference. He and the French urged that the Americans become part of their divisions. General Pershing answered by telegram that no "emergency now exists that would warrant our putting companies or battalions into British or French divisions." Convinced that American aviators must also serve in American units, Mitchell wrote in his diary in February 1918, "I could see no reason why we could not assemble a large mass of aerial maneuver and strike one day opposite the British front and the next day opposite Verdun, or clear into Germany as far as the Rhine."

Studying German tactics, he found that their pursuit flights (*jagdstaffel* or squadrons) were composed of eighteen planes, divided into *ketten* (chains) of five or six ships that acted together and attacked in echelon, one after the other. This policy was changed to "aviation in masses, sending it over all at once into enemy territory, or putting large groups into the air over a locality that they believed would be attacked." Their standard pursuit plane was the Albatros, but they were always experimenting with new types. The rear of the German army was well covered with good flying fields and airdromes, connected by telegraph, allowing their air forces to be quickly shifted along the line to where they were most needed.

Shortly after establishing himself in his new headquarters, Mitchell was told of a German Rumpler reconnaissance plane operating in the vicinity of the American base near Neufchâteau. Deciding to "try to get it," he climbed into a Spad and ascended to twelve thousand feet but was unable to find the Rumpler. While taking off, a wheel of his Spad had shattered, requiring him to land with "great caution" while an ambulance stood by and officers and men were "bustling about in a great state of excitement." Putting the weight of the Spad on the intact wheel, he set it down with "no particular inconvenience" and without turning the plane over. A few days later, he was airborne again, this time in the company of Lieutenant General Stewart Heintzleman, the acting chief of staff of the I Corps. Flying over the 1st Division at Menil la Tours and then out over German lines, they entered aviation history. It was the first time that an American General Staff officer had flown over hostile territory. The airplane was also historic because it was the first to have an American insignia—concentric circles of red, white, and blue.

Two days before Mitchell arrived at his headquarters at Neufchâteau, he noted a change in command of the Royal Flying Corps in France. His friend Hugh Trenchard was replaced by Major General Sir Hugh Salmond. Mitchell noted in his diary that Trenchard's judgment and his views on strategic and tactical use of air power had inspired confidence that the airplane was destined to be a greater force than that of sea power and that "the only way to handle air power is to unify it all under one command." The British had already moved in that direction on January 2, 1918, by forming an Air Ministry, while the United States retained the air service as part of the Signal Corps and promised through Secretary of War Baker on February 21, 1918, that American "battle planes are en route for France, nearly five months ahead of schedule." The truth was that not a single plane had been loaded on a ship. Although the first would not be on its way toward Europe from a pier in Hoboken, New Jersey, until March 15, the Germans took seriously the trumpeting from Washington, D.C., that

U.S. planes were forthcoming rapidly and in large quantities. To prepare to meet and defeat this promised onslaught, the Germans had commenced an urgent program of warplane manufacture called the *Amerikaprogram*.

The German army high command, meanwhile, planned to launch a powerful strike at the Allied ground forces before the American forces under Pershing could tip the balance of forces. This strategy had been made possible by a sudden shift in Germany's favor on the Eastern Front with the withdrawal of Russia from the war following a revolution that had deposed the czar and created a new government that was in turn overthrown by a coup d'état by Communists calling themselves Bolsheviks. This resulted in an announcement by a new "Soviet" government that it desired an immediate "peace." Succinctly summing up the impact of this in *The First World War: A Complete History* (1994), Martin Gilbert wrote, "The war-making power of Russia, hitherto the eastern arm of the Allies, was broken." Rejecting calls for an armistice, France's new prime minister and also war Minister, seventy-six-year-old Georges Clemenceau, told the French Chamber of Deputies, "War, nothing but war."

Eighteen days after the Soviets signed a peace treaty, the Germans struck hard against the British. Disaster was averted when France's chief of staff, General Ferdinand Foch, rushed troops into the fight from Italy. Offering to help, Pershing told Foch that he was prepared to put any or all available American troops in the lines. On January 8, the 1st Division arrived in the Ansauville sector of the St.-Mihiel salient, but took no offensive action. The Germans, hoping to demoralize the untested Americans, raided a listening post and killed two Americans, wounded two, and captured one, then ambushed a patrol in no man's land and killed four Americans, wounded two, and captured two.

Three and a half years after Europe went to war, and ten months after the United States had joined it, American troops were in battle. Among those at the front were young men assembled into a division drawn from National Guard units in twenty-six states and the District of Columbia.

A major who would serve in it, Douglas MacArthur, described it as stretching "over the whole country like a Rainbow." Officially designated the 42nd Division, it began arriving in France in October 1917. The leading division entered the line of the French VII Corps in the Luneville sector on February 21, 1918. There to welcome them was the commanding officer of the U.S. Air Service. For Colonel William Mitchell it was a reunion with the boyhood friend whose father, Arthur MacArthur, had been in the same regiment with John Lendrum Mitchell in the Civil War, and under whom William Mitchell had served in the Philippines. Five days later, as chief of staff of the Rainbow Division, Douglas MacArthur became so excited observing a French raid near Rechicourt that he joined in it and helped to capture several German soldiers. For this the French presented him the croix de guerre, making him the second American officer (Mitchell being the first) to receive the medal.

A consequence of Secretary of War Baker's boast that large numbers of American planes would soon be added to the war effort was a prediction by French and British newspapers that U.S. aircraft would soon "darken" the skies of the front lines. But at that moment, as Pershing pointed out to his superiors in Washington, there was not one plane in Europe that had been made in the United States. The first American air unit to enter into hostilities, on February 26, was an observation balloon. Watching its deployment in the company of General Liggett, Mitchell was horrified as a sandbag used for ballast broke loose and smashed to the ground close to Liggett. "Had it hit him," Mitchell noted, "the 1st Army Corps would have been minus a commander."

A week after the general's close call, Mitchell traveled to Villacoublay to look over new French-built airplanes—two-seater Spads—of the U.S. Air Service and to observe the mounting in a Breguet plane of the first American-designed-and-built Liberty engine. Judging it "good-looking," he understood that many things about the seventeen-hundred-rpm (revolutions per minute) motor would have to "be attended to" before it could be taken to the front. Regarding the Spad with its Hispano engine, he felt that it was "a dangerous airplane." He had recommended the French Salmson, but was overruled by General Foulois. Learning that the Germans had begun their assault against the British Fifth Army opposite the Amiens sector on March 24, 1918, Mitchell decided to visit the scene of operations, stopping on the way to inspect the airdrome at Villeneuve where the first American pursuit group was being formed. Their planes were Nieuports that he considered "second-class stuff." During this visit, he met a heroic American citizen who had served with the French, but was now a member of the fledgling U.S. Air Service: Raoul Lufbery.

Born in France on March 15, 1885, Lufbery moved as a child with his father to Connecticut and was raised by a grandmother. Enlisting in the U.S. Army at nineteen, he served in the Philippines and became an American citizen. While in Indochina in 1912, he met a famous French aviator, Marc Pourpe, and worked for him as a mechanic. In Africa in 1913, Pourpe made the first round-trip flight between Cairo and Khartoum, with Lufbery along to arrange for fuel, maintenance, and spare parts. With the outbreak of the war, Lufbery joined the French foreign legion as an infantryman, but was promptly transferred to France's aviation service as Pourpe's mechanic until Pourpe's death in combat. Joining the group of volunteer American pilots known as the Lafayette Escadrille, Lufbery savored his first victory on July 30, 1916, over Verdun. By October 12, he had shot down three more, and in subsequent air battles in which he shot down seventeen over German lines, he earned the title "Ace of Aces." Commissioned a major in the U.S. Air Service in January 1918, he was assigned to work with new American squadrons at the 1st Pursuit Organization Center near Toul at the front.

Impressed with Lufbery's achievements and his dapper and confident demeanor, Mitchell left the base at Villeneuve and proceeded to Le Bourget, the French airdrome outside Paris. He found everyone "agog over the great battle that was taking place in the north." On a cold, dark, and cloudy next day, with flakes of snow in the air, he took off alone to observe the fighting for possession of the town of Noyon. After watching the German infantry sweep into the town, he speculated that if the Germans had possessed a more powerful air force that could have been thrown ahead of the troops, followed by a few divisions of cavalry, the war might have been over.

As German long-range artillery began hitting Paris in the first weeks of April 1918, the first of Mitchell's 1st Observation Squadron airmen made their maiden patrol of the enemy lines on the eleventh of that month. Also on hand at Toul were the 91st Observation Squadron and 94th Pursuit Squadron, soon to become famous for its toll on the German air force, its squadron insignia (an Uncle Sam hat inside a ring), its nickname ("Hat-in-the-Ring Squadron"), and the man who would become its most famous pilot, Eddie Rickenbacker.

"By the end of the month," Mitchell noted, "we were in full action on the front and each day our men showed up to better and better advantage." He looked back on an April in which Lieutenants Douglas Campbell and Alan F. Winslow of the 1st Pursuit Group brought down the first two enemy airplanes credited to the AEF (April 14) and the debut of America's top racing-car driver as a combat pilot when Eddie Rickenbacker scored his first victory.

Flying over the front lines himself almost every day, Mitchell kept track of each flight, each commander, and the pilots, while pondering how much fun it would have been if he could have been one of them. With flowers blooming across the parts of France that were not marred by trenches and pockmarked with artillery craters, he commanded two observation and four pursuit squadrons and a bombardment group that was almost ready for deployment. "We were now not only using our squadrons on the front," he wrote of this period, "but were having maneuvers and aerial instruction with the ground troops at schools and in training areas. Our infantry divisions were beginning to come up, one after another. We had all the equipment that money could buy, but lacked what money could not buy—experience and a good corps of officers."

The most nettlesome of those whom Mitchell dismissed as "non-flying officers" remained Benjamin Foulois. Caught in the middle of their battles over strategy and tactics, Pershing had listened patiently to Mitchell's complaints and to Foulois' description of Mitchell as having a "childish attitude" that made him "mentally unfitted for further field service" and "incapable of working in harmony with myself." Finally fed up with the bickering, Pershing decided to call on a West Point classmate, Brigadier General Mason Patrick, to take over as chief of the air service. Although not an aviator (he was an engineer), Patrick answered Pershing's appeal, reorganized the air service command structure to end "a chaotic condition of affairs," and fashioned a truce to quell what he called "a clash of personalities" between Mitchell and Foulois. This left Mitchell where he wanted to be and in a position that Foulois finally agreed Mitchell belonged because of his "high fighting spirit" and his efficient service "in the organization, battle training, general supervision, and guidance of the Air Services" in the Château-Thierry area.

One of the most widely known and admired Americans in France, Mitchell was described at this time by a Washington newspaper's war correspondent, Clinton Gilbert, as having a "touch of the picturesque to his person." Full of dash and color in a uniform with "marvelous patch pockets" and "unusual pink breeches," he was a figure out of Alexander Dumas' novel about the three musketeers, except that Mitchell wielded a "joystick" rather than a sword. He embodied the wartime aviator that Americans at home romanticized, encouraged by news reporters such as Gilbert, Alexander Woollcott, Irwin Cobb, Harry Hanson, Heywood Broun, James Hopper (famed for his coverage of the San Francisco earthquake and fire), and Peggy Hull, who had paid her own way to France when her newspaper, the El Paso Times, could not afford to do so. In the eyes of correspondents covering the air war, Billy Mitchell was as newsworthy for fancying fast automobiles as his former driver, Eddie Rickenbacker. Concerned by all this attention, Mitchell worried that his frequent trips to the front would be construed as of "little military use" while he was "having a good time."

Seated in his office at Toul on May 19, 1918, Mitchell heard an alarm signaling that a German airplane was near. As antiaircraft guns opened up, he looked out a window and saw a two-seater Albatros so close to the ground that he expected it to land. When it suddenly rose, he told his aide to alert the U.S. planes at the airdrome that the Albatros was heading their way and dashed to his car. As he arrived at the airfield, a plane with Major Lufbery was already in the air to intercept the German. Deciding it was too late to go up himself, Mitchell returned to his office. A few minutes after his return, he was informed by telephone that Lufbery had crashed about six miles from Toul and was dead. His body was found in the garden of a house near a stream. As Lufbery's plane hurtled down in flames, he had no parachute but jumped in the hope that he would hit the water. Examination of his body revealed that he had been shot through his left hand, a wound that made control of his burning plane impossible. Eddie Rickenbacker wrote in an account of his World War I service that he and Lufbery had discussed which they believed was the better way to die in such a circumstance—by staying in the plane and burning to death or by jumping with no parachute in the certainty of quick death. Lufbery had said that he would jump.

Buried in a small cemetery beyond the Sebastapol Hospital, Lufbery was eulogized by two generals and Mitchell and then saluted by planes of the 1st Pursuit Group, led by Rickenbacker. That life had to go on was exemplified a few days later when Mitchell learned that one of America's most famous and beloved actresses and singers, Elsie Janis, was in the area. Locating her, he asked her to do her show for the men of the 1st Pursuit Group. "Although she had given three performances that day," he noted, "she came to the Toul airdrome." On a stage made of boards held up by gasoline trucks in an old prewar hangar, she gave "a remarkable performance which was thoroughly appreciated by our men."

Less than a week after losing Lufbery, Mitchell was at lunch at the Café Bosquet in Toul and looked up to see his adjutant, Captain N. P. Kelleher, approaching with a "very perturbed look on his face." Sensing that "something serious had occurred," Mitchell braced himself. "I have some bad news," Kelleher said. "Your brother has crashed."

Mitchell asked, "Is he dead?"

"Yes. It was an accident."

The crash had occurred at an air depot at Colombey-les-Belles. As John came in to land, he had too much speed. His wheel hit the ground and he bounced. Apparently deciding to make another turn of the field, he gunned the motor and started to make a circle, but the back portion of the fuselage broke and the plane slammed to earth. He was killed instantly.

"This was his first campaign," Mitchell wrote, "and it seemed to me that if either of us had to be killed, I should have been the one, because I had been in several campaigns before." He continued, "It is a tradition of our family that every male who is able goes to war immediately on the outbreak of hostilities. My mother had both her sons and four sons-in-law in the services. She had contributed every male family member she could. She was getting old now and I was afraid my brother's death would have a very bad effect on her, although she would never complain." Mitchell blamed his brother's death on "defects in his worn-out French ship."

Lengthy grieving of the loss of his brother and Lufbery was neither in Mitchell's nature nor an indulgence that the tide of the war in the spring of 1918 permitted. March and April had been disastrous. The Germans had crossed the Somme and threatened to drive a wedge between the British and French. Between March 21 and May, British casualties totaled two hundred eighty thousand, and France had lost more than three hundred forty thousand. At a meeting with Pershing in Abbeville on May 2, Lloyd George told Pershing, who refused to "fritter away" his troops by placing them piecemeal into battle under French and British control, "If France and Great Britain should have to yield, their defeat will be honorable, for they would have fought to their last man, while the United States would have to stop without having put into the line more men than little Belgium." Pershing's reply was a pledge to commit one hundred thirty thousand U.S. troops then aboard ships en route to France to join the Allied line in May and a further one hundred fifty thousand in June. The Americans already in France and all others in the future would fight only under American command. Left with no alternative but to agree to Pershing's terms, Lloyd George wrote to Britain's ambassador in Washington, "It is maddening to think that though the men are here, the issue may be endangered because of the short-sightedness of one General and the failure of his Government to order him to carry out their undertakings."

While the Americans who joined the conflict comported themselves admirably, taking the village of Cantigny, Germany's westward thrust continued and reached the Marne near Château-Thierry on May 30. With Paris in range of German guns forty miles away, General Foch renewed the appeal to Pershing for more troops, exclaiming during a meeting at Versailles, "The battle, the battle, nothing else counts." Pershing stood his ground.

Two days later, on June 3, at Belleau Wood near Château-Thierry, Marine Corps Sergeant Dan Daly and his men were pinned down and would soon be chopped to pieces by German machine guns. Ordering an attack, Daly lept forward, reportedly yelling to his men, "Come on, you sons o' bitches. Do you want to live forever?" When the day ended with the marines losing 1,087 men, one of their officers was asked if the marines intended to withdraw. He replied, "Retreat hell! We just got here."

As commander of the American Air Service at the front, Mitchell coordinated with the French air chief, Major Gerard. Arriving at French headquarters in Château-Thierry, Mitchell found the officers of the French

Third Army "more stunned" than any group of people in his experience as a soldier. After constant attacks they acted as if "they had been hit hard in the head with clubs."

To carry out the first movement of the air service from one part of the front to another, Mitchell organized the transfer in three echelons consisting of a part from each air group going ahead to the airdromes to prepare for the second echelon, the movement of the planes. A "rear party" would follow by truck with equipment, spare parts, and other material. Estimating the odds his airmen faced at five-to-one against them, Mitchell knew that they would be going up against "the best groups of the German aviation." Its Jagdstaffel (squadron) 1 was the famous "Flying Circus" of the "Red Baron," Manfred von Richthofen, although Germany's greatest ace had been killed in combat in April. Jagdstaffel 2 was "equally as good," and occupied an airdrome at Coincy. The third squadron was in the vicinity of St.-Quentin. Each had from twenty-five to fifty aircraft, including the Fokker D-VII, a plane that Mitchell regarded as "probably the best pursuit ship on the front." The Americans still flew the Nieuport 28, most of which were wearing out. Mitchell had requested the more powerful Spads but was offered "a lot of British Sopwith Camel planes" that were "very tricky machines" and no match for the fighting Mitchell anticipated. He advised that the Sopwiths be used for training and continued pressuring the French for Spads.

During reconnaissance flights taken alone across the front, Mitchell saw "tremendous movement of German equipment, temporary railroads, motor trucks and other transport" that convinced him that the Germans had "a great supply point" at the town of Fère-en-Tardenois. He proposed to Major Gerard that by the addition of a bombardment squadron and "massing" it with all the pursuit planes, "we could deliver a united attack against a key point in the area, which the Germans would have to defend." The French replied that they had no bombers available, but a request by Foch to the British resulted in the deployment of three bombardment units and four pursuit squadrons. Commanded by an aviation general, this force that Mitchell called "formidable and efficient" landed near the base of the 1st Pursuit Group at Saintes. The next day, they joined the Americans in a daylight attack on Fère-en-Tardenois that caught the Germans by surprise and blew up several ammunition dumps. Mitchell jubilantly noted, "It was the first case on record where we, with an inferior force, were able to put the superior force on the defensive and attack whenever we pleased, without the danger of the Germans sending great masses of the pursuit aviation over to our side of the line." He wondered, "What we could have done if we had one thousand good airplanes instead of a measly two hundred and fifty!"

Established in headquarters south of Coulomiers in a country home borrowed from the owner of large Parisian department stores on July 9, 1918, Mitchell reported to General Foulois, "The Air Service of the First Corps is now operating in a manner which I believe will meet the present conditions of warfare and will serve as a model on which to build in the future."

CHAPTER ELEVEN

"MILITARY PRECISION AND BRAVERY"

The American flyers at Château-Thierry, Mitchell would write years later, were children in the kindergarten of aviation, learning and growing. Hurled into the midst of the struggle, he recalled, "We had to evolve our own system and salvation as best we could." At a cost of 75 percent casualties (killed, missing, and wounded), Mitchell's American pilots had employed his tactic of concentrating a large number of planes in attack to challenge Germany's domination of the sky. Appointed chief of the air service of the American First Army on July 27, Mitchell felt that even though there were "many things left to be desired," the work of U.S. aviation was "remarkable."

Anticipating German air strategy during a planned Allied attack on St.-Mihiel, he estimated that within three days after the start of the assault, the Germans would mass around two thousand planes. To match them in numbers, he asked the French for all the aircraft they could spare and drew up a plan for each segment of his command, detailing what would be expected of pursuit, bombing, and observation. Moving into headquarters in a public school building at Ligny-en-Barrois on August 27, 1918, he found that his aide, Lieutenant Miller, had set up "an amazing relief map" of the entire St.-Mihiel salient that had been constructed on information provided by French balloon companies, showing each hill, ravine, woods, road, building, and rail yard.

"General Pershing was now in high spirits," Mitchell recorded. He continued:

Mitchell family patriarch Alexander Mitchell made his fortune in banking and railroads. *National Archives*

Billy Mitchell's father, John Lendrum Mitchell, represented Wisconsin in the U.S. House and Senate and opposed the Spanish-American War, but did not object to Billy enlisting in the 1st Wisconsin Volunteers. *National Archives*

Mitchell's mother Harriet often provided Billy financial help throughout his army career. *National Archives*

Known as Willie as a boy, Mitchell left home at age ten to attend Racine College, an Episcopal boarding school. *Library of Congress*

Photographed in Cuba, Mitchell is in the front row
(right) with his men of the Signal Corps and their goat
mascot. *National Archives*

General Adolphus Greely, a Civil War
veteran and famous for exploring Alaska,
became Mitchell's army mentor.
Library of Congress

Cuba veteran and rebel-hunter in the
Philippines, Frederick Funston became a
major influence on shaping Mitchell's
attitude toward "mossback" Army officers
who refused to accept modern ideas.
Library of Congress

First Lieutenant Mitchell supervising construction of Alaska's first telegraph line in 1903. *Library of Congress*

The army's youngest captain and member of the Army General Staff prior to World War I, William Mitchell is shown here in full dress uniform. *Library of Congress*

Major William Mitchell was the first U.S. officer to come under fire in France in 1917 and was awarded France's highest military medal, the Croix de Guerre. *National Archives*

Mitchell and American Expeditionary Force commander General John J. Pershing appear together in a 1920 photo. *U.S. Army*

Mitchell poses in flying gear with a French-built pursuit plane. *U.S. Army*

Mitchell was famous for his non-regulation uniforms.
This was his idea of the well-dressed 1918 fighter pilot.
U.S. Army

Shortly after the armistice that ended the
war, Mitchell took the Prince of Wales,
England's future King Edward VIII, on a
flying tour of battlefields. *U.S. Army*

Brigadier General William Mitchell, 1918.
U.S. Army

The first phosphorous bomb dropped
on a military target, in a test of air power
against a ship, the decommissioned
battleship *Alabama* in September 1921.
National Archives

Mitchell (center) surveys damage done by a thousand-pound bomb dropped by an airplane to the deck and superstructure of a battleship.
National Archives

A direct hit and near miss by Mitchell's bombers in a test-attack on the confiscated dreadnaught *Ostfriesland* in 1921. Following the Battle of Jutland, where she had survived eighteen hits by large shells, the German navy considered this ship "unsinkable."
U.S. Army

Satisfied that he had proved the vulnerability
of battleships to air power, Mitchell was sad
that he had to sink such "a beautiful ship" as
the *Frankfurt*. *Library of Congress*

Billy Mitchell is seen here aloft and observing his pilots sinking ships. *Library of Congress*

The obsolete battleship *New Jersey* was blasted and sunk by Mitchell's "special squadron" in a demonstration of bombing effectiveness in 1923. *Library of Congress*

Admiral William A. Moffett (left) and Assistant
Secretary of the Navy Theodore Roosevelt, Jr., were
photographed with Mitchell in 1924. Moffett bitterly
opposed Mitchell's call for an independent air force.
U.S. Army

Mitchell inspects a new pursuit plane design, the
Thomas-Morse MB3SA, before taking it up for a test
flight in 1923. *U.S. Army*

Top and bottom: The crash of the Navy's dirigible *Shenandoah* in Ohio in early September 1925 during a storm while on a publicity tour of state fairs, killing forty-three officers and crew, provoked Mitchell into publicly accusing the civilian leadership and top brass of the Navy and War Departments of "almost criminal negligence." The Army responded by charging him with insubordination. *National Archives*

Brigadier General William Mitchell
at the time of his court-martial. *National
Archives*

While Mitchell's court-martial was being organized,
he took Will Rogers up for the beloved humorist's
first airplane ride. Rogers suggested a caption for
pictures a throng of cameramen were snapping: "Last
Photograph of the Deceased." *Library of Congress*

Camera shutters click and newsreel cameras grind as Mitchell arrives for the court-martial with his wife Betty and military legal aides. *Library of Congress*

For the most famous court-martial in U.S. history, Mitchell's legal team consisted of civilian and military attorneys and chief counsel Congressman Frank Reid (far right). The woman in the hat is Mitchell's wife. *Library of Congress*

Mitchell pleaded not guilty to all charges and set out to put the government on trial on the basis that his accusations were true. *Library of Congress*

A strong witness for Mitchell was America's World War I "Ace of Aces," Eddie Rickenbacker. *U.S. Army*

The extent of national interest by the public and the press in the court-martial was reflected in articles in the *New York Times* and the line of would-be spectators that showed up each day by the hundreds hoping to get into a makeshift courtroom that seated only eighty. *Library of Congress*

The wedding of Brigadier General William Mitchell and Elizabeth Trumbull Miller, 1923. It was his second marriage. *National Archives*

Billy and Betty Mitchell's daughter Lucy, born in 1925. A son, William Jr., was born in 1928. Mitchell's first marriage produced three children, Harriet, Elizabeth and John Lendrum III. *Library of Congress*

A rider since boyhood, Mitchell became such an accomplished equestrian that he published a book on horse-jumping techniques. *Library of Congress*

No longer in the army, Mitchell remained informed about
army aviation through longtime friends and allies, such
as Henry "Hap" Arnold, who became commander of the U.S.
Army Air Forces during World War II. *Library of Congress*

Medium bombers built by North American Aviation and
named the Mitchell B-25 attacked Tokyo and other Japanese
cities on April 18, 1942, in retaliation for Japan's sneak attack
on Pearl Harbor, Hawaii, on December 7, 1941. The planes
took off from the aircraft carrier *Hornet*, with Mitchell's former
aide James "Jimmy" Doolittle leading the raid in the first
B-25 to lift off. *U.S. Army*

We were getting our American army together and our air people, who for a long time had felt that Pershing did not know, or care to know, very much about aviation, were beginning to change their minds, as he was helping us in every way. I guess he could not swallow the whole hog to begin with, had to take it easy, but it had put us back a good many months. One had to expect that in the organization of a new outfit, and from now on I hoped he would do better. I was sure he would if we delivered the goods.

Our old air units were now becoming well organized, and, although they had only been on the front two or three months, they were going like clockwork. No better working organization ever existed in the American armed services.

Under Mitchell's command on September 1, 1918, was a force of 1,476 planes and twenty balloons. Thirty thousand officers and men were disposed on fourteen flying fields and three large supply points. American, French, British, and Italian pilots and ground personnel had been assembled to form the greatest concentration of air power operating in coordination with ground forces in a broad strategic plan. It contemplated not only supporting the advance of troops, but "spreading fear and consternation" into the enemy's line of communications, men, and supply replacement and the cities behind them. In the shape of a horseshoe, the St.-Mihiel salient had been occupied by the Germans since 1915. Mitchell's air warfare plan provided for alternating attacks on the two sides of the salient in brigade strength to exploit air superiority for at least two days before the Germans could concentrate their response.

"Nothing like this had ever been tried before," Mitchell wrote of his plan for air strikes behind enemy lines and against German cities. "It marked the beginning of the great strategical air operations away from the troops." Describing the preparations, he continued, "We moved our air forces into their airdromes with the greatest secrecy possible so as not to let the Germans know how many airplanes were assembling. We were careful not to make too great a display over the front; but on the other hand, we kept our pursuit patrols working up as high as they could go, about twenty thousand feet, so as to prevent German reconnaissance."

A quarter of a century before deceptions were put in place by the planners of D-Day to trick Adolf Hitler into believing the June 6, 1944, landings at Normandy were a feint, and that the real invasion would occur at Calais, Mitchell had fake hangars constructed with fake planes in front to create the illusion for German observation flights of a larger American air fleet. Positions of the bogus planes were changed each day to create the illusion of activity. On September 13, the day of the attack by the greatest army to that time assembled under the American flag (four hundred thousand men and three thousand cannon), Mitchell would be in command of the largest armada of planes to take to the sky in France until the even larger bombing raids of World War II. He commanded 701 pursuit planes, including 366 for observation; 323 day bombers, with 91 for night operations; and a score of balloons. To make a personal reconnaissance of the situation, he was joined on September 10 by his French aide, Major Paul Armengaud. They found Germans withdrawing from the salient. Reporting this to Pershing, Mitchell ventured his opinion that there "was not going to be much of a battle at St.-Mihiel" and "all we had to do was to jump on the Germans, and the quicker we did it, the better."

Pershing chose to adhere to the original plan for an attack on September 12. The day dawned dark and cloudy, with intermittent rain making for poor visibility. During hours of many combats, Mitchell's pilots forced their scant German opponents to fight thirty miles away from the American ground positions. By attacking German trains carrying troops away from the field of battle, and destroying vehicles on the roads, American aircraft created so much debris and wreckage that the U.S. Infantry captured Germans by the thousands. In an effort to stop these attacks, the Germans threw great numbers of planes into the fight from air bases, which were then raided by the British, under the command of Mitchell's mentor on the subject of massive air power, General Trenchard. In one aerial combat that lasted forty minutes, eighteen French planes were shot down, but during the fight they had maintained formation, furnishing an example, said Mitchell, "of military precision and bravery which is required of all airmen."

An admirer of tanks and a believer that they represented the future course of warfare on the ground, Mitchell was glad to see that the U.S. tanks did so well in the attack. He was especially impressed by a brash tank commander, Lieutenant Colonel George S. Patton, for riding into St.-Mihiel on the back of one of his tanks, "away ahead of any ground troops in the vicinity."

Mitchell found himself congratulated by a "tremendously pleased" General Pershing. Calling Mitchell's airplanes "the eyes of the army" that had "led it on to victory," he praised "the very important part taken by the Air Force under your command in the first offensive of the First American Army." He cited its success as "a fine tribute to you personally." Mitchell confided to his diary that while St.-Mihiel had been "a great victory," the offensive "had actually advanced only two or three miles," and he had not had to move any of his airdromes or change any of his plans. "The army might fight for a month and not get too far away from our present aircraft locations," he wrote. "This was not getting into the interior of Germany. What did it amount to, except killing thousands of our men and the enemy's?"

To prepare for the next offensive, Mitchell moved his headquarters to Souilly to be near Pershing's command post. The attack being planned in the Argonne sector presented a different challenge than that at St.-Mihiel. "There we had a salient which had projected into our lines," Mitchell noted. "Here we had a more or less straight front, except on our right flank at Verdun, which was sloped back and to the right." This gave an excellent opportunity for German planes to attack from that direction. With half a

million troops and more than four thousand pieces of artillery in the line—
the greatest massing of cannon in history—along a fifty-mile front, Mitchell
planned to mass his force in the center and launch aerial attacks on the
German supply routes, stores of ammunition behind the line, and assault
infantry reserves and at the same time force German aviation into a fight in
their own skies. With the offensive scheduled for September 26, he planned
a briefing for his officers on the afternoon of the twenty-fourth and asked
Pershing to address them. No longer reticent about the role of aviation in
warfare, the commander in chief of the AEF expressed gratitude for the
work of the air service at St.-Mihiel and declared that he was relying on the
airmen to be the eyes of the army and to take a lead in attaining victory in
the Argonne.

When Pershing's artillery opened fire on the morning of September 26,
the thunderous volleys were so powerful that windows shattered miles away
and fuel tanks of some of Mitchell's speedy Spads sprang leaks. To have
artillery fire loosen the seams of gasoline tanks, he noted, "was an unusual
occurrence." A misty morning quickly cleared to provide good visibility as
the airborne alliance of American, British, and French pilots drove into
German territory. Observing from his own plane, Mitchell found that the
Germans had more planes in the air than they had put up at St.-Mihiel,
and that the shape of the front was such that it was extremely difficult to
keep them from flanking the attackers from one flank or the other.
Although "many incursions were made on our side," he reported, "we kept
the air fighting, generally speaking, well away from our ground troops."

Among the Americans in the air that day, Eddie Rickenbacker was
flying for the first time as commander of the 94th "Hat-in-the Ring"
Squadron. His orders called on them to attack enemy observation balloons
along the entire front and continue the attacks until the infantry's
operations were concluded. Last to take off at 5:20 a.m., he found himself
gazing in wonder at a display of "extraordinary fireworks" produced by a
"terrific barrage of artillery fire" ahead of him. He recalled in his memoir of

his World War I years, "Through the darkness the whole western front was illuminated with one mass of jagged flashes. The big guns were belching out their shells with such rapidity that there appeared to be millions of them shooting at the same time. Looking back I saw the same scene in my rear. From Luneville on the east to Rheims on the west there was not one spot of darkness along the whole front."

Both Rickenbacker and Mitchell wrote with dismay about the frustration they felt about not only a lack of understanding by ground troops of the role of aviators, but resentment on the part of the doughboys of the "soft life" of the men winging above them. Rickenbacker wrote, "To see an airplane cavorting about over their heads fills them with bitterness at the thought that these well dressed men are getting paid for that pleasant sport, while they were forced to work like beasts of burden in the rain." Noting that it was impossible to impress the men in the ranks as to the value of aviation, Mitchell was astonished to learn that the soldiers "did not even know what the insignia on our planes was." They had been taught in the United States that American planes would have a star on the bottom of the wings, but this had been changed to accord with the markings of all Allied aircraft in the form of concentric circles in each country's colors. In an attempt to educate the troops on the subject of aviation, Mitchell had Colonel Dodd prepare a message addressed to "the American scrappers on the ground" from "the American scrappers in the air." Scattered over the lines by low-flying planes, it explained that while they were "giving the Boche hell on the ground, we are helping you to the limit in the air" by attacking enemy troops, preventing German observation planes from directing artillery, and carrying supplies and ammunition.

Mitchell was equally disturbed by the course of the Argonne offensive. Deeming it "not a particularly interesting one from an air standpoint," he lamented that the infantry "just knocked its head against a stone wall." From the air he saw uncoordinated, disorganized, and "more or less detached combats." The American offensive that began on September 26 would not succeed in its objective of taking the Argonne Forest until October 10. During those weeks of intense struggle, Mitchell's tactics were directed at thwarting the German goal of forcing U.S. aviation to be split to provide protection everywhere: in Mitchell's words, the Germans hoped to force the Americans "to spread a thin veneer of airplanes all along the front through which they [the Germans] could break easily at any point with a large group formation." By concentrating his air power and attacking the enemy's rear, he was able to forestall German counterattacks. When the 5th Division attacked across the Meuse River on October 9, the way had been cleared by a formation of 332 bombers dropping thirty-nine tons of explosives on ammunition dumps and troops, followed by British planes unloading forty-two tons, for a total of eighty-one tons in one day. A German counterattack ended at the cost to them of a dozen downed planes but no losses for the Allies.

Three days after this historic demonstration of effective use of air power in the offense, General Mason Patrick extolled Mitchell's "excellent work" to Pershing, with a recommendation that Colonel Mitchell be promoted to brigadier general. With the star came appointment to the new post of chief of air service of the Group of Armies in an expanded AEF. In General Order No. 19, dated October 21, 1918, Mitchell relinquished command of First Army Air Service to his aide, Colonel Thomas DeWitt Milling, and told the officers and enlisted men of his appreciation of the manner in which they had performed their duty:

> You came into full battle a new and untried organization. You served shoulder to shoulder with our French, British and Italian Allies. You have shot down two hundred sixty-one airplanes and thirty balloons. You have covered the whole army while it has been attacking, marching and holding its positions. Your reconnaissance has extended over the enemy's whole position to a great depth, both night and day, and you have worked smoothly and

energetically with our Allies, and have met the best air troops the enemy possesses, and destroyed them.

While lauding his airmen, he did not forget the ground forces. He called on his aviators to remember that while they as pilots were "freezing in the air," the men below them "are wading over the battlefields deep in mud and debris." While the flyers were "getting the enemy's tracer bullets and antiaircraft fire" through their planes, the troops "are going through the artillery and machine gun fire below you. Their losses correspond to yours. You must protect them and show them the way forward."

Citing "low-flying system attack in echelon, massing of bombardment on the field of battle, and night pursuit operations" as "new and efficient departures in air tactics on the western front," he felt that his task of providing the American armies with a good air service had been accomplished. He was confident that "if the war lasted, air power would decide it."

Expecting the war to continue into 1919, the newly minted brigadier general met with Pershing on October 17 and described to the commander in chief of the largest American army to be fielded since the Civil War a plan for carrying the fight deep into Germany. The proposal impressed Black Jack with a boldness and daring that could only be called revolutionary. Confident that he would be receiving airplanes that were being produced by British, French, Italian, and American factories at a rate of one hundred thousand per year, Mitchell projected that by the spring of 1919 he would have "a great force of bombardment airplanes." By converting some of these large, long-range aircraft into troop transports, with each plane carrying ten to fifteen soldiers, he explained to Pershing, a force of twelve thousand infantrymen, each armed with two machine guns and bandoliers of ammunition, would be parachuted at an altitude of three thousand feet behind German lines. Assembling at a prearranged strong point, they would fortify the position and be resupplied with food and ammunition, also by parachute. Provided cover by low-flying attack planes, day and night, the troops would then attack the German rear in coordination with a massive assault from the front. The "simultaneous attack from front and rear, and on both flanks from overhead, a fire which no body of troops could withstand," he continued, "would throw open a pathway" for the American army into the strategic city of Metz and hasten the end of the war.

Fully converted to the use of air power, Pershing agreed with Mitchell's assertion that the plan was "perfectly feasible" and gave his approval to commence the planning. The commander in chief was also so impressed with Mitchell's heroism as a combat aviator that he approved awarding him the Distinguished Service Cross. Presented on November 7, 1918, it cited him for "displaying bravery far beyond that required by his position as Chief of Air Service, 1st Army," thereby "setting a personal example of the United States Aviation by piloting his airplane over battle lines since the entry of the United States into the war."

Four days later, Mitchell's plan for dropping American troops into Germany by parachute was rendered moot by the signing of a document in a railway coach at Compiègne that was called an armistice, but amounted to a German surrender. Effective use of paratroopers dropped behind enemy lines prior to an attack would not be demonstrated until two decades later, when German airborne troops parachuted into Poland to commence the Second World War, and with even more dramatic results when American and British paratroopers landed in the inland fields of Normandy on June 6, 1944.

Mitchell's report to Pershing on the morning of November 11, 1918, listed 740 airplanes in the hands of Americans at the front, of which 528 were French built, 16 made by the British, and 196 manufactured in the United States. He noted ruefully that in one year and eight months his pilots had done "practically all our fighting with foreign machines, the airplanes manufactured in America being inferior." His figures also showed that from the time American units entered into combat in March 1918 to November 11, they shot down (and had official confirmation of) 927 enemy planes or balloons, with a loss of 316 planes—a ratio of three to one and much greater in proportion than any of the other Allies. The reason for this, he believed, "was that we had remarkable pilots and our tactics and strategy were superior to any employed elsewhere."

When Hap Arnold visited Mitchell a few days after the guns fell silent and the roaring of airplanes in combat ceased, he observed the respect and adoration shown to Mitchell by not only his own men, but the British and French pilots. He wrote, "The fliers around him would have done anything for him, and so would the boys out in the squadrons. Billy was clearly the Prince of the Air now."

Politely rebuffing a proposal by Arnold that General Billy Mitchell return to the United States and assume the post of chief of U.S. air services, Mitchell argued that his airmen were going into the Rhineland with the army of occupation and he wanted to lead them "to see this thing through." Arnold took Mitchell at his word, but speculated that the real reason was Mitchell's desire "to drive the fastest Mercedes" down Berlin's most famous boulevard, Unter den Linden. In the meantime, Mitchell joined victory celebrations in Paris and heard himself hailed by a group of French pilots who had fought at St.-Mihiel. As he passed them on the Champs-Elysées in his Mercedes, they yelled, "*Vive notre general americain!*"

Driving into Germany a few days later, he inspected bomb damage that had been inflicted by his airplanes and examined the wreckage of German planes that his aviators had smashed on the ground. Setting up headquarters overlooking the Rhine in Coblenz, he installed a bust of Julius Caesar and spent many hours translating Caesar's account of how the Romans "whipped the Germans" without the benefit of air power. He took time to explore German airdromes and to see up close the red-nosed aircraft of Richthofen's Flying Circus and the massive Gotha bombers, only a dozen of which were in condition to be flown. He dined one evening with members of the Hat-in-the-Ring Squadron who were traveling without official permission "on a rubbernecking expedition" that they called "a tour of observation." The man who had once repaired the motor of Mitchell's stalled automobile, and then served as his chauffeur, Eddie Rickenbacker, was now America's "Ace of Aces." Having downed twenty-six German aircraft between March 29, 1918, and the end of the war, he was now America's most famous combat pilot.

As Mitchell left the men of the 94th Squadron to continue their holiday, he worried that these men were "the last of our pursuit aviation," and that, "as we had no real air force such as other nations possessed, it would soon fade into oblivion, and probably never be resuscitated until time came for another war." Then the United States would have to "start again by making terrible mistakes" and be defeated before it began—if the air service were "left under the army and not made entirely independent of it."

"The great adventure was over," he wrote, "and it remains for us to reap the benefits for our country, if this great catastrophe is to leave any in its wake. I feel that I have done my duty to my country in every possible way, physically and mentally."

A few days after the reunion with Rickenbacker, on January 6, 1919, Mitchell was summoned with other U.S. officers to General Pershing's headquarters to stand at attention as France's Marshal Pétain awarded the American aviator the Legion of Honor. Having fulfilled his pledge to accompany his airmen into defeated Germany, Mitchell reconsidered Hap Arnold's proposition, telephoned him in Paris, and declared, "As soon as you get back to Washington, have orders issued getting me home. I want to get back as fast as possible. Right away. Can you do that?"

Arnold said that he could and would, but Mitchell was not in such a great hurry that he wished to depart without a stop in London to consult with General Trenchard and other officers of Britain's air service "to see what the result of creating a separate branch of aeronautics has been."

PART III

WINGED
DEFENSE

CHAPTER TWELVE

"THE FLYING TRASH PILE."

Nearly two years after Major William Mitchell had rushed from Spain to Paris to present himself for duty in a world war that no one at the time expected to be preceded in history books by the adjective "first," General Billy Mitchell returned to the United States aboard the ocean liner *Aquitania* to be celebrated as a hero by the public, along with General "Black Jack" Pershing, Captain Eddie Rickenbacker, Sergeant Alvin York, "Wild Bill" Donovan, Father Francis Patrick Duffy of New York's "Fighting 69th," and the Rainbow Division's Douglas MacArthur. As he stepped onto the dock, he was saluted by an overflight of planes from Mitchel Field, named for the mayor of New York from 1914 to 1917, John Purroy Mitchel. He found a confident nation that had sent its doughboys "over there" to win the war to end all wars and to make the world safe for democracy, eager to put the ugliness behind it.

When he headed for Washington, D.C., in March 1919 to assume his post as director of military aeronautics, he found the government in a fervor to dismantle the mightiest army in the world. In this rush to return to peace, the number of officers in the air service would plummet from twenty thousand to barely thirteen hundred. He also learned that the job of director of military aeronautics that he had been promised had been abolished and that the chief of the air service would be General Charles Menoher. An infantry officer who had never flown, Menoher had commanded the Rainbow Division. Mitchell's post was as Menoher's chief of G-3 (training and operations), with the permanent rank of colonel.

Recalling the temper of the times, Hap Arnold wrote that Mitchell "came away from the first great war with the conviction that a new weapon vital to modern warfare had come into existence." According to Arnold, Mitchell found a nation that was "tired of war, not a fertile soil for his teachings and pleadings for air power." Ironically, the dismissal by high-ranking government officials of the future importance of military aviation stood in vivid contrast to the public's embrace of airplanes, along with automobiles, as the wonders of their world. On December 4, 1918, the first army transcontinental flight had left San Diego, California, to arrive at Jacksonville, Florida, on December 22, followed by a second cross-country trip in ten days in January. While its pilot, Major T. C. Macauley, was winging between the coasts, the secretary of the treasury sent to the Congress recommendations for legislation to regulate air commerce, license pilots, provide inspection of aircraft, and set rules for building and operating landing fields.

Five days after Mitchell began his new job, Acting Secretary of the Navy Franklin D. Roosevelt invited him to meet with the Navy General Board on April 3 on the subject of future air policy. Eager to expound his view that the airplane would alter the nature of naval warfare, Mitchell told the assembled admirals that unless the navy developed an air service, their beloved battleships were in danger of being destroyed by airplanes. In a wide-ranging, three-hour give-and-take, he told dubious admirals that "a direct attack on ships from the air" was not only possible, but that "we will get a missile" capable of this "whether it takes a ton or two tons." Calling for the transfer of coastal defense from ships to aircraft, he proposed to stone-faced officers of the fleet a "Ministry of Defense, combining Army, Navy, and Air Force under one direction."

A newspaper reported:

General Mitchell announces that in his opinion the creation of a single Department of National Defense with a sub-secretary of Air, on an equal basis as sub-secretaries for the Army and Navy, is the only possible way to meet the ever expanding demands of aviation, which, as all the leading nations recognize, will in the future play a part of the very first importance both in national defense and in commerce.

England and France are already far ahead of us. European air routes are being planned on a grand scale and some are already in operation. America must not lag behind.

General Mitchell's plan provides for 5,100 planes of all types, 1,700 in active commission, 3,400 in reserves, with a proposed establishment of 1,923 officers and 21,853 men.

To carry his message and crusade beyond Washington conference rooms, the man whom newspaper aviation writers now invariably identified as "Billy" visited McCook Field near Dayton, the hometown of the Wright brothers, to inspect and test a new fighter plane designed by Thomas Morse. After flying "faster than any general in any army had ever flown before" in the "best all-around fighting single-seater in the world," Mitchell told Morse to put the plane into production. He spoke on his favorite subject to large audiences in Chicago and his hometown of Milwaukee; inspected an airplane manufacturing plant on Long Island; took to the air again at Bolling Field, Maryland; consulted with aviation pioneer Glenn Curtiss; inspected mail planes; and told his boss, General Menoher, that he wanted a fleet of bombers capable of non-stop crossings of the Atlantic to carry out "offensive expeditions." He also proposed building two army "aircraft carriers" with decks of nine hundred feet. He asked for torpedoes, armor-piercing bombs, and bigger cannons and machine guns for planes. When he asked a General Staff officer what was being done with these proposals, he was told, "We're filing them."

This growing collection of memorandums, Mitchell learned, became known in the War Department as "The Flying Trash Pile." Undaunted, he wrote a magazine article that was published a few weeks after his meeting with the navy board, which declared, "The United States must organize to lead in aerial development so that the country that invented the airplane may also be a leader in its expansion and use."

An ally on Capitol Hill was Congressman Fiorello H. La Guardia. A rambunctious, liberal representative from New York City, he had been a major in the U.S. Air Service in Italy, flying Caproni bombers and constantly protesting that the inferior planes being supplied to his men were "flying coffins." As a member of the House Military Affairs Committee, he arranged for Mitchell to testify in May. Together they made the point that the U.S. Air Service suffered from the lack of leaders who knew how to fly airplanes, including General Menoher and Secretary of War Baker.

In a letter to a friend concerning this time, Mitchell confided his view of the capital city's post-war political atmosphere. "After the World war, having commanded the organization that I did," he wrote, "to enter a life of political intrigue and four-flushing, where the person with the most glib tongue and softest handshake could get away with things he had not the courage to do against the enemy or the ability to devise in time of peace, was not to my liking, nor to that of the men around me." His opponents were "self-centered, ambitious politicians." To them, as one of his admirers wrote, Mitchell talked too much and too loudly. An objective observer, L. J. Maitland, thought Mitchell was "the type of man who thinks fast, acts fast, talks fast." Maitland continued, "Of medium height and aquiline features, he walks with quick, impatient steps. His personality is such that it is easy for him to make friends if he wants to and equally easy to make enemies. General Mitchell is averse to neither friendship nor enmity. It would be as impossible for him to suppress his convictions as it would be for a lion to turn tail in an attack."

Mitchell found friends not only among the aviators with whom he had served and those who admired him, but in Washington social circles, especially people who shared his enthusiasm for riding. The author of

"How to Jump a Horse" in the September 1916 *Country Life* magazine, Mitchell impressed them by winning ribbons for riding at the 1919 Arlington, Virginia, horse show and acting as their host at frequent dinner parties. Finding the costs of entertaining higher than before the war, amounting to $30,000 a year, he wrote to his mother that he could either "get out of Washington or leave the service and make more money." To help lessen the financial strain, his sister Harriet Mitchell sent him $15,000. Between courting potential allies at parties, riding, and performing official duties, he found time to enroll at George Washington University to complete the work on his degree that he had interrupted in 1898 to help kick Spain from Cuba. He was also at work writing accounts of the contributions of the air service at St.-Mihiel and in the Argonne-Meuse offensive for publication by *World's Work* in August and September of 1919.

Aware that members of Congress were being quietly lobbied by his opponents in the War Department, and especially those in the navy, to reduce the air service to what General Benjamin Foulois, now a Mitchell ally, saw as "less dignity and a lower status than that accorded to the Dental Corps, the Veterinary Corps, or the Army Nurse Corps," Mitchell was determined to force the issue of air power into the national consciousness by speaking to the public, writing articles, and cajoling such aviation-friendly members of Congress as La Guardia. To another sympathizer, James V. Martin, a navigator and inventor of airplanes, he spoke of waging "our own private war" by using the press to gain and hold the attention of newspapers in order to tell "the people what is going on." Mitchell said, "We will have to attack those inside the government who are already subordinating the airplane to all other arms of war. After we have aroused the country we'll be ready to demand laws to wipe out the [army and navy] monopoly. We'll have the public with us."

Evidence that Mitchell's campaign had claimed the attention of Secretary of War Baker came with an announcement by Baker that he was appointing an eight-member commission to study European aviation.

Heartened by this development, Mitchell immediately notified all the American air attachés in Europe to "befriend and guide" the commission. He felt confident that when the commissioners talked with Sir Hugh Trenchard in London, his English wartime teacher and mentor would endorse creation of a large, powerful, independent U.S. air force.

Mitchell was optimistic that the commission would return to file a report supportive of all that he had been strenuously advocating since coming home. Secretary of War Baker's expression of "hope" that the findings of the commission would prove useful to "any committee of Congress" interested in promoting commercial and military aviation gave Mitchell confidence that his quest had made great progress, if not achieved a total victory.

CHAPTER THIRTEEN

"AVIATION IS JUST A LOT OF NOISE."

When the commission to study the state of aviation in Europe sailed from New York in May 1919, Secretary of War Baker's selection of its leader was universally praised. He picked his assistant secretary, fifty-year-old Benedict Crowell of Cleveland, Ohio, who had been a successful leader in the steel and mining industries before the war. Commissioned a major in the Reserve Officer Corps in 1916, he served in Washington and rose to brigadier general as a member of a board named to conduct a survey of American industrial capacity for producing war material. This work resulted in his appointment by President Woodrow Wilson as assistant secretary of war and director of munitions. Other members of the seven-man commission were either aviation experts or leaders of the Manufacturers' Aircraft Association (MAA). Often described in the press and Congress as "the air trust," the MAA was headed by Howard E. Coffin, a member of the Council of National Defense with a reputation as a "progressive" industrialist. Aviators on the commission were Captain H. C. Mustin, who was the first officer to serve as aviation chief in the navy, and Colonel Halsey Dunwoody, a wartime associate of Mitchell, who had been assistant AEF air chief in France.

Because Crowell was not only assistant secretary of war, but a longtime friend of Baker, he was not surprised that Baker asked to review the commission's final report before it was released to the public. Although Crowell's answer was noncommittal, Baker was confident that the commission was a "safe" group and that Crowell understood that he went to Europe with an unwritten and unspoken order to toe the official War Department line of opposing an independent air force. Rather than conduct their investigation of European aviation as an entity, each member would follow his own line of interest or specialty and contribute findings and recommendations to a report that would be prepared in a shipboard conference on the voyage home in mid-July. With such a group of strong personalities, Crowell anticipated fireworks of disagreement, but he was astonished that the panel expressed unanimity about Europe's advantage over the United States in commercial and military aviation and a conviction that the imbalance must be remedied. The way to do this was to concentrate American air activities, "civilian, naval, and military," in a single government agency created for the purpose, "coequal in importance and in representation with the Departments of War, Navy and of Commerce."

Furthermore, urged the report, "Immediate action is necessary to safeguard the air interest of the United States, to preserve for the Government some benefit of the great aviation expenditures made during the period of the war, and to prevent a vitally necessary industry from disappearing." This danger was evidenced, said Crowell, by the fact that 90 percent of the aviation industry had vanished, and the rest was in danger.

Presented with a report that "flew in the face" of orders and seemed to have been written almost entirely by Billy Mitchell, the Secretary of War was horrified. He promised Crowell that he would make it public promptly, but saw that the document stayed a War Department secret. The explanation for the report being "immediately shelved," said Commission member Howard Coffin five years later before a House committee, was the "unsatisfactory, antagonistic attitude" toward its contents by the general staff. It would be alleged later that the Crowell report had been "thrown into the nearest waste basket."

When Crowell and Coffin called on Chief of Naval Operations Admiral Charles Benson soon after their return from Europe, Benson told them, "The Navy doesn't need airplanes. Aviation is just a lot of noise." In a confidential order issued on August 1, Benson abolished the Aviation Division of the Navy, apparently without the knowledge of Assistant Navy Secretary Franklin Roosevelt. In a defensive mode a few days later before the Senate Military Affairs Committee, Roosevelt described army aviation as "shot to pieces" and naval aviation "non-existent as an arm." He later conceded that aviation "might conceivably even in the Navy become the principal factor" and that "in the future aviation may make surface ships practically impossible to be used as an arm."

Senator Harry New of Indiana asked, "Isn't that practically agreeing with what General Mitchell says?"

"No," replied Roosevelt. "His intimation is that it is going to happen right away. I think it is so far in the future that when it comes the Navy will automatically be transferred to the air, the whole Navy."

New responded, "I think, with all respect, that the Navy ought to adjust its binoculars and look searchingly into the future. I think that they will discover . . . that something is coming, and it is almost here, and it is coming very rapidly, something for which we must make better provision than has yet been made by this government."

"It is inconceivable," said Roosevelt, "that under certain conditions at the present time the naval aircraft branch might be more important than the battleship branch."

Feeling personally under attack by Roosevelt in the hearings, Mitchell wrote a memo in reply to one from his immediate boss, General Menoher, asking who was right, Roosevelt or Mitchell, about naval aviation. Referring to the order by Admiral Benson abolishing the navy's air service, Mitchell wrote to Menoher, "Mr. Roosevelt undoubtedly did not know that this order existed when he appeared before the committee."

Wherever the Crowell report was kept in the War Department proved to be an insufficient hiding place. In what latter-day Washingtonians would routinely call "a leak," the contents fell into the eager hands of Fiorello La Guardia. Five months after Secretary Baker's suppression of the document, the feisty Congressman used his position as acting chairman of the Subcommittee on Aviation to schedule a hearing on a united air service. The first witness in December 1919 was Crowell. Relating that members of the commission had interviewed the leading statesmen and military leaders of the wartime allies in Europe, including Marshal Foch and Winston Churchill, and presenting evidence of British and French enthusiasm for independent air forces, Crowell testified, "I find that the more study given by an officer of the army, the greater his tendency to swing in the direction of an outside, independent department of the air." He would later inform the Military Affairs Committee, "A year ago, I was thoroughly convinced that the army ought to retain all of its aviation activities. But an intensive and careful study of the subject during all of last summer has made me change my mind entirely."

One of the country's wartime flying heroes, General Benjamin Foulois, told the Senate Committee on Military Affairs that the Amy General Staff, either through "lack of vision, lack of practical knowledge, or deliberate intention to subordinate the air service needs to the needs of other combat arms, had utterly failed to appreciate the full military value of this new military weapon, and in my opinion, has utterly failed to accord it its just place in our military family."

Taking a stance that appeared to be an invitation to the army to convene a court-martial and try him for insubordination, the man who had often engaged in disputes with Mitchell over organization of the air service in France, and had once demanded that Pershing send Mitchell home, now went beyond Mitchell's position on whether a separate air force should be structured as a free-standing executive-branch department with cabinet status. Foulois believed it ought to be, as did Colonel Hap Arnold. Mitchell thought it should be equal to the army and navy but as part of the War Department.

Foulois did not have to stand trial, but was left wondering, as he wrote many years later, why Mitchell had "very carefully avoided the controversial issues" on which Foulois was ready to risk his military career by daring the army to convene a court-martial. What is clear in the record of Mitchell's statements to Capitol Hill committees and his speaking in civic forums and writing is that he did not want a showdown on the matter until he was certain he had popular support. To win the American people to his side, he believed, he had to educate them and show them that the airplane was not simply a fascinating and thrilling attraction at county fairs, carnivals, and air shows, with daredevil pilots doing loops and dives and wing walkers defying death high in the air. While he strove to persuade politicians that the airplane was essential to national defense, he stressed in public appearances and magazine articles that the airplane was for everyone. "The commercial traveler," he wrote in an article titled "The U.S. Air Service" in early spring of 1919, "henceforth will read the new air time table and find that the distance is not measured in miles, but that Chicago is four hours from New York, or that Los Angeles is twenty-eight hours from Boston." The Atlantic Ocean, he said, "is going to be crossed and within a short time we shall have regular airplane mail transportation between America and Europe."

At a time when there was no such thing as an "airline," the government's division of civil affairs created a system of radio communications for future intercontinental flights and drew up plans for a nationwide network of landing fields and support personnel. The former Signal Corpsman who had built Alaska's first telegraph line told Hap Arnold, then an air force officer on the West Coast, that he was "very anxious to push through a flight to Alaska with land planes." The goal was achieved in 1920, but between New York and Nome. Having proved by this accomplishment that "we could go across the United States" and demonstrated "that we could establish an airway to Alaska and Asia," he informed a Senate committee of plans to connect Alaska by air routes to Panama. To further his goal of firing-up public enthusiasm, he inaugurated a "transcontinental air reliability" contest in which thirty army planes started from San Francisco and thirty from New York. The purpose was to show how fast an air force could be mobilized for war and moved to where it was needed quickly.

When one of the contestants, Major Carl Spaatz, who would lead American aviators in World War II, was asked after completing the first leg how he felt, he replied, "I feel like a drink of whiskey." The winner of the race, Lieutenant B. M. Maynard, who was also a Baptist minister from North Carolina, and called "the flying preacher" by the press, noted that there had been nine deaths in crashes and blamed them on "too much booze." Congressman La Guardia attributed the deaths to "obsolete discarded" airplanes. Hap Arnold looked back from the perspective of years and pronounced the reliability contest "the foundation of commercial aviation in the United States." Mitchell declared, "There can no longer be any doubt that complete control of the air by any nation means military control of the world." But, for the world's military leaders at the dawn of the 1920s, the most pressing armament issue for the future was not airplanes, but the world balance of naval power and the role of the mightiest weapon of the high seas, the battleship.

Yet, Americans who read the *New York Herald* on December 21, 1919, found Mitchell proclaiming not only that the air service should be "of greater importance than the naval organization," but that "air power will prevail over the water in a very short space of time." This outrageous claim, in the view of America's admirals, was followed on February 3, 1920, by Mitchell's assertion to the House subcommittee on aviation, with illustrative charts, that a ship at sea would be easier pickings for airplanes than "an object on land." A thousand planes built and flown "for about the price of a battleship," he said, could employ "projectiles up to one ton in weight," along with torpedoes and other weapons, to blast battleships out of the water. The policy of all navies, he said, was to "look with abhorrence" on a system of attack against their vessels, "because it will mean eventually the diminution or entire elimination of their strength."

Not since Assistant Secretary of the Navy Theodore Roosevelt had swaggered into the nation's capital in 1897 to insist that the country build a powerful fleet of battleships had one man created such a stir by fomenting a debate over what was required for national defense. Many Washingtonians saw echoes of Teddy Roosevelt in Billy Mitchell. He was, as one observer put it, "everywhere at the same time." Restored to the rank of brigadier general, Mitchell was for the press the kind of figure around whom legends were built. A reporter who heard him address a meeting of the National Geographic Society in Philadelphia wrote, "General Mitchell has speed written all over him. He talks, thinks and practices speed."

Looking about ten years younger than his actual age of forty-two, continued the reporter, "the most competent and intrepid pilot in America is as trim and as fit as a college halfback." In his brown gabardine uniform and Sam Browne belt and with embroidered silver wings and "row on row of campaign ribbons" on his tunic, he wore his dark hair parted and had a "strong, stern face and compelling eye."

An admiring army pilot who watched his boss taking off almost daily from Bolling Field to keep an appointment at a near or distant place thought of Mitchell as "the hard-riding cavalryman of the air." He was known to give an address in the evening and be a thousand miles away in the morning, always carrying the message of building an American air force. The only trip he took in which he appeared anxious about how he would be received by his audience was at the request of his boyhood friend Douglas MacArthur. Now superintendent of the U.S. Military Academy at West Point, he invited the friend who had gone to war as a private in the Wisconsin Volunteers in 1898 and was now a brigadier general in the Regular Army to speak to the cadet corps and faculty about aviation in the world war. Greeted by MacArthur and the entire academy staff at the train station, he masked his nervousness with a stride that his critics considered cocky. He entered the assembly hall to a roar of cheers that was surpassed in enthusiasm at the conclusion of his address by a standing ovation that brought him to tears. Among the listeners to his hour and a half of tales of the air battles of the First World War were cadets who would command troops in the Second, including Maxwell Taylor, Lyman Lemnitzer, and Hoyt Vandenberg, destined to be chief of staff of the Air Force and namesake of an air base in California that would become a launching pad for rockets to go into space for military and scientific purposes and a landing field for space shuttles.

When Mitchell visited West Point, he was a father for the third time. Born on January 20, 1920, the son was named John Lendrum Mitchell III, in remembrance of Mitchell's brother. A child among many thousands that were fruit of reunions of wives with men who had gone "over there" to "beat the Huns," avenge Germany's sinking of the ocean liner *Lusitania*, and make the world safe for democracy, the infant was seen by friends of Billy and Caroline Mitchell as the confirmation of their continuing devotion. Upon Mitchell's return from the war they had been welcomed warmly into the Washington social scene of glittering dinner parties and the Virginia "horsey set." But his absences as he made frequent flights to distant places in his campaign on behalf of air power were taking a toll on Caroline. As he became an even more famous figure for his blunt criticisms of his superior officers, and earned a reputation for being "good copy" among journalists, the marriage suffered. Before John's second birthday, it would end in divorce.

In the meantime, General Billy Mitchell was hurtling ahead with rhetorical guns blazing as though he were in a Spad chasing a German in the skies of France, but in actuality he was speeding hellbent to a dramatic confrontation with earthbound and seafaring men at a time when his country was in love with speedy airplanes, racy automobiles, and fast living while they launched a decade-long binge of self-indulgence and excess that even then would be called the Roaring Twenties.

CHAPTER FOURTEEN

"DESTROY OR SINK ANY SHIP
IN EXISTENCE"

Probably because Alexander and John Lendrum Mitchell had been distinguished Democratic members of the U.S. Congress, their scion, William, looked at the candidates to succeed Woodrow Wilson in the 1920 presidential election, Republican Warren G. Harding and Democrat James Cox, and cast his vote for Cox. Mitchell arrived at this decision even though Cox's running mate, Franklin Delano Roosevelt, as assistant secretary of the navy, had defended the navy's opposition to making the air service an independent military branch. While the debate raged in congressional committee rooms, echoed in Capitol Hill corridors, and caught the attention of journalists early in 1920, the dominant issues of the national conversation in the summer and autumn were the terms of the peace treaty decided at Versailles in May and June, an appended "Covenant of the League of Nations" that would create a world organization to keep the peace, and fierce opposition to the league in the Republican platform and from powerful leaders in the U.S. Senate. Cox and Roosevelt were for the league. Preferring to sidestep the issue of a world body and appeal to the war-weary voters by calling for a "return to normalcy," Harding won almost double the popular vote of Cox and 404 electoral college votes to Cox's 127. The Republicans' victory would result in a change in the civilian leadership of the War Department and the departure of Mitchell's most determined opponents in the offices of the secretary and assistant secretary of the Navy Department. However, there would be no similar turnover in the bevy of admirals who believed the airplane was of no consequence in a world where peace would not depend on terms of a "covenant of nations," but on battleships that they insisted were so massive and armor-plated that they were invulnerable to attacks from airplanes.

Yet, as these American naval voices sought to drown out those of Mitchell and his allies, a dissonant chord added to the debate from an unexpected quarter. Admiral William F. Fullam stated in a widely reprinted article that because of the advent of both the airplane and submarine, "immense and costly ships" such as battleships and cruisers "will be driven from the sea." The future of warfare and usefulness of the navy, he said, "will largely be dependent upon control of the air, and that fleet that secures this control in future battles must win, other things being approximately equal." A sufficient number of airplanes properly armed with bombs, he went on, "could hold off an attacking fleet." He stated, "Sea power will be subordinated to or dependent on air power." From beyond the Atlantic at the same time came the voice of Britain's first sea lord in the first year of the war, Admiral Lord Fisher. Beloved by his sailors as "the old sea lion" and to the adoring English as "Jackie," he asserted, "By land and by sea the approaching aircraft development knocks out the present fleet, makes invasion practicable, cancels our country being an island, and transforms the atmosphere into a battle ground of the future. There is only one thing to do to the ostriches who are spending these vast millions on what is as useful for the next war as bows and arrows. Sack the lot. As the locusts swarmed over Egypt, so will aircraft swarm in the heavens, carrying inconceivable cargoes of men and bombs, some fast and some slow. Some will act like battle cruisers and others as destroyers. All cheap—and this is the gist of it—requiring only a few men as crew."

To answer these dire predictions, and to silence Mitchell, confident American admirals who believed that their battleships were the unbreakable backbone in defending a nation standing between two oceans decided to prove they were right by conducting their own test. The dates of the test were to be October 28 and November 3, when the nation's attention was centered on the final days of the presidential campaign. The head of the navy's General Board, Admiral Charles J. Badger, named Captain Chester Nimitz to do the planning. The object of the experiment was to be the battleship USS *Indiana*. More than a quarter-century old and a relic of the 1898 Spanish-American War, the ship would be subjected to a series of explosions to simulate actual wartime conditions, but these were to be the result of underwater charges and one nine-hundred-pound bomb placed on the deck. Although airplanes would attack the *Indiana*, they would not drop live ordnance, but sandbags. The submerged explosives broke the battleship's seams, sinking it. After the planes dropped their dummy bombs, the real one lying on the deck blasted apart superstructures.

What this massive damage showed was that if real bombs had been dropped from the air and the *Indiana* had been attacked by torpedoes from a submarine, it would have been sunk, and along with it the navy's claim that battleships could withstand these new devices of warfare. To avoid revealing the truth and facing embarrassment, the Navy Department issued a statement, written by Captain William D. Leahy, who was then the director of naval gunnery and in the next war would serve as aide to President Roosevelt and a senior member of the Joint Chiefs of Staff. It stated, "The entire experiment pointed to the improbability of a modern battleship being either destroyed or completely put out of action by aerial bombs."

What the navy could not prevent was publication in the *London Illustrated News* of two photographs of the *Indiana* with most of its torn hull underwater and its upper works a tangle of wreckage. To make matters worse, on the same day the photos were published (December11, 1920) in an edition of the *London Times*, Admiral Sir Percy Scott, esteemed as "the father of modern naval gunnery," fired a salvo that shook the halls of the British Admiralty and echoed around the world's oceans. "What," he asked, "is the use of the battleship?"

Six weeks after the London publication of the photos, the *New York Tribune* printed seven pictures of the destroyed *Indiana* and said in an editorial, "The Navy Department, for reasons best known to itself, has not published the result of the *Indiana* experiment, nor has it invited or encouraged a free and thorough discussion as to the effect of new weapons upon naval warfare by officers of the navy who are best qualified by their recognized ability, study and experience to give intelligent opinions on the subject."

How the newspapers obtained the pictures was a mystery, but because Mitchell had been allowed to watch the test, suspicion quickly settled on him. In January 1921 he was again before a House committee, summoned by its airpower-friendly chairman, Daniel R. Anthony of Kansas. Charging that the navy had tried to avoid a showdown between the airplane and the battleship with the "subterfuge" of the *Indiana* test, Mitchell told the committee that he could "destroy or sink any ship in existence." Denying that he had "pushed open a door" to obtain the photographs and give them to newspapers, Mitchell said that he and his aviators had "watched the experiment on the *Indiana* with the greatest interest and care." They did so, he said, because they had tried but failed "to get targets of actual ships to develop our methods of attack" Appearing before the House Appropriations Committee in late January, he pleaded to be allowed to demonstrate the effectiveness of air power by bombing an obsolete battleship at any time Congress "wanted to do it—tomorrow if you wish."

Through adroit exploitation of opportunities afforded by widely publicized appearances before congressional committees called by sympathetic chairmen, and by giving the journalists who covered them dramatic and colorful stories, peppered with phrases that would fit easily into headlines, the portrait that emerged of General Billy Mitchell was that of a dashing, lone crusader for modern ideas who was preparing to assure victory in the next war, should one come, against an entrenched, stodgy old guard. Speaking past Congress to a forward-looking nation of people with their feet on the gas pedals of their new cars and fascinated eyes on exploits of daredevils in the skies, he argued that government must have no more urgent priority in allocating money than spending on national defense in the form of a powerful, independent air force. "The army," he said, "fights on land, a navy on the water, but an air force over both." All that Congress had to do was give him the warships to attack in a demonstration of air power and "come watch."

With Mitchell's ally, Senator New, declaring that his Military Affairs Committee had "faith" in Mitchell and vowing to offer an amendment to the army appropriations bill to compel the navy to turn over an obsolete battleship for Mitchell's demonstration, Secretary of the Navy Josephus Daniels fired a broadside at Mitchell. Asserting that Mitchell had distorted the results of the *Indiana* test and disparaged a sister branch of the armed services as part of a "propaganda campaign" for a separate air force department, Daniels warned that if Mitchell ever tried to aim bombs on the decks of naval ships, he would be "blown to atoms long before he gets close enough to drop salt upon the tail of the Navy." Daniels accompanied this boast with a pledge that he would be glad to stand bareheaded on the deck or at the wheel of any battleship Mitchell "tried to take a crack at" from the air.

When it was proposed that Mitchell be allowed the use of the battleship *Iowa* as a target while the crewless ship was moving by radio control, Daniels responded, "I am so confident that neither Army nor Navy aviators can hit the *Iowa* when she is under way that I would be perfectly willing to be on board her when they bomb her, provided they were kept at an altitude which they would be compelled to maintain in battle." This flash of bravura was answered the next day by a derisive chorus of newspaper editorials. The *Baltimore Sun* opined, "It would thrill many a heart to witness the duel that he proposes, with Daniels himself at the ship's wheel. Even the cup races would pale in comparison with a dispute to the death in which the Secretary of the Navy wielded the awful engine of modern destruction, the warship." A writer to the *New York Tribune* called the offer "the most sensible and graceful suggestion that the admiral has made during the last eight years," adding, with a reference to the recent election of a new president, who would be appointing a new secretary of the navy, that the whole navy "will vociferously applaud this gallant act of Admiral Daniels [this was sarcasm; Daniels was not an admiral, but a former newspaper editor] in throwing himself as a sacrifice upon the altar of his country only twenty-two days before he is billed to retire." An editorial in the *Tribune* upbraided Daniels for "undignified and gratuitously offensive" criticism of Mitchell for speaking his mind and stated that "the country owes General Mitchell a vote of thanks."

Support for Mitchell came not only from newspaper editors and readers, but within the navy from two of the country's most honored admirals. The president of the Naval War College, W. S. Sims, told the House Naval Affairs Committee, "One of the strongest defenses against an enemy fleet will be an air force." Asked if the time had come for the navy to scuttle reliance on the battleship, he answered that he preferred to put money into airplane carriers and development of airplanes. Bradley Fiske, inventor of the torpedo plane, testified, "If there was to be a fight on the ocean between an airplane carrier on one side and two battleships on the other side, and I had to be on one side or the other, I would rather go on the airplane carrier than be on the two battleships."

Following Sims and Fiske in testifying, Mitchell gave the Military Affairs Committee a vivid picture of what he expected from direct hits on decks and superstructures. The blasts, he said, "will break every electric-light globe on the ship, throwing her into absolute darkness below decks; disrupt telephone, radio, and interior communication systems; fill fire rooms, engine rooms, and all compartments ventilated by a forced draft system with noxious gases; cause shell shock to the persons within a radius of three hundred feet; disrupt ammunition hoists; dislodge or jam turrets; dish up upper decks at least; kill all persons on the upper decks (antiaircraft crews and fire control parties in tops); cause fires to break out; and explode all antiaircraft ammunition. Detonations of bombs beneath waterline will sink or disable battleships."

On February 1, 1921, he handed the chief of the general staff a formal proposal that five ships, including a battleship, be provided for bombing tests. Included in the material was a draft of a letter Mitchell wanted to be sent by Secretary of War Baker to Daniels, asking for captured German warships as targets. Baker declined to endorse the letter. On February 7 he got a letter from Daniels informing him of the navy's desire to carry out its bombing tests "jointly with the army, or representatives of the army should witness these experiments." Baker turned the matter over to the Joint Army and Navy Board. Its recommendation that the test be under control of the commander in chief of the Atlantic Fleet was approved by Baker four days before he and Daniels would be replaced by appointees of the new president, Warren G. Harding. That the brand-new administration would bring a new outlook on the issue of the structure of the armed forces was signaled by Harding on March 1 with a statement to the press that he intended to create a single Department of National Defense, with equal secretaries of the army, navy, and air service serving under Secretary of the Army John W. Weeks and Navy Secretary Edwin Denby, whose assistant secretary would be Theodore (Ted) Roosevelt. He was the eldest son of the late president and a distant cousin of Franklin Roosevelt, both of whom had held the position—his father under McKinley, and FDR under Wilson.

The place of the air service in the new structure and whether it would be a union of army and navy aviation and become a co-equal with the army and navy, said Harding, would depend on the outcome of the matchup between airplanes and warships. The targets would be German. Turned over to the United States Navy under terms of the Versailles peace treaty, they were of "comparatively recent design" and included the dreadnaught *Ostfriesland*, which the Germans had declared "unsinkable" after the 1916

Battle of Jutland. To sink such a monster, Mitchell recognized, he would need an equally monstrous bomb. The Army's biggest was eleven hundred pounds. Wanting a two-ton bomb, he turned to Major W. A. Borden, chief of the aircraft armament division, and two of his assistants, Captains C. H. M. Roberts and S. R. Stribling, and asked them to deliver it in June. In a feat of new bomb design and breakthrough engineering, which would not again be attempted until World War II's Manhattan Project produced the atomic bomb, Mitchell's team devised and built a TNT weapon, in Captain Roberts' words, "to insure a complete and effective detonation." Assembling the largest air force ever seen in the United States at Langley Field, Virginia, Mitchell directed what one historian called "an atmosphere of war, of crusading fervor, and of dynamic activity." With his wartime aide, Colonel Thomas DeWitt Milling, as chief of staff, Mitchell's unit, known as the 1st Provisional Air Brigade, trained and practiced attacks on land and sea targets of the dimensions of the actual ships they were expected to destroy.

They began with one-hundred-pound dummy bombs and moved up to live ordnance dropped on the wrecked hulks of the *Indiana* and *Texas* at Tangier Island, about fifty-four miles from Langley. Flying new, two-engine Martin bombers that had never been in service and using navigational gyroscopes loaned by Lawrence Sperry of the Sperry Aircraft Company to fly through ground- and horizon-obscuring fog, they found the ships and rained twenty tons of bombs on them, led by Mitchell at different altitudes and with devastating results. The tests also had repercussions far from Tangier Island. Always keenly appreciative of the value of the press, Mitchell had allowed newsreel cameras to film preparation for the test, including the loading of dummy bombs on planes. Onto the side of one of them someone had scrawled, "Regards to the Navy." Infuriated by this, as well as by a newspaper cartoon showing a bomber attacking a battleship with the caption "Count Two Against the Army—in Navy Eyes," the secretary of the navy shot off a protest to Secretary of War Weeks that was forwarded to Mitchell's boss, General Menoher, with an order to Mitchell to cease the offending publicity.

A few weeks later, on Saturday, May 29, 1921, Mitchell found himself on the defensive amid a flurry of demands that he be fired, not because of his activities in planning the bombing test, but as the result of a display of bombing squadrons for the benefit of the French air attaché. It ended with the crash of one of the planes during an electrical storm near Indian Head, Maryland, killing its seven-man crew. It was the country's worst airplane disaster. When Menoher appeared ready to acquiesce to the demand by Weeks that Mitchell be dismissed, and amid fears that the airplanes-versus-battleship showdown would be canceled, Mitchell's allies in civil and military aviation and the press rallied to his defense. The *New York Globe* cited his "courage, energy, and convictions." The *New York Times* recognized him as "a brilliant, active, positive, outspoken officer, who is quick to take the initiative and assume responsibility." This pro-Mitchell barrage, and the public's intense interest in the outcome of the drama set for June 21 off the Virginia Capes on Chesapeake Bay, forced Weeks to retreat with an announcement that the test would be held "under all circumstances." Mitchell's only punishment was a dressing down by General Menoher and an order to keep his mouth shut. Noting that there had been no adequate experiments "to determine the relative worth of warships and airplanes," the Cleveland *Plain Dealer* observed, "How nearly right Mitchell may be will be better known after the forthcoming army and navy tests."

CHAPTER FIFTEEN

"THE MENTION OF YOUR NAME"

"You are throwing the Navy into convulsions," wrote Associated Press reporter Herbert Corey in early June 1921 in a note to Brigadier General William Mitchell at the Langley Field headquarters of the 1st Provisional Air Brigade. Corey had returned from observing a navy training cruise. "The entire fleet," he informed Mitchell, "trembles with rage at the mention of your name."

To assemble the brigade at what had been a tiny army air training school with seven instructors and a handful of students near the small town of Hampton at the mouth of Chesapeake Bay, Mitchell had scoured the country to gather 250 planes and a thousand pilots and mechanics. To curious newsmen the base was shrouded in so much mystery that a Norfolk, Virginia, paper headlined, "VEIL OF SECRECY OVER PREPARATIONS OF ARMY AIRMEN." The base attracted the attention of the press in the same way that a secret air base and testing ground during and after the years of the Cold War in the Nevada desert, known as Area 51, would inspire conspiracy theorists to claim that its black hangars held the bodies of space aliens and their flying saucers. When reporters asked Mitchell for details of what was going on in the black hangars at Langley, the general with a reputation for talking to the press answered with a Cheshire Cat grin and kept walking. The newsmen were luckier with Mitchell's aide, Major Davenport Johnson. Nicknamed "Jam," he told them, "Our men think bombs, talk bombs, and expect to make the Navy eat bombs. Our biggest trouble now is getting targets. My men are blowing them up so fast, the government is having trouble keeping us supplied." Another officer, Major

William Hensley, bragged, "Our crews can hit a moving target 50 percent of the time in a thirty-mile gale. With a little more practice we'll be able to pick the crow's nest off any ship in Uncle Sam's Navy."

As reporters probed for information about Mitchell's mysterious air base, they and the American public were able to plumb the mind of its commander in the pages of Mitchell's first book, published in the spring and titled *Our Air Force*. A reviewer for the *New York Times* wrote that Mitchell's critics "will not like it," and that its author was "either in advance of his time or misconceives and exaggerates the scope and value of aviation." Writers for newspaper society pages observed that in the midst of training pilots to prove that airplanes could sink battleships, the controversial general remained a star personality at horse shows and at the dinner parties of the social and political elite of Washington and New York. Even sports writers found him good copy. When Mitchell and his sister Harriet went to a baseball game with Mrs. Babe Ruth and were introduced to the "Sultan of Swat," shutters of Press Graphic cameras clicked and the crowd roared its pleasure. Harriet saw her famous brother as a "magnetic, dynamic personality with a sense of humor" and "fun to be with." Like their father, he was also a history instructor, but at the controls of an airplane flying Harriet over Civil War sites and lecturing her about battles waged on them.

History and historic places were also elements in Mitchell's training program for the men who were to put his beliefs to the test. Addressing pilots and crews, he spoke of the history of Virginia, from the Jamestown settlement and Hampton, the oldest continually inhabited town in colonial America, to Cornwallis surrendering to George Washington's army at Yorktown and the duel between the Civil War ironclads *Monitor* and *Merrimac*. He also lectured on the stubbornness of generals and admirals and challenged his men to teach the doubters of air power a lesson.

Although he was tight-lipped with reporters about giving details of activities at Langley, he retained his appreciation of the value of photographs and newsreels in promoting the cause of military aviation and his belief that airplanes had rendered battleships obsolete. As planning for the testing of air power over sea power proceeded, he flew to McCook Field in Ohio to talk with the head of its photographic studio, General George Goddard. Mitchell told Goddard, "I'm going to bomb some ships and I've got to have a photography man who knows his stuff."

Finding himself installed in an office next to Mitchell's in the Munitions Building in the nation's capital, Goddard learned that he would be responsible for more than photographers. He was to "handle the newsreel and movie people." Calling them "temperamental," Mitchell said, "We've got to get all we can out of them. I want newsreels of those sinking ships in every theater in the country, just as soon we can get them there." Understanding that he was engaged not only in a contest between planes and ships, but in a battle for public opinion, Goddard assembled his own air armada of eighteen de Havilland photographic planes and borrowed a small dirigible from the Aberdeen Proving Ground in Maryland to record the outcome of the first war games matching two arms of the military so that there could be no doubt about the victor.

As practice flights continued, Mitchell's 1st Provisional Brigade was plagued by a lack of finances. When a request for money to trim tall pines trees at the end of a runway was denied, the result was several crashes, including a plane carrying four one-hundred-pound bombs, killing the two-man crew. When Mitchell requested torpedoes for use in the forthcoming tests, the navy not only rejected the plea, but directed that no information on torpedoes be given to anyone in the army without a direct order from the secretary of the navy, based on the belief that the information would "undermine the Navy."

Because the tests of air power versus warships had been placed under the aegis of the commander in chief of the Atlantic Fleet, the targets, means of attack, places, and dates were set by the navy. The first on June 20, 1921, was to be an anchored German submarine. The *U-117* would be assaulted by navy planes in three waves, dropping 165-pound bombs. Recalling the day in his book *Winged Defense*, published four years later, Mitchell described eight "majestic" battleships, several cruisers, many destroyers and auxiliary vessels, hospital ships, and tenders moving into Chesapeake Bay and anchoring at Lynnehaven Roads. Observers would be aboard the transport *Henderson*. Mitchell watched from his airplane, the *Osprey*, along with observation planes, three dirigibles, and an aircraft arranged by Goddard for newsreel crews. When the navy attack quickly blasted the submarine to pieces and sank it, Mitchell wrote, no one "except the air people had expected such a rapid termination."

With the next test scheduled more than a week later, there was plenty of time for the newsreels to be shown in theaters from coast to coast. During this period, the navy argued that the destruction of an "easily sunk" unarmored submarine was one thing; a heavy capital ship was another. Resuming bombing training the day after the submarine demonstration, Mitchell led a flight of fifty-three planes on another attack with two hundred bombs on the battered *Texas*. During this raid, two planes collided and crashed into Chesapeake Bay, killing both pilots. In a message to General Menoher, Army Secretary Weeks stated that he was "seriously disturbed and concerned over the succession of accidents." He ordered, "Most rigid instructions will be given by you [to Mitchell] for the purpose of preventing repetitions."

Mitchell assured Menoher, "Every precaution practicable is taken by the personnel whose own life depends on the proper function of this equipment."

The first test of the Provisional Air Brigade's skill in bombing a ship at sea was against the ex-German destroyer *G-102*. Eighteen pursuit ships with four twenty-five-pound bombs in three waves were followed by a dozen heavy Martin bombers in V formation. In recalling the first attack against a ship by a large air force, Mitchell wrote, "As we approached the target vessel we could see the whole Atlantic fleet formed in a circle around it. We wound our way in and out of cirrocumulus clouds behind which we could have concealed our approach very easily had it been actual war." Within minutes, planes plummeting from three thousand to two hundred feet in thirty-second intervals had the destroyer's decks "punctured and swept from end to end," followed by the Martin bombers, hitting close in front, behind, around, and directly in the center, sending up columns of water and smoke. As the flaming destroyer fractured at midship and sank, Mitchell believed that the "absolutely conclusive" demonstration had validated all his systems of bombing. The tests using a submarine and a destroyer had shown that planes could sink "any kind of vessel not protected by armor."

The next phase of the navy-run tests would involve an air attack on a ship protected by side and deck armor, with watertight compartments and bulkheads and "every perfection of a modern vessel of that class." The former German cruiser *Frankfurt* would be subjected to varying sizes of bombs that were not intended to sink it, so that inspectors could go on board to assess damage. When a test was made using 600-pound bombs, the blasts were so powerful that the *Frankfurt* rolled to its port side and quickly went under, proving to Mitchell that "our air bombs could destroy a cruiser as no other weapons could."

But the big question—and the real test of Billy Mitchell's boasts—remained unanswered. "Could airplanes find a battleship at sea and put it out of commission?"

The ship the navy provided for the experiment was the USS *Iowa*. Controlled by radio from the *Ohio*, five miles distant, the *Iowa* was "hiding" in a twenty-five-thousand-square mile area between Capes Hatteras and Henlopen. In the Spanish-American War, the *Iowa* had been the flagship of one of the U.S. Navy's most colorful captains, "Fighting Bob" Evans. To the delight of Jingoes, such as Teddy Roosevelt, Evans had boasted, "Give me the *Iowa* and I will see that Spanish is the only language spoken in hell for the next twenty years." On June 29, 1921, navy planes found the ship in less than three hours. Attacking from an altitude of four thousand feet, twenty-five aircraft dropped dummy bombs. When they scored only two direct hits, navy observers informed the press they could "safely dismiss" the claims by advocates of air power that battleships could not withstand attacks from the air.

Mitchell replied that the experiment with the *Iowa* had proved that navy aviators could locate a moving ship at sea and attack it, but by dropping dummy bombs had not answered the pertinent question. All the tests to this point had been conducted with targets that fell far short of the warships that had put to sea in the world war in design, armor, and durability in battle. No finer example of modern naval warship architecture existed than the German dreadnaught that had been made available to Mitchell for the final phase of the experiment in air versus sea power. Built in 1911, the *Ostfriesland* had been designed on orders from Admiral von Tirpitz and built to be unsinkable. In the Battle of Jutland she had taken eighteen hits by large shells and a mine, but made her way home. The meaning of this challenge to the future of air power, as Mitchell saw it, was clear: "We had to kill, lay out and bury this great ship."

Mitchell's aviators would have to do so before an audience of the most powerful men in government: General Pershing; observers from England, France, Spain, Portugal, Brazil, and the Empire of Japan; and an assembly of fifty reporters. They were hungry to write the ending of a story they had been covering for nearly three years in which Billy Mitchell had been cast as David and the navy as Goliath. Aboard the *Henderson* at dawn on July 20, 1921, they entered Chesapeake Bay in an armada of eight battleships and a swarm of destroyers and smaller ships in choppy waters and twenty-mile-an-hour winds. Believing that Mitchell's planes could not operate in such conditions, the navy chose not to signal him to start the test and elected and to take its ships back to port. Puzzled that he had gotten no order, and suspecting a navy trick, Mitchell signaled he wished to start "at once."

With the observer ships again in place, the demonstration opened with five planes in a column dropping five bombs in such rapid succession that it seemed as if two or three were in the air at the same time. Two hit alongside the ship and three on the deck. Fragments of battleship were blown long distances, forcing terrified observers to duck and run for cover. Water spouted hundreds of feet. Mitchell and his airmen felt jolts at three thousand feet. The navy control ship flashed frantic signals to stop the attack to allow the damage assessment team to go aboard and inspect the mangled, listing, but still floating battleship. With the weather worsening and the first day of the test program completed, reporters were ferried ashore on the fast destroyer *Leary* to file their accounts from Norfolk. Clinton Gilbert of the *Washington Post* wrote, "On the good ship *Henderson*, [Navy] Secretary Denby told us how little impression the bombs had made. High naval officers sniggered cheerfully."

Because of the unexpected stormy weather, Mitchell and his fleet of planes struggled to make it back to Langley. Setting down long after dark on a field with landing lights that did not work very well, Mitchell found all his aircraft "present or accounted for" (one was forced to land "some distance south of Norfolk" with a broken wheel). Confident the two-thousand-pound bombs that had been secretly built would finish the *Ostfriesland* the next day, he listened to a debate among his pilots as to whether they should proceed. One side held that the attack would be so terrible and devastating that it would result in the American people demanding the abolition of the navy. The other side felt the battleship must be obliterated because air power had brought an entirely new element into warfare on the water, and if the United States did not draw the proper lessons from it, other nations would, leaving the United States at a great disadvantage.

Mitchell had no doubt as to what to do. Angry that he had not been allowed to sink the *Ostfriesland* on the first try, he was, as his sister Ruth recorded in her book about him, "mad clear through," and determined that in the second attempt in the morning it was going to be "kill or die trying." Just before seven o'clock on July 21, as he and his planes took off, he warned the navy by radio that while the plan called for navy planes to participate, his men were not to be "interfered with by naval aircraft." At half past eight they found the battleship riding evenly but so low in the water that portholes at the stern of the third deck were awash.

Led by Captain W. R. Lawson, the planes broke from a V formation into a single column of seven planes. Four bombs hit in rapid succession, close alongside the ship, lifting it eight to ten feet. "When a death blow has been dealt by a bomb to a vessel, there is no mistaking it," Mitchell wrote. "In a minute the *Ostfriesland* was on her side; in two minutes she was sliding down by the stern and turning over at the same time; in three minutes she was bottom-side up, looking like a gigantic whale, the water oozing out of her seams as she prepared to go down to the bottom, then gradually she went down stern first." Recalling the historic day in *Winged Defense*, he described a mixture of emotions in killing magnificent warships:

We had been anxious to sink the submarine and destroyer, but I had felt badly to see as beautiful a ship as the *Frankfurt* go down. She rode in the water like a swan. The *Ostfriesland*, however, impressed me like a grim old bulldog, with the vicious scars of Jutland still on her. We wanted to destroy her from the air but when it was actually accomplished, it was a very serious and awesome sight. Some of the spectators on the observing vessels wept, so overwrought were their feelings. I watched her sink from a few feet above the transport *Henderson*, where the people who had observed the tests were waving and cheering on the decks and in the rigging.

Contrary to the popular opinion, that great vortices in the water are formed as a ship sinks, there were none in this case. She slid to her last resting place with very little commotion. Thus ended the first great air and battleship test that the world had ever seen. It conclusively proved the ability of aircraft to destroy ships of all classes on the surface of the water.

What Mitchell could not know as he savored his triumph on the day his planes sank the *Ostfriesland* was that he had won a battle, not the war. While the U.S. Army's chief of ordnance, General C. C. Williams, exclaimed that a bomb "has been fired that will be heard around the world," Secretary of the Navy Denby was unwilling to commit himself "as to the plane against the battleship." His Assistant Secretary, Theodore Roosevelt, Jr., reminded the world that he was the son of a famous big-game hunter by telling reporters, "I once saw a man kill a lion with a 30-30 caliber rifle under certain conditions, but that doesn't mean that a 30-30 rifle is a lion gun."

Addressing the battleship slayers as they celebrated their deed late into the night in one of the black hangars at Langley, Mitchell is reported to have said, "Well, lads. I guess we showed old Admiral Tugaboats [*sic*] today!" In the war to come, he continued, "God will be on the side of the heaviest air force. What we did to the *Frankfurt* and *Ostfriesland* is what will happen to all warships in future wars. And don't you forget it. Keep your eye on the sky!"

CHAPTER SIXTEEN

"SOMEWHAT ERRATIC AND CHANGEABLE."

"The sun rose today on a city whose tallest towers lay scattered in crumbled bits of stone."

Eighty years before Islamic terrorists flew two airliners into the twin towers of New York's World Trade Center on September 11, 2001, these shocking words appeared in a news story on the July 29, 1921, front page of the *New York Herald*. It presented a terrifying picture of what would happen if the world's greatest city were attacked by airplanes. "The sun saw, when its light penetrated the ruins, hordes of people on foot, working their way very slowly and painfully up the island," the story went on. "Rich and poor alike, welded together in a real democracy of misery, headed northward. Always they looked fearfully up at the sky."

On the previous day, Billy Mitchell's heavy bombers had flown from Langley, Virginia, to conduct a simulated attack on Manhattan. The *Herald*'s story was a grim scenario of what Manhattan might look like after an aerial attack with real bombs. The bombers flew at eight-thousand feet over the length of Broadway to the tip of Manhattan, raining imaginary bombs upon the world's tallest edifice (the stately Woolworth Building), the Treasury and Customs houses, and the other historic, governmental, and financial landmarks of America's premier city. Similar fake attacks blasted Philadelphia; Wilmington, Delaware; and Baltimore. To underscore Mitchell's point that the navy's property was vulnerable to attack, a mock air raid also hit the U.S. Naval Academy at Annapolis before returning to Langley. Adding salt to wounded egos in the Navy Department a few days later, Mitchell led four pursuit planes to the naval facility at Hampton Roads, Virginia, in a night raid on four docked destroyers in which the bombs were several million candle-power flares dropped close to the ships from five hundred feet, awakening their startled crews. Had they been bombs, Mitchell declared, the destroyers would have been sunk. This demonstration, he told the press, proved that navies were not safe in their own harbors by day or night.

The official War Department response to Mitchell's demonstration of airplane superiority to their battleships came in a report on the bombing of the *Ostfriesland*. Released in September by the Joint Army and Navy Board over the signature of General Pershing, it reported the findings of the chief inspector of the damage inflicted. He stated that the *Ostfriesland* was already sinking at the time of the air attack, and that if there had been a crew on the ship, they could "easily have kept the ship almost free of water." The report concluded, "The battleship is still the bulwark of the nation's sea defense and will remain so long as the safe navigation of the sea for purposes of trade or transportation is vital to success in war."

Infuriated, Mitchell shot off his own analysis of the test to General Menoher. The lengthy document said in part, "Aircraft now in existence can find and destroy all classes of sea craft under war conditions with a negligible loss [of airplanes]. Aircraft acting from suitable floating airdromes can destroy any class of surface sea craft on the high seas. The problem of destruction of sea craft by air forces has been solved and is finished. It is now necessary to provide an air organization and a method of defending not only our coast cities but our interior cities against the attack of hostile air forces."

Asserting that no real aerial defense was possible so long as aviation was "buried in the Army and Navy," Mitchell called in the document for a revision of the structure of national defense "at once," said a solution "will not exist until a department of national defense is organized," and called for a separate air force. Menoher sent the report to Secretary of War Weeks with the notation that Menoher did "not concur" with the demand for the "creation of a 'Department of Aeronautics.'" While the top leadership of the War Department intended to keep the Mitchell document secret, its contents exploded on the pages of the *New York Times* on September 13. It was a "sensational chapter" in the controversy that "flatly contradicted" the report and a broadside aimed at "battleship admirals."

Four days later, Menoher notified Weeks that unless Mitchell was disciplined by Weeks himself, Menoher would resign as chief of the air service. Weeks agreed that Mitchell should be rebuked, but he also suggested that if Menoher could not handle his subordinate, Mitchell, Menoher had better take another command. Menoher quit on September 17. So did Mitchell. Explaining his request to be "relieved from my present post and be assigned some other duties," he wrote that he felt "the conditions with respect to the development of aviation, as they now exist in the War Department, make my presence in the executive organization more a source of irritation than a means of progressive advancement."

Unaware of Mitchell's request, newspapers praised Weeks for accepting Menoher's resignation and called for Mitchell as his replacement. To the editors of the *Philadelphia Public Ledger* Mitchell had become not only a symbol of the air force, but a figure who "looms large in the public mind as a restless, relentless, energetic, studious and yet smashing enthusiast." The *New York Globe* advised Weeks that he would "make a mistake if he does not give the command of the army air service to General Mitchell." News editors found themselves under bombardment by expressions of praise for Mitchell from the lower echelons of the air service. Evidently in a public relations campaign either orchestrated by Mitchell or with his approval, the press releases claimed that air service officers "over the whole U.S. are unanimous in their demand" for a commander "who will fly with them" and also in their "fear that there will be much useless expenditure and loss of life if their new chief is selected from some other branch of the service." This support in the press and from the public for the dashing war hero and peacetime battler in the cause of air power, combined with plans for other bombing tests on September 20, persuaded Weeks to ask that Mitchell "remain on your present duties at least until after completion of the bombing experiments." These involved three days of trials in which the target was the old battleship *Alabama*. The bombs were "chemical missiles" consisting of phosphorous and tear gas. A night attack illuminated by flares dropped as markers sank the ship with one-ton bombs from twenty-five hundred feet and proved that airplanes could locate and destroy a naval target at night.

Eager to provide other demonstrations, Mitchell was denied permission to continue the operations by the Army-Navy Board. The order read: "Disapproval recommended. It is desired that the [1st] Provisional Air Brigade be disbanded and that the personnel return to their proper stations and normal functions without delay."

Suddenly without an air force as newspaper headlines blared the brigade's success, he returned to Langley and his office to learn that General Pershing had gotten himself out of a personnel problem by tapping the man he had turned to during the war in the dispute between Mitchell and General Foulois. Pershing brought in General Mason Patrick as Menoher's replacement. Although Mitchell's impulse was to resign, he spent a weekend thinking it over and decided to stay, but on the condition that his powers and duties as Patrick's assistant be put in writing. Recognizing that Mitchell had "a better knowledge of tactics of air fighting than any man in this country," Patrick assented, but expressed his expectation that his new deputy "would lose no opportunity to take a fling at the navy," if for no other reason than Mitchell's "undoubted love for the limelight." In the propaganda war between Mitchell and the admirals and some sympathetic generals, few observers in the capital and interested citizens and newspapers across the country did not give the advantage to the colorful general who backed up his words with successful actions.

Coincidental with this tug of war with Mitchell, the Navy Department suddenly faced the prospect of reductions in its number of battleships. On December 14, 1920, U.S. senator William Borah had introduced a resolution requesting that the United States call for a conference of the world's naval powers to draft a treaty to limit the size and power of their fleets. Attached to a naval appropriations bill, it required Secretary of State Charles Evans Hughes to invite Great Britain, France, Italy, and Japan to talks on balancing of naval armaments. When the conference opened with Hughes chosen as its chairman, he proposed not only limitation of future warship construction, but substantial scrapping of existing ships and those being built. The United States proposed abandoning ships totaling displacements of eight hundred forty-five thousand tons and asked that Britain give up five hundred eighty-three thousand tons and Japan four hundred eighty thousand. The program was accepted in principal. It was then agreed that the formula for ships of more than ten thousand tons be a ratio of 5 for the United States, 5 for Britain, 3 for Japan, and 1.67 for France and Italy. There would also be a ten-year "naval holiday" in which no new capital ships were to be built. In a separate four-power treaty on the subject of the Pacific and the Far East, the United States, Britain, France, and Japan agreed to respect each other's rights over Pacific island possessions and provide for "consultations" in the event of "aggressive action" in the region. The U.S. Senate ratified all nine of the resulting treaties with the reservation that the United States made no commitment to the mutual use of armed force and that there existed "no alliance, [and] no obligation to join in any defense."

As the disarmament talks commenced, General Mitchell found himself sailing off for a study of European aviation. Although he was certainly the man for the task, his appointment to lead the study mission was not based entirely on his qualifications, fame, and the high esteem in which he was held in European aviation circles. State and War Department officials worried that as air adviser to the American delegation he might complicate the disarmament talks. Mitchell's friends and colleagues were concerned that his struggle with the navy and a strenuous campaign of public appearances and writings on behalf of his cause were having a negative effect on him, physically and mentally. This was also a concern of Mitchell's wife. Complaining of his "recent erratic conduct," she asked Secretary Weeks to rescind Mitchell's participation in the European mission. Weeks ordered him to report to Walter Reed Hospital for a psychiatric examination.

Objecting to hospitalization and protesting that he could "convince any fair-minded person within a few minutes that there is nothing wrong with me," he proposed an examination in his own quarters by army doctors. After several interviews, Major W. L. Sheep of the Medical Corps reported Mitchell to be "oriented in all spheres," neither depressed nor elated, and with "no disorder of apprehension or apperception." Although Mitchell had admitted he liked "to take a drink with a crowd of congenial companions and at times imbibes too freely," he was deemed by the doctors to show no signs of acute or chronic alcoholism and no evidence of mental or physical disease. His only problem, they reported, was being "greatly worried over his domestic situation," but that he stated that he could not "afford to let worry" about the state of his marriage "get the best of him." When the examiners reported him "fit for full military duty," Secretary Weeks ordered him to resume his plans for the European inspection tour.

It began with Mitchell standing on the bridge of the ocean liner *Rotterdam* with the ship's captain and watching an aerial "bon voyage" overflight by planes from New York's Mitchel Field. His fellow mission members were his aide in the war and thereafter, Captain Clayton Bissell, and an aeronautical engineer, Alfred Verville. When they reached Paris, Mitchell had a reunion with Benjamin Foulois, now the air attaché at the U.S. embassy. Invited to a conference of French air officers, he told war stories, discussed the future of flight, and found himself teasingly hailed as the "hero of Chesapeake Bay." Observing him moving in the midst of the Parisian social life, Verville saw "something so strongly magnetic about him that he drew attention no matter where he was." The women seemed especially attracted and "couldn't keep their hands off him."

Early in January 1922 Mitchell traveled to the south of France to his birthplace in Nice. With Verville in tow he went to Place Grimaldi and posed for a photograph on the second floor balcony of the house that would later be marked with a bronze plaque stating:

Here was born William Mitchell, Brigadier General
U.S. Army Air Service. December 29, 1879.

At a naval station in Toulon he examined an experimental aircraft carrier, the *Berne*, and was taken to sea on it. He came away impressed but found the French "dubious" about the value of carriers because of vulnerability to air attack. Moving on to Rome, he was feted at a dinner party by King Victor Emmanuel. After passing through Paris, he gave Verville a tour of Verdun and Château-Thierry and the locations where he had commanded air squadrons. In the cemetery at Thiaucourt where his brother John and Raoul Lufbery lay he placed two bronze wreaths. By the time the three-man mission arrived in Coblenz, Germany, he had developed influenza but did not remain in bed long. On route to Berlin he observed the people in towns and cities of the country he had helped to defeat in 1918 and discerned that the "military spirit of Germany is by no means crushed." He would note this in his report and warn, "At the first opportunity, Germany may ally herself to any nation that is willing to help her." If Austria were to join Germany, he wrote, the joining "of all the Germanic people will give them 100 million population." He also observed that although Germany was forbidden by the peace treaty to have an air force, a group of war pilots was an air reserve that practiced flying in gliders. His belief that Germany was serious about building an air force was validated at a luncheon given in his honor by the German Aero Club, where he met and listened to Germany's leading aviation figures,

Ernst Udet, Erhard Milch, and the successor to Baron von Richthofen in leading the Flying Circus, Hermann Göring, talk of the rebirth of a German air force. Verville thought Mitchell, Bissell, and the Germans were "like a bunch of boys, like opposing ball teams who had gotten together after a ball game." He noted, "There was a seeming admiration, an affable feeling on the part of these men toward Mitchell. They all liked him. I could see that."

In Holland, Mitchell met the designer of some of Germany's best planes during the war, Anthony Fokker. He replied to Fokker's expressed desire to move to the United States and go into the aircraft business by urging him to do so. (The company that Fokker started in the United States would be eventually bought by General Motors and become the basis of an airline company headed by Eddie Rickenbacker and subsequently transformed into Eastern Airlines.) The final stop on the European tour was England. The visit included a review of the cadets at the new Royal Air Force College at Cranwell, a meal with Winston Churchill, a formal reception and dinner given by Sir Hugh Trenchard and Aviation Minister Freddie Guest, and test-flying new R.A.F. fighters.

After more than three months, he was back in Washington in March 1922. His mission's report noted, "All the great nations have assigned definite missions to their air forces, to their armies, and to their navies. In the United States we have not done this, and, at this time, if we should be attacked, no one can tell what the duties of these three arms are."

In his absence the disarmament conference agreed to scrap sixty-eight capital ships, but set no limit on numbers of aircraft. Encouraged by this acknowledgment of the importance of military aviation by the conference, he began a tour of army aviation centers and launched himself into the work of developing new plane designs, giving his encouragement to inventors, plotting new airfields, and organizing air races.

Feeling bitter that his wife had gone to Secretary of War Weeks and suggested that he was mentally unfit for the European mission, he flew to

Milwaukee and filed for divorce. She brought a countersuit and sought custody of the children. The court sided with her.

During a visit to Selfridge Field, Michigan, in the early summer of 1922, when he was separated from his wife, he took time to attend the Detroit Horse Show and was introduced to a young woman rider, Elizabeth Trumbull Miller. Called Betty, the daughter of prominent Detroit attorney Sidney Miller had served as a nurse in France during the war and had heard of General Billy Mitchell, but had never seen him. She also knew his name because of his articles on how to jump a horse. Small, slender, dark-haired, with blue eyes, and dressed in riding habit, she had also written on the subject. When Mitchell learned that she had never been up in an airplane, he insisted that they go flying that afternoon. Mitchell's sister Ruth in her chatty biography of him called the meeting "love at first sight, on his side at least." The "ideal mate" for a "stormy petrel," Betty was "beautiful, with a charm that enchants prince and peasant alike," and a "fine horsewoman without horsiness, a crack shot without bravado, a skilled hostess, warmhearted, gay, infinitely encouraging, and loyal." Mitchell's civilian friends and military associates noticed a calmer and more temperate mood, but he remained impatient about progress in building an air force, weary of fighting for funds, bitter about having to fend off the navy, and needing to grapple with "some idiotic committee with an ax to grind."

As he engaged in ground battles in War Department offices and Capitol Hill hearings, he showed that at the age of forty-two he had lost none of the daring that had made him famous in the air. Flying over the Potomac River with aide Captain St. Clair Streett in another plane, he abruptly broke formation and headed his plane for the Washington Monument and circled closely around it. Not to be outdone, Streett did the same. On a flight from Aberdeen, Maryland, to Philadelphia with mechanical inspector Harry Short in the rear seat, Mitchell pointed down to tracks of the Pennsylvania Railroad and asked Short, "Do you suppose we can land on them?" Before Short could advise against trying it, the plane was zooming down. In a maneuver pilots called "touch and go" he set the plane's wheels between the rails of a straight stretch of track and instantly took off, with the plane's only damage a dent in the tail skid.

On October 18, 1922, at an air meet in Detroit he established a speed record of 224.38 miles an hour. The Mitchell publicity office promptly sent out a press release that boasted, "In bringing the world's speed record to America by this flight the assistant chief of army air service has once again demonstrated not only his ability as a pilot, but also further endeared himself to the flyers of the army by being willing to lead in any contest in which the air service takes part."

Two months after garnering this praise from his own publicity office and similar accolades in the press, the general who was recognized and lauded around the globe as Billy Mitchell, but still called Willy by his mother, lost his most enthusiastic supporter. On the eve of his forty-third birthday, seventy-year-old Harriet Danforth Becker Mitchell died in his house in Washington. She and his sister Harriet had moved into it to "take care of him" after he moved out of the home he shared with his wife and children. Although he was the country's most famous army aviator and had built a public image as swashbuckler of the air by wearing a flashy uniform, he remained a dutiful son. When his mother saw him wearing a riding outfit of bold black-and-white plaid, she scolded, "Now, Willy, didn't I tell you never to wear those horrible breeches? Don't let me see them on you again." Mitchell meekly replied, "Yes, mummy." The pants were never worn again.

The Mitchell penchant for eye-arresting uniforms would also invite a rebuke from Eddie Rickenbacker. Although America's Ace of Aces had been no slouch in sporting non-regulation army attire during the war, he drew the line one night in 1920 in New York's new Biltmore Hotel. Now a successful businessman in both aviation and the automotive industry, Rickenbacker had invited Mitchell to come up from Washington to join him and a group of mutual friends to take in a World Series game between the Brooklyn Dodgers and the Cleveland Indians. According to Rickenbacker, Mitchell appeared in full uniform with "six rows of ribbons and a swagger stick," looking "hotter than a firecracker." After the game Mitchell proposed that they all go out on the town. "Nuts to that," Rickenbacker retorted. "I'm not going out with a billboard like you." He insisted that Mitchell change into "civvies" and provided suit, shirt, tie, socks, shoes, and hat.

Through the autumn of 1922 Mitchell had been working on a plan for a flight around the world and mapping a route of "stepping stones" that were no more than four hundred miles apart. He also envisioned a series of three flights across Central America and over the Caribbean to show "the ease with which the approaches through the West Indies Islands may be guarded by aircraft as a defense of the Panama Canal." The former Signal Corps officer who had brought the telegraph to Alaska proposed and then led an expedition to Canada in February 1923 to test ski-equipped planes. In a report titled "Aeronautics in Canada" he appealed for the designation of a "suitable person" to deal directly with the Canadians on the subject of opening air routes for "commercial intercourse with Canada, through Canada to Europe, and through Canada to our own possession of Alaska," and onward to Asia.

Turning his attention to the future of military flight along the Mexican border, he went to El Paso, Texas, and found the U.S. air squadron stationed there "in just about as poor condition as could be and still be called an observation squadron." Pointing out the lack of a command system, suitable equipment, and liaison system, he could not resist reporting to General Patrick the irony that the dining facilities and barracks were fine, the officers and enlisted men were "well turned out," and "they have the championship basketball team in the cavalry division."

While Mitchell was exploring the future of aviation north of the border and its sorry state in Texas, General Patrick created a board to investigate the overall condition of the air service. Headed by General William

Lassiter, it found the situation "is actually alarming" and "critical." Should a national emergency confront the country within a few years, Lassiter's report warned, "the air service would not be able to play its part in meeting that emergency." It recommended a ten-year rebuilding plan at an annual cost of $25 million, establishing an officer corps of four thousand, a body of twenty-five hundred flying cadets, twenty-five thousand enlisted men, and a fleet of twenty-five hundred planes. Although it did not advocate an independent air force department, it proposed an autonomous air combat arm that would be "attached" to ground troops. Approved by Secretary Weeks, the report was sent to the Joint Army and Navy Board, where it languished.

Although Mitchell was not surprised by the inaction, he was shocked by a remark by a new occupant of the White House. Soon after Calvin Coolidge became president upon the unexpected death of President Harding on August 2, 1923, of a mysterious illness during a goodwill trip to Alaska and the West Coast, Coolidge complained to dinner guests about imprudence in federal spending and cited "those aviators" who "just run around and burn a lot of gasoline." He went on to name "that Mitchell fellow," who "thinks nothing of flying in a government plane to Michigan to visit the girl he's engaged to marry."

Pressing General Patrick to exert pressure on the navy to provide obsolete ships for new bombing experiments, Mitchell found Patrick not only sympathetic, but a man willing to take the issue to General Pershing. Accusing the navy of "stalling," Patrick opined to the army chief of staff that the secretary of the navy's explanation that ships could not be made available until after ratification of the disarmament treaty was "simply and solely an excuse." Having gotten his way in employing the AEF in the war, Pershing used his forceful personality and prestige to bring the navy around. It released two twenty-year-old battleships, the *Virginia* and the *New Jersey*. But the time for preparation of Mitchell's bombing tests was short. The date was set at September 5, one day after the scheduled maiden flight at the

Naval Air Station at Lakehurst, New Jersey, of the navy's airship ZR-1. Named *Shenandoah*, it was the first Zeppelin-type dirigible to abandon dangerous, inflammable hydrogen for lift and use non-flammable helium.

In a "spectacular show," in the words of an Associated Press observer, Mitchell's planes sank the *Virginia* in twenty-seven minutes. Because the attack on the *New Jersey* was made from ten thousand feet with lighter bombs, its destruction took a little longer. The magazine *Aviation* reported "a revelation in bombing accuracy." The *New York Times* said, "There can be no doubt that those who say the *Virginia* and *New Jersey* went to the bottom of the sea so quickly after vital hits were scored are deeply impressed with the necessity for command of the air in modern naval engagements." Pershing was still not persuaded. He praised the "air bombers' aim," but said that the tests did not prove that modern warships "can be sunk." A later article in *Aviation* revealed that Black Jack had evidently surrendered to a plea by Admiral William E. Shoemaker. "My God," Shoemaker was reported to have exclaimed, "we can't let this get out or it would ruin the Navy."

Worried about having to deal with another Mitchell broadside and noisy public tirade, General Patrick seized an opportunity to send Mitchell abroad. Aware of his impending marriage and plans for a honeymoon abroad, he invented another mission to inspect foreign air power, this time in the Pacific and Asia. The itinerary would allow Mitchell to fulfill an expressed desire to hunt tigers in India. Accordingly, after the wedding ceremony in the bride's church in Grosse Point, Michigan, on October 11, 1923, the couple sailed from San Francisco on the *Cambrai* for Hawaii, and on to the Philippines, China, India, and Japan, with the cost of their travel paid for by the U.S. government. Mitchell gave Patrick an outline of objectives that was far-ranging:

> In addition to the regular inspections I shall study the whole Pacific problem as far as it concerns us both from an offensive and

defensive standpoint across the Pacific–taking into consideration any alliances or assistance one Power may gain from another in this area. It will comprise: (a) The problem of destroying the enemies' armed forces–land, water and air. (b) Destruction of their power to make war, including production and supply of war material, transportation, etc. (c) Destruction of their morale. And I believe that we can arrive at a solution of the Pacific problem which will allow us to carry on an offensive campaign across the Pacific Ocean.

Welcomed to Hawaii by a flight of eighteen airplanes from Wheeler Field, Honolulu, and a throng of reporters on the dock, he was also greeted by former adversary General Menoher, now in command at the army's Schofield Barracks. After observing maneuvers with no participation by aircraft and inspecting the state of defenses all over the island of Oahu, he wrote a report to Patrick describing Hawaii's vulnerabilities to an air and sea attack that "a boy fifteen years old, who knows about air power and had a simple military training in high school" would see and know how to correct. Defense of the islands, he said, would depend on an air force being able to "prevent landings on any islands and to destroy any force either in the air, on the water or under the water within the radius of their operations." His assessment of air force readiness was grim. Finding "only two little squadrons of pursuit aviation," a few "ill equipped bombers," planes with no machine guns, no reserve pilots, and no one trained for combat, he warned that Hawaii was "hopelessly unable to ward off any decided attack."

On a nine-month journey that included the U.S. islands of Guam and Midway and the Philippines, he had a reunion with General Douglas MacArthur, at the time army commander in the Philippines, and took the now docile, aged, former rebel leader Emilio Aguinaldo for a ride in an airplane. Defenses in the islands, Mitchell reported, were no better than in Hawaii. Moving north to the Asian mainland, he achieved his tiger-hunting ambition as the guest of an Indian maharajah, found Siam "one of the pleasantest places" in the Far East (with an air force of 260 planes), and during a tour of China predicted that once the country's population was organized, its potential would be "unlimited." From Japan he reported a military effort centered on an air force that was "rapidly approaching the second in size in the world, being exceeded in number only by France," and with "many more men, more machines and more factories working on an air force three times over what has the United States."

Mitchell greatly expanded on this assessment of a growing Japanese military during the long voyage home. He forecast that a war between Japan and the United States would begin with a Japanese sneak attack on the U.S. naval, air, and army bases at Pearl Harbor, Hawaii, with a concurrent invasion of the Philippines and attacks on British and French colonies to quickly eliminate all opposition to the conquest of the Pacific and ensure ultimate Japanese domination of the Pacific and the Far East. Offering a prediction that would become a horrifying reality on December 7, 1941, he said that in perfect Hawaiian weather, starting at half past seven o'clock on a quiet Sunday morning, one hundred Japanese bombers launched from aircraft carriers would swoop across the main island of Oahu to destroy the Pacific Fleet at Pearl Harbor. Simultaneously, sixty pursuit planes would attack the army's Schofield Barracks and Hickam airfield.

When he presented the 323-page report to General Patrick in October 1924, it combined practical knowledge, expert observations, and the sum of his experience as a soldier and aviator with intuitive vision. Patrick said he would review it "in due course." A reader in the War Plans Division dismissed it as nothing new and greatly exaggerated in its conclusions. "Since he so notoriously overestimates what could be done with air power by the United States," the reader wrote in an assessment of the report, "it is not improbable that he has likewise overestimated what Japan could do and would be able to accomplish with air power."

Others in the War Department also found faults in the report and in the character of the author, whom many regarded as a trouble-making, egotistical, arrogant, and dangerous personality with his head literally and figuratively in the air. He was widely viewed as "somewhat erratic and changeable." In an efficiency report shortly after Mitchell's return, General Patrick said, "He is impulsive, and in dealing with subordinates frequently shows evidence of temper and a tendency to use measures unnecessarily harsh. His recommendations frequently fail to take into account conditions actually existing and which must be, in a measure, controlling. He is erratic and his opinions on many matters are frequently biased."

Having submitted his report of his Pacific and Asia survey to a cool reception by men who harbored grave reservations about it and him, Mitchell sat down for lunch in his Washington home with Thomas B. Costain. The editor of *The Saturday Evening Post*, Costain solicited from Mitchell a series of articles on all aspects of aviation that would then be published as a book titled *Winged Defense* by George P. Putnam. During a meal of brook trout seasoned by Billy Mitchell's tales of airplanes in combat and the promise of aviation in war and peace, Costain found a dramatically different personality than the one seen by generals and admirals. "I can recall," he would write of that day, "how quiet and modest Billy Mitchell seemed to me. There was something boyish about him. He had no feeling of his own importance, but he was burning with zeal." His articles and book would trigger a chain of events that would rattle the War Department, Congress, and nation with the force of a direct hit on a battleship by a one-ton bomb.

PART IV

"THIS AIN'T A VAUDEVILLE SHOW!"

CHAPTER SEVENTEEN

"MITCHELLISM."

A s Brigadier General William Mitchell returned from nine months of assessments of the American military in relation to the nations of the Pacific and Asia, the United States was going through its quadrennial ritual of electing a president. For the third time since 1868 the incumbent was a Republican who had been thrust into the office upon the death of a president. Lincoln and McKinley had died by assassination, and Harding's death from a sudden illness was attributed to eating tainted seafood but suspected by some Americans to have been suicide or even murder because of the worst government corruption scandal since the administration of Ulysses S. Grant. Involving the granting of oil exploitation rights on three U.S. Navy petroleum reservations through bribery and favoritism in the Interior Department, the "Teapot Dome Scandal" got its name from one of the oil reserves. Untainted by the scandal, Harding's successor, Vice President Calvin Coolidge, found himself in a crowded field of contenders in the 1924 presidential election, from the Democratic Party's nominee, John W. Davis, to Senator Robert M. La Follette (Progressive), W. J. Wallace (Commonwealth Land Party), and Frank T. Johns (Socialist Labor), to Judge Gilbert O. Nations (American Party), William Z. Foster of The Workers' Party (Communist), and Herman P. Faris, Prohibition Party.

While none of the presidential candidates made the future of aviation an important issue, Coolidge and Mitchell's War Department nemesis, Secretary Weeks, had been ostentatious in greeting American pilots and crews on September 8 at Bolling Field upon their completion of the first round-the-world flight. Four specially designed Douglas biplanes named

"World Cruisers" had begun the flight. One had crashed in Alaska and another dropped out with engine problems. The route covered 26,350 miles and took 363 hours over 175 days, averaging 74 miles an hour. Although the feat was a great accomplishment by Americans that received accolades in the press, it was not Coolidge who lauded the achievement at a National Aeronautical Association meeting in Dayton in October, but Mitchell as "the president's representative."

He used the occasion to renew his campaign to win public support of aviation as the only reliable bulwark of national defense, forcefully forecasting that in future wars there was a "great probability that the armies will never come into contact on the field of battle" and asserting the true weapons of future sea warfare would be submarines and aircraft carriers. These were themes he planned to explain and champion in the series of articles for *The Saturday Evening Post*, but because he was an active army officer, governmental permission was needed to publish them. To seek it, editor Thomas B. Costain decided to go straight to the top and was granted a meeting with Coolidge that Mitchell attended on November 12, 1924. Later that day Mitchell received a letter from Coolidge:

My Dear General Mitchell:

Confirming my conversation with you this morning, I do not know of any objection to your preparing some articles on aviation, so far as I am concerned. But, of course, I can not speak for your superior officers. The matter should be taken up with them and their decision in relation to the articles followed.

Accordingly, Mitchell discussed the matter with General Patrick and received permission, but he did not tell Patrick of Coolidge's letter specifying superior *officers*, meaning not only the chief of the air service, but Secretary of War Weeks. With General Patrick's assent, Mitchell began work on the first article. An expansion of his Dayton remarks on unrestricted future warfare in which air power would be decisive and pilots like "armored knights in the Middle Ages," the article was published a few days before Christmas. By Easter 1925 the series of five articles would state the Mitchell vision for commercial aviation, with America in a better position than any other nation to develop it; organization of an independent air force; and air power as "a dominating factor in the world's development."

He also continued his assault on the army and navy leaders who looked to past wars and models for conflict that were "dead." Those who did so were "psychologically unfit" to assess and judge the promise of aviation:

> They always fear to change, to do away with or eliminate anything which had long been a part of their organization or system. Unless the public and the legislatures periodically inspect and overhaul the professional organizations maintained for national security, increased expenditures, adherence to obsolete and useless principles of defense, and an inexact knowledge of military conditions are always the result.

Published in the wake of the international disarmament conference, the articles appeared at the very moment that another test of bombing a battleship was in the planning stage. The target was to be one of the ships that had been under construction, the USS *Washington*. Terms of the agreement required it to be scrapped. Because it consisted of only the hull, it was to be towed to a spot off the Virginia coast and subjected to aerial attacks with fake bombs, then sunk by naval gunfire. Because the experiment was done in secret, the navy announced that the *Washington* had withstood bombing and for safety reasons had to be destroyed by naval guns. Mitchell exposed this deception in testimony before a House committee, chaired by Congressman Julian Lampert of Michigan, in questioning by an aviation-friendly committee member, Frank L. Reid.

Born in Aurora, Kane County, Illinois, on April 18, 1879, Congressman Reid attended the public schools, the University of Chicago, and the Chicago College of Law. Admitted to the bar in 1901, he set up practice in Aurora and served as prosecuting attorney of Kane County and State's attorney (1904–1908), assistant United States attorney in Chicago (1908–1910), member of the state house of representatives (1911–1912), and chairman of the Kane County Republican Central Committee (1914–1916). Elected to the 86th Congress, he would serve from March 1923 to January 1935, and retire to general law practice in Chicago and Aurora.

Employing his prosecutorial skills to the questioning of Mitchell in December 1924, Reid permitted, and often led, his famous witness to present his views at length in a scathing attack on the "conservatism" of "desk admirals" who clung to a navy whose "usefulness" as "a defensive agent on the surface of the water along our coasts" was gone.

"You see, the army and navy are the oldest institutions we have," he explained to Reid and the Lampert committee about why aviation was being restricted. "They place everything on precedent. You can't do that in the air business. You have to look ahead."

"If you suffer any criticism," Reid told Mitchell, "I think this committee will want to go on the record to say that you have helped the country to be greatest air republic in the world."

Mitchell's longtime friend and ally, Hap Arnold, now on General Patrick's staff as the director of information, worried that Mitchell was going too far and courting retribution from the admirals and generals he criticized. He pleaded, "Billy, take it easy. We need you. Don't throw everything away just to beat out some guy who doesn't understand. Air power is coming." He begged, "Stop saying all these things about the independent air arm that are driving old Army and Navy people crazy."

"When senior officers won't see the facts," Mitchell replied, "you've got to do something unorthodox, perhaps an explosion. I'm doing it for the good of the air force, for the future of the air force, for the good of you fellows. I can afford to do it. You can't."

Frequently a star witness before numerous congressional committees with an interest in the debate over aviation, Billy Mitchell was an even more fascinating figure for reporters on the Capitol Hill beat and source of delight to editors and headline writers looking for a catch phrase. In a burst of creativity the *New York Evening Post* coined the term "Mitchellism." The definition of its practitioner, in the words of the *New York Times*, was "militant reformer." To provide avid readers a portrait of the firebrand at his desk in the Munitions Building, an edifice that seemed to be aptly named as headquarters for someone who was interested in setting off an explosion, Oscar Cesare of the *New York Times* ventured a visit. He found a "carefree museum." The desk was a litter of papers, charts, photographs, sample plane parts, and a shard from a one-ton bomb. Model airplanes dangled from the ceiling. A wall displayed the steering wheel of a Zeppelin that had been shot down in France. Another held the brass name plate of the bomb-sunk *Alabama*. A huge tiger skull adorned another. A hat rack held a pair of rubber fishing waders. The occupant of the office often preferred to wear golfing knickers and buckskin shoes rather than a uniform. What Cesare was not shown was the content of a black notebook marked "secret" that contained the number and location of every airplane belonging to the army. The record was the only account of military readiness in the government.

With Mitchell's four-year appointment as General Patrick's assistant chief of the air service due to expire on March 26, 1925, Secretary of War Weeks was bristling with resentment of Mitchell's incendiary congressional testimony and the combative magazine articles, published without Mitchell having sought Weeks' permission. Evidently hoping that Patrick was equally fed up, he asked Patrick, "Do you want him reappointed?" If Patrick did not, Mitchell would have to be replaced and have to give up his temporary rank of brigadier general and return to colonel. Conceding that

Mitchell was frequently difficult, but noting that he "carried out in a fairly satisfactory manner his agreement to work for me," Patrick replied, "I do."

Despite problems with Mitchell, Patrick had been an ally, although quietly. Four months before Weeks posed the provocative question of Mitchell's reappointment, Patrick had sent his staff a confidential memorandum to prepare for his signature legislation to achieve much of what Mitchell advocated. He also urged that President Coolidge back creation of a united air force. To Patrick's surprise, and Mitchell's, an ally surfaced in the person of Admiral William A. Moffett, the navy's chief of aeronautics. In an appearance before the Lampert committee, Moffett admitted that at least three-fourths of the navy's aircraft were either obsolete or unfit for effective use. He also asserted, "If you have enough planes and the battleship is within reach, you can sink it." In the next war, he said, safety of ships "is going to depend, to a great measure, on aviation."

Feeling battered not only by Mitchell, but by the navy's chief of aeronautics, Secretary Weeks flung down the gauntlet. At the end of January 1925 he shot at Mitchell a charge on the subject of "objectionable parts" of Mitchell's testimony "which seriously reflect upon the War Department's efficiency and management." An accompanying questionnaire asked for answers to substantiate Mitchell's statements. When members of the investigating committee and the press learned of this, they termed it an "Inquisition." Representative Charles Curry, whose legislation to create an air force had been bottled-up for years, blasted a "determined effort" to silence anyone who differed and to subject "America's only fighting flying general of the world war and one of the outstanding figures in world aeronautics to humiliation, demotion and discipline." A world war veteran who had taken a leave of absence from Congress to fly Caproni bombers in Italy, Fiorello La Guardia denounced the navy's secrecy about the conditions of the sinking of the *Washington* and accused Weeks of intimidating witnesses.

On February 19 the air force general who had mastered the skills of headline-grabbing by testifying at congressional hearings, providing provocative press releases, chatting with reporters, and arranging unattributable information known as leaks found the tables turned. In a capital city where it appeared that much of government business was transacted by the manipulation of the press to promote an idea or scuttle someone else's, somebody in the White House or in the War Department offices in the building next door whispered to the press that Secretary of War Weeks and Secretary of the Navy Curtis D. Wilbur had given the president of the United States a stark choice. Coolidge could keep their services or Billy Mitchell's. The story also stated that Coolidge intended to summon Mitchell and offer him a choice: resign as assistant air chief or be demoted and replaced. When these reports reached the ears of Congressman La Guardia, the noisy former bomber pilot immediately announced he would introduce a bill providing that no army or navy officer that Congress called to testify could be ordered not to comply or be transferred or demoted.

As the story of the threat by Weeks and Wilbur percolated, the attention of the excited press turned to the Washington social calendar. Scheduled for that evening at the White House was the annual army and navy reception. As formally uniformed, medal- and ribbon-adorned generals and admirals sprinkled a reception line with the politically powerful to be greeted by President and Mrs. Coolidge, they and an observant, eager cluster of reporters and photographers whispered in anticipation of the answer to a question that had been buzzing across the gossipy city all day: "Would Billy Mitchell be there?"

With Mrs. Mitchell on his arm, he arrived early and made what a society columnist saw as "a sort of triumphal progress through the drawing room." Stopping every few feet for greetings by friends, he accepted hearty handshakes. The account in the next day's newspaper gushed, "He's a romantic sort of personage, this flying general—with his swanky air and the rows on rows of decorations, foreign and domestic, pinned on his chest.

Mrs. Mitchell looked like a bride, all in flowing white." A less feverish but equally colorful reporter wrote that Mitchell "moved among the other officers of the two armed services like a flagship." Everyone in the press noted that the talk at the reception was about the general and his testimony.

More than a few of the socially astute guests had a question that only time could answer. It rested on the fact that General Mitchell was chairman of the committee in charge of organizing the Charity Ball on March 4 to celebrate the inauguration of the president who had on his desk an ultimatum from two of his cabinet members that he side with them or Mitchell. Along with a rumor that Weeks and Wilbur vowed not to attend the ball if Mitchell were still in his post as assistant chief of the air service, the question loomed in the air like a pair of Mitchell's world war observation balloons for three days. The answer came on Washington's Birthday. Mitchell announced that because "the work I am now engaged in might seriously affect the success" of the ball, he was resigning from the committee. Conspicuously absent from the ball on March 4, he created a sensation at a gala masquerade thrown by the Italian embassy. He arrived with his wife and sister Harriet in the uniform of a navy enlisted man.

Back in his own uniform two days later at Fort Monroe, Virginia, Mitchell was to take part in another Navy Department attempt to demonstrate that his challenges to the viability of naval defenses were unfounded. The purpose was to show that naval antiaircraft artillery could shoot down attacking airplanes. Three of Mitchell's aircraft were to tow targets measuring ten by four feet while three-inch guns fired from the ground. With members of Congressman Lampert's Select Committee of Inquiry into Operations of the United States Air Services, army and navy officers, and the press observing, the naval gunners missed thirty-nine out of thirty-nine shots. Targets that were subjected to thousands of rounds of machine gun fire were found to have one bullet hole.

What the witnesses did not know as they watched the navy's failure at Fort Monroe was that back in Washington the secretary of war and his

Navy Department ally had won in their struggle with Mitchell. As the gunnery tests continued, Weeks announced that Mitchell was out of his job and reduced in rank to colonel. But even in their victory, Mitchell got in the last word and another dig at his enemies. Anticipating that Coolidge would side with his cabinet officers, Mitchell had prepared a statement. Calling reappointment as assistant chief of the air service "a small matter," he said, "The question of reorganization of our national defense is a big matter."

In an outburst of outrage at Mitchell's firing that would not be equaled until President Harry S. Truman relieved General Douglas MacArthur of command of U.S. forces in the Korean War in 1951, the shocked American public, sympathetic members of Congress, and irate editorial writers bombarded Washington with protests. Calls upon the president to step in and reverse the decision were unavailing. Coolidge lived up to a reputation for keeping his own counsel that had earned him the nickname "Silent Cal."

As reliably outspoken as ever, Mitchell said at a farewell luncheon arranged by Major Hap Arnold at Washington's Racquet Club, "I found it impossible to do anything in the War and Navy Departments on the matter of air defense, so I took it to Congress and the people, and will continue to take it to them until it is recognized."

It was a brave assertion, but he would have to do so from a post far away from the capital. His next assignment, the army announced, would be air officer at Fort Sam Houston in Texas. Entitled to a furlough, he made his way to the place that his friend, humorist Will Rogers, called "some mosquito post," by way of Milwaukee. Telling an adoring hometown crowd that his and their problem was "to jar the bureaucrats out of their swivel chairs," he vowed, "I have not even begun to fight."

CHAPTER EIGHTEEN

"ALL IN A DAY'S WORK"

Three-quarters of a century ago, nervous and explosively angry civilian officials of the War Department believed they had succeeded in ridding themselves of a general who was widely popular with the public, but a troublesome link in the chain of command, by "busting" Mitchell down to his permanent rank of colonel and banishing him to Texas. Today, such a sensationalistic event would be ripe pickings for panels of "talking head" commentators and military analysts on TV news programs and grist for one-liners tossed off by smart-aleck comedian-hosts of late-night television shows. In 1925 all of these were combined in a twangy-voiced, rope-twirling, easy-going, Oklahoma-born former cowboy and aviation-minded humorist named Will Rogers. Starring in the Ziegfeld Follies on Broadway, he claimed that all he knew was what he read in the newspapers. Blazing the trail for a host of latter-day jokesters with "topical" subjects torn from the day's headlines, he pondered the controversy surrounding the firing of Mitchell and told his audiences, "France gave Mitchell the Croix de Guerre, England the Order of the King, and the Republican Administration gave him the Order of the Tin Cup."

Before departing Washington on the furlough that would begin with a visit to Milwaukee, Mitchell had taken Rogers for the humorist's first airplane ride. Thronged by reporters as they climbed into Mitchell's *Osprey*, Mitchell asked, "Have you got cotton in your ears, Will?"

Rogers replied, "I just use that in the Senate gallery."

As photographers snapped them in the plane, the humorist suggested a caption for the pictures: "Last Photograph of the Deceased." Later, he said to eager reporters concerning Mitchell's plight, "It does seem a strange way to repay a man who has fought for us through a war, and who has fought harder for us in peace, to be reprimanded for telling the truth."

Newspaper cartoonists gleefully enlisted in the fray. One depicted Mitchell in an airplane dropping a bomb on a battleship and shouting, "Sailor Beware!" Another showed Mitchell barging into the bedroom of an army officer and yelling, "Boss, your house is on fire!" The corpulent, reclining officer replied, "You're fired." The theme of slumbering defenders of America was repeated in a cartoon of two figures representing the War and Navy Departments snoring as the sun rises and a fleet of war planes roars toward them over the horizon.

Out of power and out of Washington, Mitchell had other matters weighing on his mind. He was soon to be a father again. Rather than subject pregnant Betty to the rigors of army life at Fort Sam Houston, he insisted that she stay with her family in Detroit. He also had the task of disposing of the estate where he had grown up. With his parents and brother dead, sisters living elsewhere, and he having settled onto a Middleburg, Virginia, farm named Boxwood, the old homestead, Meadowmere, was to be subdivided for small home sites and the mansion preserved for public use. During the disposition of the property, the Wisconsin Legislature asked him to run for Congress. The grandson and son of distinguished House and Senate members declined.

When Colonel William Mitchell arrived in San Antonio in late June, he was assigned comfortable quarters on the Fort Sam Houston Parade Ground, with no troop command and no specified duties. But he and a secretary, Maydell Blackmon, had plenty to occupy them. Their small office was inundated with correspondence to be answered and requests from publishers and editors for articles. He elected to write one for an August issue of *Liberty* magazine that he titled "Exploding Disarmament Bunk: Why Have Treaties About Battleships When Airplanes Can Destroy Them?" Those he had written for *The Saturday Evening Post* had been compiled as a book entitled *Winged Defense* that was scheduled for publication in September.

Equally in demand as a speaker, he accepted an invitation to give an address in San Diego during a trip that would include an inspection of the Douglas Aircraft plant. The July 14 talk was on his persistent theme of American unreadiness for modern warfare. Declaring the air force "almost extinct," he spoke of the urgency to "educate the people to the need of air power by telling them what it [America] can do, not what it cannot do." His visit to the airplane plant included examining new navy PN flying boats. With maximum speed of seventy-five miles an hour, the planes were to take part in an attempt to fly from California to Hawaii. Convinced the perilous, unprecedented flight over thousands of miles of Pacific Ocean was a navy publicity stunt meant to counter his campaign for an independent air force, he worried that the PN planes would be unwieldy and too weighty with fuel and crews, that the refueling stops to meet picket ships were spaced too far apart, and navigators were inexperienced in long flights over water.

When the *Liberty* magazine article was published in August, the author was in Detroit for the birth of a daughter, Lucy. The occasion of visiting the automotive capital of the nation was an opportunity to meet Henry Ford and inspect an aircraft engine designed by Mitchell's companion on the European aviation junket, Alfred Verville. Offered a job by Ford, Mitchell replied that it would never work out. "We're two forceful individuals," he explained. "You'd want me to do something one way and I'd want to do it another. I'm not the man for the job. Furthermore, I have a big job to do—a big unfinished job, to carry on this fight to reorganize aviation and build up national defense."

Predicting to Detroit reporters that New York–to–Paris flights of thirty-seven hours would soon be regular events, he urged the United States to beat the French in making the first trans-Atlantic flight. This bold assertion came as his book was being distributed nationally. Described by the publisher, George Putnam, as "a bomb in the lap of American complacency," the 223 pages had eleven chapters, with titles such as "The Aeronautical Era," "Leadership in Aeronautics Goes to the United States," "How Should We Organize Our National Air Power?" "The Effect of Air Power on the Modification and Limitation of International Armaments," "The Obtaining of the Aircraft and Equipment for the Flyers," and "Conclusions." A preface set the tone of the book. Because of airplanes, he wrote, "The former isolation of the United States is a thing of the past."

As the book was being read by the public, press, book reviewers, aviation enthusiasts, and the top brass and civilian leaders of the War Department at the end of August, its author was busy assessing progress in converting an old cavalry section of Fort Sam Houston into an airfield. At 7:30 a.m., Monday, August 31, 1925, he decided to take a flight with his friend and mechanic Harry Short, in a Consolidated PT-1 biplane trainer. Although the engine was found to have a couple of leaking valves, it performed as expected, turning over at 1,650 rpm. To be certain that the plane was airworthy, they performed eleven takeoffs and landings. On the twelfth they were shocked and alarmed when the engine shut down at eighty feet. With not enough altitude or speed to turn back to the field, the airplane came down to ten feet, narrowly missing wagons and teams of mules, and slammed to earth at the corner of a fenced field. The landing gear collapsed and it nosed over. Upside down, Mitchell and Short unbuckled their safety belts and crawled free.

Mitchell later discovered that the engine had stopped because its right fuel tank was empty, although a gauge had indicated it was half full. Anxious observers rushed to the wrecked plane and found Mitchell grinning and waving. When reporters flocked to his office, he shrugged and said, "It's all in a day's work."

That afternoon he went riding, and on Tuesday morning was airborne in a de Havilland DH-4 biplane with a full 110-gallon tank for a spin over the post. After dictating letters into the afternoon, he drove a Packard that the maker had sold him at a discount to join a group of local citizens for dove-shooting. They bagged none of that quarry, but garnered a pair of buzzards, three armadillos, and six skunks.

In Ruth Mitchell's breezy biography of her famous brother, he had been shunted to Texas by enemies and was sitting "like a shackled tiger," never to be stationed near Washington again. The intent was to keep him safely out of reach of a voracious capital press corps that was always in his corner, if only to sell more newspapers by keeping his fight with the admirals and civilian hierarchy of the War Department going another round. Publication of *Winged Defense* caused a flurry of hope that the battle would flare up. A report circulated that it was being "carefully examined" in pertinent government offices. Intimations of revenge in the form of a court-martial, noted one observer, were floating around the War Department like the navy's dirigible *Shenandoah*.

The pride of the admiralty and described as a "battleship of the skies," the 682-feet-long offspring of Germany's fleet of world war Zeppelin airships had been built for $2.7 million and based at Lakehurst Naval Air Station in New Jersey in a specially-designed hangar that cost $3 million. So much ballyhoo had surrounded it that its skipper, Lieutenant Commander Zachary Lansdowne, had become a national celebrity. Handsome as a motion picture star, with an attractive wife, he was a descendent of the Scottish Protestant Reformer John Knox and was such a favorite of Calvin Coolidge that he had received several admiring letters on the presidential stationery. Although Coolidge had declined invitations to fly in the *Shenandoah*, Lansdowne had taken numerous government officials on flights to view the wonders of New York City from the air. With Lansdowne at the helm, the graceful dirigible had created a national sensation in 1924 by wafting from east coast to west and back again. The voyage had been so successful as a Navy attention-getter that when it was announced the *Shenandoah* would make overflights of Midwest state fairs in early September 1925, scores of governors and mayors pleaded to have their states and cities added to the proposed route.

At a time when Americans seemed to have gone crazy in their enthusiasm for dirigibles, even Billy Mitchell was optimistic about the lighter-than-air craft, military and commercial. Discussing civilian dirigibles in *Winged Defense*, he envisioned five running continuously from New York to Chicago and carrying as many people as all the fast trains then in service. The scion of a man who had pioneered and championed railways and built the foundation of the Mitchell family fortune wrote of operating airships without the expense of upkeep of tracks and other costs in the operation and equipment of railroads. "Our figures show that in the larger airships, with a full load," he noted, "passengers can be carried for distances of over five hundred miles at about three and one-half cents a mile." Noting that satisfactory progress was being made in the use of helium, rather than inflammable hydrogen to float the giant airships, he saw a "sure, safe, and reliable" means of transportation. He also predicted that a third means of aerial locomotion, the helicopter, from both a military and commercial standpoint, would eventually be of "great value."

Being in Texas did not prevent the nation's most vigorous and vociferous proponent of the military potential of airplanes from keeping well informed on the activities and motivations of his naval adversaries, nor from expressing himself on those subjects. During his inspection of the planes the navy had chosen for a pioneering flight from San Francisco to Hawaii, he had voiced doubts concerning structural and fuel limitations of the PN-9 flying boats. He also surmised that this three-plane flight, two PN-9s and a Boeing PB-1, and demonstrations by the *Shenandoah* were part of the navy's public relations effort to prove that naval aircraft were capable of defending America's coasts against seagoing enemies without the help of the Army Air Service.

Consequently, he felt that his forebodings were justified when he learned that one of the planes was unable to take off because of its heavy load and another had been forced to set down a few miles offshore soon after taking off. With the last plane winging westward, he kept track of its progress through reports on radio broadcasts. Late on September 1, he heard that the captain, Commander John Rodgers, signaled that the plane was running low on gas three hundred miles short of Hawaii. It was the last contact with him and the three-man crew. As a search was in its thirtieth hour, Mitchell went on a San Antonio radio station to ask for prayers "for the American flyers, down in the Pacific." With no expectation that survivors were likely to be found, he said they were "martyrs to the progress of civilization."

While Mitchell was on the air, Zachary Lansdowne and a crew of forty-three officers and men were going aloft in the *Shenandoah* at Lakehurst. Their ultimate destination was Minneapolis, with cruises above twenty-seven cities and towns along the route that had been alerted to the time that the majestic ship would arrive. As the dirigible flew at fifty-five miles an hour, reports on weather conditions ahead provided by radio from Lakehurst alerted the ship's weather officer, Lieutenant Joseph Anderson, of thunderstorms over the Great Lakes. Confident that the storms were too far to the north to be a factor, Lansdowne left the helm to get some rest. A few hours later, a crew member awakened him to report that storms were closing in on the ship. Anderson urged a turn to the south. Lansdowne replied that the storm was "a long way off" and that he wanted to stay on the course he had been ordered to follow "as long as I can."

When the ship reached Caldwell, Ohio, a squall that had formed ahead of a fast-moving cold front caught it in a violent upsurge that carried it higher and perilously close to the limits of pressure in the dirigible's helium bags. Ground observers gazing at the ship against a shelf of angry gray skies watched in horror as it swung back and forth, as one witnessed reported, "like a huge pendulum." Buffeted from side to side and jerked up and down, it buckled and broke into two pieces. The forward portion and control car floated to earth in a wide circle. The tail section split in half just before slamming to earth. Lansdowne and thirteen others were killed.

Informed by friends in the air service in Washington of this second disaster involving naval aircraft in two days, Mitchell resisted requests by the Associated Press and other news agencies for a statement. Rather than immediately expressing outrage at what he thought was a double tragedy in the name of the navy's political agenda, he chose to spend the remainder of the day shooting at targets on a firing range and riding and fence-jumping his two horses, Eclipse and Boxwood. His schedule for the evening required attendance at a chamber of commerce banquet at the Alamo Country Club, seated with the mayor of San Antonio and consul general of Mexico. But when he arrived at his desk on Friday morning, he called Maydell Blackmon into his office with her stenography book to take down a statement for the press that he had been composing in his mind while shooting, riding, dining, and lying in bed during a troubled and sleepless night.

Reporters crowded into his office at five in the morning on Saturday, September 5, were rewarded for the delay with exactly what they had hoped for, and in plenty of time for the story to make it into the country's Sunday newspapers. Explaining that he had given "mature deliberation and after a sufficient time had elapsed since the terrible accidents to our naval aircraft to find out what happened," he leveled an accusation that would be set in eye-catching typeset in headlines stretching the width of scores of front pages. "These accidents," he said, "are the direct results of incompetency, criminal negligence and almost treasonable administration of the national defense by the War and Navy Departments."

Standing before the journalists, he described the conduct of the two government branches as "so disgusting in the last few years as to make any self-respecting person ashamed of the cloth he wears." His six thousand-word blast continued with phrases that realized every newsman's desire for electrifying quotes.

"All aviation policies, schemes and systems are dictated by the non-flying officers of the army and navy who know practically nothing about it [flying]. The lives of the airmen are being used merely as pawns in their hands.

"The great Congress of the United States, that makes laws for the organization and use of our air, land and water forces is treated by these two departments as if it were an organization created for their benefit.

"Officers and agents sent by the War and Navy Departments to Congress have almost always given incomplete, misleading or false information about aeronautics, which either they knew to be false when given or was the result of such gross ignorance of the question that they should not be allowed to appear before a legislative body.

"The airmen themselves are bluffed and bulldozed so that they dare not tell the truth in the majority of cases, knowing full well that if they do, they will be deprived of their future career, sent to the most out of the way places to prevent them from telling the truth, and deprived of any chance of advancement unless they subscribe to the dictates of their non-flying bureaucratic superiors. These either distort facts or openly tell falsehoods about aviation to the people and to the Congress."

The Hawaiian flight was meant to "get publicity." The *Shenandoah* had crashed during a "propaganda mission." The War Department held on to outmoded planes that were nothing but "old flying coffins."

"The bodies of my former companions in the air molder under the soil in America and Asia, Europe, and Africa, many, yes, a great many, sent there directly by official stupidity.

"We would not be keeping our trust with our departed comrades were we longer to conceal these facts."

During a Labor Day weekend during which the nation's press expected to offer only coverage of parades, patriotic speeches, baseball games, pictures of girls in bathing suits sunning themselves one last time before the onset of autumn, and the parade of beauties in the annual Miss America pageant in Atlantic City, news editors and composing rooms suddenly had a startling story that promised to result in fireworks worthy of a Fourth of July. No one doubted, as intimated by Secretary of War Dwight Davis, who had taken over when Weeks resigned because of ill health, that Mitchell would face severe repercussions, quite likely in the form of a court-martial. The center of this sudden storm thought so. Speaking to a reporter as he set out for a day of fishing in the Gulf of Mexico, Mitchell said, "I expect the War Department to arrest me, but I doubt they'll get to it before Monday."

Vacationing at Swampscott, Massachusetts, the president of the United States validated the nickname "Silent Cal" by saying nothing. Secretary Davis, tracked down in New York at a tennis match that awarded to the winners a silver cup that bore his name, told reporters that it was not the place or time to argue publicly with a subordinate, but that Mitchell would not be kept in suspense about his fate for long.

Newspaper editorials from coast to coast chose sides. Many were with Mitchell. To the *New York Times* he was guilty of "insubordination and folly." In the view of the *New York Herald Tribune* he was "opinionative, arrogant, and intolerant." The *Kansas City Star* wrote that he was "a zealot, a fanatic, a one idea man," but also a man "who may be a prophet without honor only because he came a decade or two decades ahead of time."

Presently, Coolidge emerged from his New England retreat with an announcement that he was creating a board to investigate the entire field of aviation and naming New York banker Dwight Morrow as chairman. Although a blue ribbon panel on the subject had been an idea in Coolidge's mind for six months, and Morrow had been alerted to such a possibility, Coolidge's decision to proceed appeared to be accelerated by Mitchell's outburst. Coolidge's original intent was to wrest the issue of the control of aviation from Congress to the Executive Branch. Members of the panel, immediately named the "Morrow Board" by the press, appeared to be a guarantee that the president would not be disappointed by the outcome regarding Mitchell. Morrow was a longtime Coolidge friend, and the members were either conservative on aviation issues or navy men and navy allies in Congress. Disappointed that the establishment of the Morrow Board meant that there would be not be an immediate court-martial, Mitchell gamely said of the Morrow panel, "I am confident of its integrity and am most hopeful that much good will result from its inquiry and findings."

As he said this, a War Department investigator arrived in San Antonio to gather evidence. Mitchell saved him time and effort by acknowledging everything that was attributed to him in the newspapers. He added to the furor by asserting to eager reporters, "The investigation that is needed is of the War and Navy Departments, and their conduct in [the] disgraceful administration of aviation." But Admiral Moffett, chief of naval aviation, shot back, calling Mitchell a man of "unsound mind and suffering from delusions of grandeur." He went on to warn against the example of military officers "making a political appeal, over the head of Congress, to the people" that might be "the opening wedge for military dictatorship in the United States."

Amid these conflicting stories reported by the press, the American people received a bit of good news. After being considered lost at sea for nine days, the men of the navy plane that had gone down near Hawaii were found alive in the flying boat, which had been forced to set down on the sea after running out of fuel. Located and picked up by a navy submarine, Commander John Rodgers and his four crewmen became national heroes. By month's end they would be feted at San Francisco's city hall and guests of honor at luncheons and dinners. Rodgers would then be escorted across the country in early October to be celebrated further for surviving the ordeal and to testify at the court-martial of Billy Mitchell that the War Department planned to begin after the Morrow Board had completed its broader investigation into aviation.

Meanwhile, Mitchell headed east to keep his date with the Morrow Board. He planned to travel by car from San Antonio to Washington, but a storm forced him to switch to a train at Muskogee, Oklahoma. When a reporter asked if he was afraid to appear before the committee, he replied, "Piffle." Joined by Betty at St. Louis, he arrived at Washington's Union

Station on the evening of September 25, 1925. Greeted on board by Hap Arnold, he was alerted that awaiting him in the huge station and outside were ten thousand well-wishers, an American Legion drum and bugle corps, and a throng of reporters and photographers. As Mitchell stepped from the train, several men hoisted him onto their shoulders. The *Washington Post* reporter found "as usual a picturesque character," but not in uniform. He wore a gray suit very much in need of pressing and "somewhat soiled by the long journey." The "stoop of his shoulders, accentuated by many weary hours of flying, was a trifle more noticeable than usual, but that was all."

Barely audible over the din of cheers, blaring bugles, and pounding drums, he said, "What I am here to do is to tell the truth and to present irrefutable facts and figures which will awaken the people of the country to the breaking down of their national defense system." Shepherded out of the station by Arnold, the Mitchells were barely settled into a suite at the New Willard Hotel when another crowd of reports and photographers appealed to him to have a press conference in the lobby. He permitted questioning in his suite by one, Charles Palmer of Universal Services. Standing at a window with a view of the Washington Monument, he said to Palmer, "They sent me to Texas, far away, but not so far that I couldn't come back and talk. Now I'm back in Washington. Say, it's great the way life turns out, isn't it?"

Told that the legionnaires who met him at Union Station were having a barbecue the next evening and hoping he would attend, he replied, "You bet I'll go." To his surprise and delight he was conveyed to the party at Eighteenth Street and Benning Road by a colorful, noisy parade as he and Betty rode in an open horse-drawn carriage on Pennsylvania Avenue, within hearing of the occupant of the White House. A *Washington Post* wag ventured in print, "Colonel Billy Mitchell is willing to come to Washington to tell all even at he risk of getting his name in the papers," and "Colonel Mitchell's testimony will be somewhat delayed, as it is understood that all the arrangements for the movie rights have not been completed."

Four days after this tumultuous reception, another crowd overflowed from a hearing room of the House Office Building. Within, the witness was Benjamin Foulois, telling the Morrow Board of having had to spend $300 of his own money in 1910 to keep the army's "one plane going" while he "begged, borrowed and stole from the Quartermaster Corps." He placed blame for "the lack of teamwork today" on the "utter ignorance of the General Staff of 90 percent of the air service problems." His comments were interrupted when Mitchell entered the room to a thunderclap of applause from the audience. Foulois would continue for nearly an hour.

Anticipating an exciting performance by the most famous, glamorous, and controversial general to testify in his own defense since George Armstrong Custer was the defendant in a court-martial at Fort Leavenworth, Kansas, in 1867, observers of Mitchell were disappointed. Instead of lively assertions and combative style, they heard a droning recitation of words from the pages of *Winged Defense* and watched a listless, obviously exhausted figure. Hap Arnold's wife, Beatrice, discerned "coldness" in the members of the Morrow Board and thought the cause that had brought Mitchell to Washington was "just sunk." Her husband recalled, "We squirmed, wanting to yell: 'Come on. Billy, put down that damned book! Answer their questions and step down. That'll show them.'"

Longtime Mitchell journalistic observer Clinton Gilbert wrote that no one felt that he was the "sorehead or a crank" they wanted to hear. Conceding that Mitchell had "nothing new to say," he wrote, "A man who has talked so much and written so much as he has in the last couple of years becomes an old story." It was impossible that Mitchell could be "the star witness unless he had some new evidence in reserve, and Colonel Mitchell is not the kind of man to have anything in reserve." The only flash of the Billy Mitchell everyone desired occurred the next day when a board member, Congressman Carl Vinson, questioned the army officer asking if Mitchell was "putting a far-fetched interpretation on the law" restricting navy air activities and claiming that the flight of the *Shenandoah* had not been legally authorized, Mitchell again called the flight a "propaganda mission." Although the law had not been "exactly disobeyed," he said, it was "evaded" by non-flying officers.

The judgment of the *Kansas City Star* of Mitchell's questioning was that the Morrow Board had made "a studied effort to have the Mitchell testimony appear as only an incident of the probe—not the central spot." Far more riveting testimony would come from beyond the grave in the form of letters from the skipper of the *Shenandoah*, Commander Lansdowne, to the Department of the Navy. Prior to the disastrous flight, he had pleaded with the navy for a postponement until the weather conditions would be "reasonably safe." He had also objected to the chief of naval operations, Admiral E. W. Eberle, that the first leg of the flight (to Des Moines, Iowa) was too ambitious and that there was a lack of fueling and helium gassing facilities and mooring masts along the route. A result of these revelations was a chorus of demands in the press for Navy Secretary Wilbur's resignation.

Always keen to the value of a sympathetic press, Mitchell scored a publicity coup when *Liberty* magazine, for which he was contributor of articles on air power, awarded him a $1,000 prize given each month for "distinguished moral courage." Mitchell turned the money over to the widow of Commander Lansdowne for dependents of the enlisted men killed in the crash.

Into this tempest stepped President Coolidge. Addressing an American Legion convention in Omaha that Mitchell had been unable to attend due to orders to appear before the army inspector general, the president made it clear that he expected Mitchell to be punished. "Any organization of men in the military service bent on inflaming the public mind for the purpose of forcing government action through the pressure of public opinion," he asserted to an audience that was largely in support of their world war comrade, "is an exceedingly dangerous undertaking and precedent."

Having heard from ninety-nine witnesses, the Morrow Board adjourned to ponder what it heard, consider the law, and explore any precedents. When it would announce findings and offer its recommendations was anyone's guess. What the president of the United States had decided on the question of Billy Mitchell was announced four days after his speech to the legionnaires. Ordering a court-martial to convene on October 20, he set the trial's opening date at October 28, with a dozen high-ranking generals sitting as inquisitors, jurors, and judges.

Demanding "a court of flying officers," Mitchell told reporters, "No man should sit in judgment on me who doesn't know flying." Asserting that he was "not afraid of what the court will do to me," he vowed, "I'll fight on to get a real department of national defense, no matter what happens."

CHAPTER NINETEEN

"MOST AUGUST TRIBUNAL"

Seven years after General Billy Mitchell and victorious doughboys returned from fighting "over there" to make the world safe for democracy, the return to normalcy that 1920 Republican presidential candidate Warren Harding promised had become a half-decade of economic boom. Optimism about the American way of doing things had produced "Coolidge Prosperity" and a nationwide illegal-booze-fueled frenzy of jazz music, wild dancing in places called "speakeasies," cigarette-smoking and bobbed-hair young women known as "flappers," sporty cars, buying goods on the "installment plan," and "playing the market" by investing "on margin." And why not? Silent Cal himself had trumpeted the simple catechism of the United States in the Roaring '20s: "The business of America is business."

Examining the attitude of Americans in the "Jazz Age," social historian Frederick Lewis Allen wrote in *Only Yesterday: An Informal History of the 1920s* that "they gave their energies to triumphant business" and were in "a holiday mood." Ready and eager for "any good show that came along," the citizenry of the United States found it possible to enjoy any exhibition of human achievement and failure, triumph or tragedy, foolhardiness and folly, the daring and dumb, the majestic motivation and the mean-spirited, and the sad, stupid, or funny. "It was now possible in the United States," Allen recorded, "for more people to enjoy the same good show at the same time than in any land on earth or at any previous time in history."

Americans had always had newspapers, but with the 1920s had come coast-to-coast radio. It enabled people in California to feel that they were in ringside seats at the big heavyweight-title boxing matches in New York's Madison Square Garden, front and center in evening garb for a symphony concert half a continent away, a juror in the trial of a Tennessee schoolteacher for teaching Darwinism, or the judge in a Chicago murder case, listening to the same lawyer who had defended the schoolteacher. Clarence Darrow made an impassioned plea to spare the lives of a pair of obviously crazy young thrill-killers, Nathan Leopold and Richard Loeb. In both trials Darrow had turned the issue from the defendants to putting the accusers on trial. In the Scopes case he questioned the literal truth of the biblical story of creation. In Leopold and Loeb he laid down a challenge to the morality of the death penalty. Each proceeding had been covered by newspapers as "the trial of the century" and found no disagreement from readers, hungry for the next sensational event.

"The result was that when something happened which promised to appeal to the popular mind," Lewis wrote, "one had it hurled at one in huge headlines, waded through page after page of syndicated discussion of it, heard about it on the radio, was reminded again and again in the outpourings of publicity-seeking orators and preachers, saw pictures of it in the Sunday papers and in the movies, and (unless one was a perverse individual) enjoyed the sensation of vibrating to the same chord which thrilled a vast populace. The country had bread, but it wanted circuses—and now it could go to them a hundred million strong."

With the 1925 World Series behind the populace (Pittsburgh Pirates over Washington Senators in seven games) and the next election for president three years away, the question that surged like a charge in an electric chair from one end of the country to the other three days before Halloween was, "What will happen to Billy Mitchell once those generals get their hands on him?"

Mitchell foe Frank Kent of the *Baltimore Sun* wondered in print, "Has the army got the guts to kick him out? Has Colonel Mitchell created a condition that makes his dismissal inexpedient and which will compel a compromise verdict?"

Americans who had never heard that there was a code of military justice learned that it was not the same as the civilian system of criminal trials. They suddenly became conversant with the Ninety-Sixth Article of War. Pertaining to "all disorders and neglects of good order and military discipline and conduct of a nature to bring discredit upon the military service," it was, Mitchell explained to a correspondent of the *Public Ledger*, "the most embracive of all army disciplinary measures." With a chuckle, he said, "Officers are tried under it for kicking a horse."

His complaint concerning the charges against him, he continued, was that they did not allow considering the truth or untruth of his accusations against "the bureaucrats." He was being tried, he said, "for daring to remind the conservatives that there is something new under the sun, that there is a great new modern branch of the service, aircraft, which is being ignored in the administration of national defense."

Rejecting a proposal that he retain Darrow of the "Thrill Killing" and "Monkey" trials, Mitchell stayed with Congressman Frank Reid, who had not only been his counsel in the Morrow Board hearings and an adviser in Congressional testimony, but was a Mitchell believer who had been a prosecutor in Illinois and knew Clarence Darrow's tactics well. While America's suddenly most recognizable defense attorney came across in press coverage as a rumpled figure with unpressed clothing, askew necktie, suspenders stretched by a bulging belly, and a shock of unruly hair, Reid was tall and rangy, impeccably attired in a three-piece suit and bow tie, and well kempt. He had an innocent-looking expression that could abruptly turn fierce when challenging either witnesses or the manner in which a trial or hearing was being run. A non-smoker, non-drinker, and non-gambler, and known as a man who never swore, he was fascinated with unusual words that he jotted down for looking up later in a black notebook he carried in a coat pocket. Like his client, he was astute in using the press to his and their advantage.

As another "trial of the century" loomed before reporters assigned to cover it, the general expectation was that the drama would unfold in an impressive setting, possibly the House caucus room or the majestic auditorium of the Department of the Interior. This speculation was shot out of the air by Secretary of War Davis. Growling that "this is serous business," he exclaimed, "This isn't a vaudeville show—or an advertising scheme."

The site of the court-martial would be an almost derelict, unused warehouse that had been the headquarters of the Census Bureau. Known as the Emory Building, it was a low red brick eyesore at First and B streets in the shadow of the dome of the Capitol. Unoccupied for the past two years, it was described by an astonished newsman as "little short of impossible." It had no heat, and floors were littered with trash and puddles of stagnant rain water. The walls looked as if they were lined with cardboard. Given short notice that the space had to be converted into a courtroom, a team of workers scrambled to get it ready for installation of a dais for the judges and tables and chairs for prosecution, defense, witnesses, and the accused. Also, provisions had to be made for the press; cameramen for newspapers, magazines, and newsreels; and as many other observers as possible. When they were finished, the room had a capacity to seat an audience of eighty.

Given as little time to prepare as the Emory Building workmen, Mitchell began working with Reid and Mitchell's friend and aviation expert Clayton Bissell, who was acting as an assistant defense counsel, in Reid's office in the House Office Building. With a dozen stenographers on hand as needed, they interviewed a stream of Mitchell witnesses on what they planned to say and drew up a strategy based on the fact that Mitchell was on the public record admitting his guilt. Their goal, therefore, was to shift the issue from insubordination and conduct prejudicial to the service to the education of the American people on aviation and "to make national defense mean something." Bissell recalled, "It was the only way left. To do that, we knew we had to stay on the front pages of newspapers. If we slipped off for a day, we'd have to find a way back, something spectacular, new stuff every day. We knew it would be a job."

When Joseph E. Davies (future ambassador to the Soviet Union under President Franklin D. Roosevelt) recommended a guilty plea "to save time and sharpen the issue," Reid replied, "Nothing doing! So long as I'm in the case he'll defend himself. If they'll let us prove that he'd been telling the truth, and that finally he got to the point where nobody would listen to him, so that he had to go to the people, then we've got a chance."

Following Reid's decision to bring in a young lawyer from a House committee staff, William H. Webb, to research legal precedent, Mitchell rented two floors of the Anchorage Apartments as his and Betty's temporary lodgings and work space for the legal team. Costs of the travel of friendly witnesses were paid by Betty's father, Sidney Miller, a Packard Motor Company attorney. Ensconced in the apartment house at 1900 Q Street Northwest whose shape earned it the name "Flatiron Building," Reid called in reporters on the evening before the convening of the court-martial and fired the defense's opening salvo. He termed Mitchell's public utterances "mild" when compared to those of Generals Hooker and McClellan in the Civil War against President Lincoln and the blasts at President McKinley and even Theodore Roosevelt by their unhappy subordinates. Reid asked, "Could there be a greater contrast" than the wisdom of those presidents in retaining the services of their critics "and the actions of martinets in time of peace who would punish a faithful officer for timely and judicious advice on public matters of great importance?"

While reporters hurriedly recorded his words and envisioned them in bold headlines in the morning papers, Reid added, "Rome endured as long as there were Romans. America will endure as long as there are Mitchells."

Formally served with notification of the court-martial at nine o'clock in the morning of the day it was to commence, October 28, 1925, Mitchell was directed to appear at 10:00 a.m. Shrugging off the obvious insult of the

War Department's deliberate last-minute summons, he donned a uniform that displayed rows of ribbons attesting to more than a quarter of a century's service and action in two wars and the Philippine Insurrection, foreign decorations for valor, and the silver wings of an army aviator. When he arrived at the Emory Building with Betty, sister Harriet, and his lawyers, a reporter compared him to "a small boy on a picnic" and later wrote, "If his nonchalance was insincere, then Mitchell is a great actor."

As Mitchell entered an anteroom, he found the members of the court-martial waiting like the cast of a Shakespearean play listening for the cue for the curtain to rise. The panel consisted of six major generals, six brigadier generals, and Colonel Blanton Winship, serving as their legal adviser. "There were more stars in that little room," cracked a reporter, "than you'd find in the Paramount movie studio's cafeteria at lunchtime." If the mingling generals could be viewed by the press as characters in a film, the press gave top billing to Major General Douglas MacArthur. With an aloof and proud bearing that could be interpreted, according to one's opinion of him, as arrogant or heroic, he brought into the Emory Building a touch of drama and irony. Reporters had been diligent in pointing out to their newspapers' readers that "Doug and Billy" were boyhood pals in Milwaukee and that Mitchell had experienced combat years before MacArthur garnered fame for his heroics in France. MacArthur also felt the weight of their history and the twist of fate that forced him to sit in judgment of Mitchell. Being commanded to determine his old friend's fate, he later wrote, was "one of the most distasteful orders I ever received."

He was not the only member of the court with a personal connection to the accused. The president of the court, Major General Charles P. Summerall, had been in command in Hawaii during Mitchell's inspection tour and had taken issue—and offense—after Mitchell's report of inefficiencies and lack of preparedness. General Robert L. Howze had led the 4th Division in France and was one of Mitchell's postwar riding and hunting companions. In one way or another, Mitchell knew the others.

Fred W. Sladen was commandant at West Point. William S. Graves was VI Corps area commander. Mitchell did not have to be introduced to Major General Benjamin A. Poore and Brigadiers Edward R. King, Albert L. Bowley, Frank R. McCoy, Edwin P. Winans, George L. Irwin, and Ewing E. Booth. Besides the stars on their collars, these men had in common the fact that none was an aviator.

"If Bill was depressed he did not show it," wrote Ruth. "I think he was quite unconscious of the atmosphere. The showdown had come which he had chosen. His heart was firm. He smiled and greeted friends." When the judges "settled themselves with dignity at a curved table" in the courtroom, she continued, any spectators hoping that generals wearing dress uniforms would "add a note of color to the picture" were disappointed. "The generals were all in olive drab," Ruth recorded. "It was noted at once, however, that the prisoner had more decorations than any of his judges."

As in civilian trials, each side in a court-martial was entitled to challenge the fitness of jurors. In this case, with generals who would be both jurors and judges, the prosecution lawyer, Colonel Herbert A. White, with the title trial judge advocate, was satisfied that no member of the court had "a declared enmity against the accused" and accepted their participation. When he sat down, Frank Reid rose and shocked the courtroom by challenging Brigadier General Bowley on the ground of "prejudice, hostility, and animosity" toward Mitchell evidenced by a speech he had made the previous week that had mocked Mitchell's "flocks of airplanes dropping bombs on New York City" and newspaper pictures showing skyscrapers "toppling right and left." After a meeting in the anteroom without Bowley's presence, the generals returned to "excuse" Bowley from participation in the court-martial. When Reid challenged Major General Summerall, one reporter noted that the eyes of the officer with a reputation as an "Oliver Cromwell in khaki" blazed in indignation. Following Reid's presentation of proof that Summerall had grievances against Mitchell for his Hawaii report, Summerall labeled the report "untrue, unfair." Accusing Mitchell of "bitter hostility toward me," he asked to be excused.

Trailed by reporters to his office in the War Department, the distraught and embarrassed general said in a wounded tone, "I have kept an open mind on Mitchell's case. I took him into my home as a fiend when he came to Honolulu. I placed a private car at his disposal. I loaned him an airplane. Only ten minutes before court convened I shook hands with him. Now it's all over. We're enemies, Mitchell and I."

With General Robert Lee Howze taking over as court-martial president, Reid voiced a successful challenge against General Sladen, then requested a dismissal of the case on the basis of Mitchell's constitutional right of free speech. "If the First Amendment didn't apply to the Army," he asked, "why didn't it say so?" A reporter with a flair for drawing homely comparisons saw in Reid a small-town schoolteacher with an informality that seemed to irritate the generals, even when he declared, "I consider this the most august tribunal that has ever been called upon to act on any question since the Magna Carta." Whatever he may have gained through this flattery was gone a moment later with a reference to the generals as "you people" twice in two sentences in a challenge to their legal authority to put Mitchell on trial. Nor did he gain sympathy by asking if the generals were going to "invoke the old Spartan system" in which, he lectured, if they didn't like a person or his looks, they would banish him. "It's just the same idea," he said, "as challenging a truth-teller."

Ruling that the court-martial had authority to try Mitchell, the generals were ready to hear Mitchell's plea on each of eight specifications of insubordination and "highly contemptuous and disrespectful" statements intended to discredit the War Department and the navy. Mitchell said to each, sometimes before the reading of a charge was completed, "Not guilty." The two words were not simply a defendant's response, but a signal to the court and the press that the American people were about to be entertained by a drama that would last for weeks, perhaps months, and that it would not only be Billy Mitchell in the dock, but the broader issue of the proper, modern defense of the United States of America. Summing up the result of the court's first week, the *Nation* magazine opined, "Holding a bear by the tail is a pleasant pastime compared with trying Colonel William Mitchell by army court-martial." Noting that "the energetic officer and his able counsel carried off all the honors," the article mused, "How the powers that be in the War Department must be kicking themselves that they did not ask Mr. Coolidge to issue a sharp presidential reprimand and station the colonel in the remotest parts of Moroland!"

While legal warfare that raged in the Emory Building took a weekend break, Silent Cal was aboard the presidential yacht *Mayflower*, plying the waters of Chesapeake Bay. Before he left, reporters inquired during his regular Friday press conference if he had heard that Reid was threatening to subpoena him to testify. The tight-lipped commander in chief replied, "I don't care to comment on that while it is before the court of inquiry."

Weekending at Boxwood, Mitchell may or may not have taken notice that a newspaper had published a poem that took liberties with Rudyard Kipling's "Danny Deever" at the expense of Navy Secretary Curtis Wilbur:

"What are the bugles blowin' for?" Said Wilbur on parade.
"To bring you out, to bring you out," the old press agent said.
"What makes you look so pale, so pale?" Said Wilbur on parade.
"I'm thinking of the hell I'll catch," the old press agent said.
"For they're hanging' Billy Mitchell, you can hear the trumpets play;
The staff has got its thumbs turned down, they're hanging him today.
They're chargin' of his service, they'll cut his stars away,
They're hangin' Billy Mitchell in the morning."

The all-seeing eye of the press had not left women readers unrewarded. Describing Betty Mitchell as the "breezy and confident" wife, the *New York Sun* depicted her arriving for court at Mitchell's side: "Her arm unconsciously finds its way around her husband's broad shoulders. Occasionally she softly presses his arm as he sits erect during the proceedings. Her smile is magnetic, and the young officers who stand at the door of the room stiffen when they are so favored. Hard boiled high officers bow and smile eagerly when she nods." For the benefit of the fashion-conscious, reporters filed tidbits about her "silken bandana, shot with riotous colors" on her shoulders, and frequent tam-o'-shanters of black or blue. She and her husband arrived about five minutes before the court was called in session. He invariably carried a malacca walking stick that seemed to be an affectation, but was actually needed because of his slight limp. If he had been riding early in the morning, he entered in breeches, boots, and spurs. At the end of a day's session he and his sister Harriet rode in Rock Creek Park. Evenings were spent preparing for the next day, often with Hap Arnold and his wife, Commodore C. E. O. Charlton of the Royal Air Force, and Clayton Bissell. Another friend, adviser, and world war associate, now a general, Carl "Tooey" Spaatz, also dropped by to talk about what he would say when called as a witness.

Taking the stand when the court began its second week, Spaatz was thirty-five years old and no longer the young pilot whose daring in French skies had earned him the Distinguished Service Cross. Now the tactical chief of the air service, he presented a dismal portrait of the status of aviation in 1925. In a fleet of 1,820 planes, he said, 1,300 were obsolete and 400 were leftovers from the war. If he "dragged" all administrative officers from their desks, he testified, he could put 15 pursuit planes in the air. "It is very disheartening," he said, "to attempt to train or do work under such circumstances."

Next up for the defense was Captain Robert Oldys. Posted to the air services war plans division, he was a pilot. Asked by General Howze how he would constitute the general staff, he answered, "On Colonel Mitchell's plan." Reid inquired, "Now, is there any air force at the present time on the Pacific Coast?" Oldys replied, "There is not, sir."

When the name of the following witness was called, the makeshift courtroom buzzed with excited anticipation. Henry H. Arnold came to the witness chair as the air service's chief of information. The post was not for the purpose of disseminating information to the public. This "propaganda," as Reid termed it, was handled in a separate office by four army press officers. Arnold's job was gathering and distributing data on all aspects of military aviation, domestic and foreign. This made him an authority on the number of aircraft accidents, causes, and fatalities. In a grim accounting covering the past six years, he related details of 36 accidents and 517 deaths in the United States Army, Navy, Marine, and Post Office air services. Under questioning by the court on whether the United States had been deprived of its ocean defenses because other countries were ahead in developing military air power, and if "the U.S. must have just as many airships and personnel" as England and France, Arnold said, "I think that [oceans] make no difference in an aerial war, where distance is annihilated by a few hours."

Dubious prosecutor Colonel Sherman Moreland asked, "Is three thousand five hundred miles of salt water annihilated?"

"Yes, sir. It is today."

"In what respect?"

"Airships have crossed the Atlantic and Pacific."

The next morning's headline in the *Washington Post* blared:

ARMY HIGH COMMAND ON TRIAL IN MASS OF MITCHELL DATA

The court-martial and the people of the United States now found themselves marking a solemn anniversary. When the trial resumed on Wednesday, November 11, 1925, the nation took time to recall that on the eleventh minute of the eleventh hour of the eleventh of November in 1918 the most awful war in history had ended with the signatures of a few politicians. To observe Armistice Day 1925, veterans of the air war had wanted Mitchell to attend their banquet in New York as guest of honor and had conveyed this desire by telegram to Coolidge. The president was silent. The army replied to the three hundred pilots that because Mitchell was in the midst of a court-martial, he could not leave Washington. The outraged airmen had to settle for a speech by Benjamin Foulois. Just as furious, the former bomber pilot Congressman Fiorello La Guardia of Manhattan exclaimed to reporters, "Billy Mitchell is not being judged by his peers. He is being judged by nine dog-robbers of the general staff." The colorful phrase "dog-robbers," the reporters explained to readers, was army enlisted men's slang synonym for an officer's orderly. The next telegram from the veterans to Washington, D.C., was addressed to Mitchell:

GREETINGS FROM YOUR BUDDIES.
AMERICA LOVES A MAN WITH GUTS . . . WE ARE ALL
WITH YOU. AND WE DON'T MEAN MAYBE.

At eleven o'clock that morning in the Emory Building the court-martial of Billy Mitchell fell silent for two minutes, with everyone standing and facing east in tribute to the fallen. At issue as the court resumed was a demand by Frank Reid that the defense be permitted to introduce evidence and thirty-six additional witnesses to testify in mitigation of the offenses with which Mitchell was charged. After consulting in the anteroom, the generals returned with the surprise decision to grant Reid's request. Newspaper stories pointed out that if Mitchell could back up his public statements with proof that they were correct, he would be acquitted. Central to his defense was that he had no choice but to publicly criticize the War Department because it chose to ignore his official warnings about the vulnerability of Hawaii to attack and suggestions on how to improve readiness. Called to testify about what had happened to Mitchell's report on conditions in the Pacific in October 1924, Major General Gerald Brandt of the air service was asked by Reid, "When did this report reach you through channels?"

Brandt replied, "Saturday."

Reid asked incredulously, "Do you mean *last* Saturday?"

"Yes, sir."

How could it take a report more than a year for to reach his desk?

Brandt answered that the cause was "lack of a unified command," resulting in a long and circuitous routing, combined with a note attached to it by the War Plans Division stating that the "recommendations were based on Mitchell's personal opinions and therefore no consideration need be given them."

Asked about the present state of the air service, Brandt replied that the best pilots were quitting in disgust and that flying fields built during the war had been allowed to deteriorate. As he was testifying, Reid paused to gaze at the men at and around prosecution's table who had not been present previously and asked the court if everyone was entitled to be there. Among them was a well-known Kentucky attorney, Allen W. Gullion. A former teacher of military science and tactics at the University of Kentucky, he held the rank of major and had earned a reputation for boisterous conduct in courtrooms, heckling witnesses, and playing to the press. Believing that Gullion had been imported to attack Mitchell when he took the stand, Reid soon found himself in a wrangle over which of the prosecution's lawyers was entitled to interject objections. Reid also took exception to the presence of Major Francis Wilby of the War Department General Staff for whispering advice to chief prosecutor, Colonel Sherman Moreland. This also caught the attention of General Howze. When Moreland jumped to his feet to voice an objection at Wilby's urging, Howze blurted, "Sit down, colonel, sit down. Then you can get what they have to say and get the answers in a hurry."

When the spectators burst into laughter, a guard yelled, "Don't go off so loud." He then echoed the admonition made earlier by Secretary of War

Davis to the press that the court-martial was serious business. The guard shouted, "This ain't a vaudeville show!"

After further haggling about objections and who could make them and the admissibility of portions of testimony by defense witnesses Major Roycroft Walsh and Lieutenant H. W. Sheridan of the air service, the court adjourned for the day. When it resumed in the morning, nothing about the testimony provided by the next witness gave the spectators a reason for merriment.

On the morning after the day of moments of silence that had been observed all across America for the seventh time since the killing stopped in 1918, Mitchell and Betty traveled to a townhouse on M Street in northwest Washington. They went to accompany to court the widow of the skipper of the *Shenandoah*, the navy dirigible that crashed in a violent thunderstorm in September over Ava, Ohio. That disaster had propelled Mitchell to publicly brand the civilian and military leadership of the War and Navy Departments criminally incompetent and accuse them of having been the real cause of the deaths of thirteen of the forty-three men aboard, including the captain of the *Shenandoah*, Lieutenant Commander Zachary Lansdowne. Although Margaret Ross Lansdowne had appeared before a navy investigative board in October, she was prepared to tell the Mitchell court-martial that a navy captain, Paul Foley, had attempted to persuade her to give false testimony. Angry that she was asked in a note from Foley to endorse a Navy Department statement about the crash that she saw as "an insult to the memory" of her husband, she was a friend of the Mitchells and agreed to testify in the Mitchell case about this attempt to enlist her to commit perjury.

Except for Mitchell, no one entering the courtroom had inflamed the curiosity of the press and spectators to the extent of Mrs. Lansdowne's appearance on November 12, 1925. With dark bobbed hair, she wore widow's black and a black felt hat, pulled low over grayish blue eyes. The outfit seemed cruelly out of place for a pretty, lightly freckled, twenty-three-year-old mother of a young girl. As she was sworn in, flashbulbs of cameras of scores of photographers lit up the room. When the stir subsided, prosecutor Moreland asked her full name and, "Do you know Colonel Mitchell, the accused in this case?"

She replied, "I do."

As Moreland returned to the prosecutors' table, Frank Reid rose and with an unfortunate use of past tense asked, "What was your husband's name?"

With slightly quavering voice, she replied in the style of naval identification, "Zachary Lansdowne, Lieutenant Commander, United States Navy, commanding the USS *Shenandoah*."

Ascertaining that she remembered "the occasion of the [*Shenandoah*] court of inquiry" by the navy, Reid got straight to the point. "Was there a communication delivered to you purporting to come from Captain Foley, the judge advocate of the *Shenandoah* court of inquiry?"

Moreland objected that the naval inquiry was immaterial to the issue.

"May it please the court," said Reid to the presiding officer. "The trial judge advocate evidently does not understand the purpose of this testimony. Colonel Mitchell, in his statement, for which he is now on trial, charged that the navy board would proceed to whitewash the *Shenandoah* accident, and pursuant to that, would do certain things. We expect to show that they absolutely did that by trying to get this witness to give false testimony in regard to the accident."

With Morleand overruled, Mrs. Lansdowne recounted Foley coming to her uncle's house on M Street on October 7, two days before the date of her testimony at the inquiry. "He sought to impress me first with the importance of the court," she continued. He then asked me what it was I was going to say to the court and I answered that I preferred to make my statement to the court."

Describing Foley's persistence in finding out "what I had on my mind," and asking her to "rehearse the statement you are going to make to the court," Mrs. Lansdowne said she told him she wished to "lay emphasis on the fact that the [inquiry] had failed to develop the fact that my husband had been sent on this trip for a political purpose." This resulted in Foley telling her she "had no right to say that the flight was a political fight, as taxpayers the Middle West had a perfect right to see their property."

Captain Foley's unavailing mission was followed the next day, Lansdowne related, by a visit from a friend, the wife of another naval officer, who handed her a typewritten statement on plain paper prepared for her to sign. Reid asked its contents. She answered:

It began with the remark that when I at first accepted the invitation to appear at the *Shenandoah* court and testify in my husband's behalf, I had done so with the idea my husband was in need of defense, but at the present time my opinion had been changed and I was appearing simply because I said I would and that I thought the court was absolutely capable of handling the situation and [I] was entirely willing to leave it in their hands.

[The statement also said] that my husband always considered the *Shenandoah* a ship of war, and did not care to take the ship on political flights, but any time the flight was for military purposes, regardless of the landing facilities and the weather conditions, he was absolutely willing and ready to take the ship.

Reid asked, "Was that statement false?"

"False."

Reid asked how it was incorrect.

To state that her husband was willing to take the *Shenandoah* "anywhere at any time regardless of weather conditions," she said, "was an insult to his memory."

With Moreland's objections to Reid's solicitation of Mrs. Lansdowne's memory of her navy board testimony overruled, she stated that she had told the board that Lansdowne believed that the flight was made "solely for political purposes," but his protests had been dismissed. As evidence of his feelings, she read from an August 15 letter he had sent to the chief of naval operations asking for a postponement until the better weather conditions of the second week of September. The request was turned down because state fairs were held in the first week of that month, and the navy wanted the attendees to be able to see the airship. Being a loyal and dutiful naval officer and despite stating that the *Shenandoah* "should not be taken on commercial trips inland to give the taxpayers a look at their property," Lansdowne, according to his widow, did "what he was told."

In an attempt to discredit Mrs. Lansdowne, the prosecution inquired about what seemed to be a change of heart from earlier statements attributed to her in the press that she "would not for the world have it thought" she would criticize the Navy Department. Denying she had said such things, she also insisted she had not told a reporter that her husband had "premonitions" that the flight would go badly or "objected to going along." The witness held up under cross-examination and left the courtroom unscathed, having succeeded in furthering the impression, as one observer noted, that the War Department was losing the case before the bar of public opinion.

Although presenting a plausible argument about the weather risks, the commander of the *Shenandoah* was certainly naive about displaying expensive military equipment to the citizens who paid for it. Flamboyant exhibitions of paraphernalia of warfare were as old as the armies and navies that used them. From the threatening massing of warriors of Joshua outside the fortress walls of Jericho and triumphal parades in the streets of ancient Rome to Theodore Roosevelt's sending a "Great White Fleet" around the world to flex America's muscles in 1908 and overflights by the planes of Billy Mitchell's air force to drop imaginary bombs on Manhattan, publicity stunts had been vital to generals, admirals, and governments in winning public support. Throughout the decades following the court-martial of

Billy Mitchell, the U.S. government advertised "bang for the buck" with public shows ranging from victory parades in 1945 to the testing of intercontinental rockets during the Cold War, launching nuclear-powered submarines and the naming of aircraft carriers for presidents to flying a space shuttle on the back of a Boeing 747 cargo plane over cities from coast to coast, including the city that Mitchell "bombed" in a blatant grab for the headlines in the sake of his cause.

While the court-martial seemed to be going Mitchell's way, a decision by another court on Tuesday, November 17, 1925, dealt him a financial blow. The Wisconsin State Supreme Court awarded the first Mrs. Mitchell, Caroline, annual support from Mitchell of $2,000 a month for their three children, Elizabeth, Harriet, and John. She had originally sought six times that in the divorce papers, filed in August 1924. Although Mitchell was earning barely enough for himself and Betty in army salary, with another $4,665 a year from his mother's estate, and Caroline had an inheritance of $172,837 from her family, he did not file an appeal. He had been granted the right to visit their children, but Caroline made it clear that she would disown any that she caught seeing him. Settled in a rented Washington townhouse on Massachusetts Avenue off Sheridan Square, she had become a capital socialite and continued to mingle with top military figures, including two members of Mitchell's court-martial, Generals Winans and Irwin. But there is no evidence they discussed the case.

The roster of defense witnesses on November 18 and 19 bore names of two men who proved that they had "guts" by fighting Germans in the air. First on Frank Reid's list was Reed Chambers. A twenty-four year old from Memphis, Tennessee, when he reported for duty in France with the 94th "Hat-in-the-Ring" Squadron in the spring of 1918, he flew 208 hours in combat and shot down six enemy planes and one balloon without being hit. Remaining in the air service after the war, he became so dismayed by the lack of interest in the War Department in building a strong air force that in 1921 he handed in his resignation, intending to go into commercial aviation. When the papers landed on Mitchell's desk, he called Chambers in for a chat in the basement of Mitchell's house. Pouring Chambers a prohibited drink from an illegal still that produced a kind of gin, Mitchell said, "You can't do it. Too many old-timers have left, and we need you in the service. I'll give you command of the 1st Pursuit Group."

Four years after downing Mitchell's illicit booze and agreeing to stay, Chambers was no longer in uniform. In partnership with the former commander of the 94th Squadron, Captain Eddie Rickenbacker (the second name on Frank Reid's current witness list), he was engaged in running Florida Airways (later expanded into Eastern Airlines). Much of his cross-examination consisted of questions concerning the prosecution's statistics on the effectiveness of antiaircraft fire by the Germans in the war. "Are you aware," Chambers was queried, "that they averaged seventeen planes shot down with 10,273 shots, or an average of 605 shots per plane?"

Chambers said it was news to him and that it was impossible to accept such figures.

The name that rang out in the courtroom on November 19 was that of one of the most famous figures to come out of the war and be venerated by Americans as worthy of the accolade "hero," and perpetuated in newspaper and magazine articles as a dynamic and savvy businessman in the fields of aviation and automobiles. Chief executive of an airline and manufacturer of a sporty line of cars that bore his name, Edward V. Rickenbacker was by far the most well-known player in the drama of the court-martial, other than its star.

Everyone who knew of Rickenbacker had heard the story of how he had started out in the war as a wining race-car driver and mechanic who became Billy Mitchell's chauffeur. Those closest to him knew that the Rickenbacker-Mitchell relationship had often been a stormy one. Among Rickenbacker's tales was an episode involving a brand-new Mercedes automobile that Mitchell asked Rickenbacker to bring from a garage in Paris to Mitchell's headquarters in Chaumont. Knowing that a Mercedes of that type, with a double-chain drive, had won first place in the Grand Prix race of 1914, he was eager to drive one. Even more excited when he found that Mitchell had had it converted it from a racer to a sports car with four deep leather-lined bucket seats, he was soon racing at sixty miles an hour on a smooth military highway. As he went into a turn, he lost control and veered into a ditch. With the aid of a group of French mechanics who happened to be passing by, he fixed a damaged chain guard and resumed the trip to Chaumont. Arriving two hours late, he explained what had happened. Mitchell glared but said nothing. Returning to Mitchell's office, they found a French general waiting. To Rickenbacker's amazed embarrassment, Mitchell began an angry tirade that seemed to Rickenbacker to be a show for the Frenchman to demonstrate that Mitchell was a tough officer.

The episode still nagged at Rickenbacker in 1920 after he and Mitchell had gone to the World Series and Rickenbacker had called Mitchell's ribbon-bedecked uniform a "billboard" and refused to go out to dinner with him unless Mitchell changed into civilian clothes. After a few hours of touring speakeasies and illicit spas that Rickenbacker described as "one gyp-the-blood to another," and feeling "well lubricated," Rickenbacker decided that the time had come to settle the matter of the dressing-down he had endured for the benefit of the French general and Billy Mitchell's inflated ego.

As Rickenbacker was about to drag up the incident, Mitchell blurted, "Eddie, there's something I've always wanted to tell you. I owe you an apology. You remember when I bawled you out in France? I've been sorry ever since."

"Bill, goddamn it," Eddie replied, "now we're friends. I was about to tell you that you owed me an apology. Up to now we have not been friends. You may have thought we were, but I know better as far as I was concerned. Now everything is out the window. We'll start over."

Five years later, looking as trim and fit as the dashing aviator whose image had adorned the pages of countless newspapers and magazines and filled movie screens in newsreels during the war, Rickenbacker strode to the front of the Emory Building courtroom on November 19 and was asked what seemed to be a superfluous question from Frank Reid: "Are you a flier?"

"I am."

"And you have the title of 'Ace of Aces,' have you not?"

"I do."

"And for what was that?"

"The greatest number of enemy planes shot down by any American pilot . . . twenty-six, balloons and planes."

The prosecution quizzed Rickenbacker, as it had Chambers, on the effectiveness of antiaircraft fire. The intent was to undercut Mitchell's contention that air power was a superior weapon by showing that airplanes were highly vulnerable and, therefore, unreliable both as a way of defense and attack. To underscore the point, Rickenbacker was asked about the most famous—or infamous, depending on one's historical viewpoint—German aviator, Manfred von Richthofen. Known as the "Red Baron" and leader of a "Flying Circus" whose airplanes' noses were often painted red, he had shot down four-score French and British planes, more than anyone in the war, but in a period of four years, while Rickenbacker scored twenty-six victories in six months (between April 29 and October 30, 1918). After calling Richthofen "their best," Rickenbacker was asked. "How did he come by his death?"

"My understanding is he was brought down by machine gun fire on the ground in [a] trench [while] strafing during the advance on Paris." (The cause of the Red Baron's demise is still a matter of dispute as to whether ground gunners brought him down or a Canadian pilot who had been firing and pursuing him in a Sopwith Camel.)

Recalling his support of Mitchell and the cause of aviation in an autobiography published in 1967, Rickenbacker wrote, "I spoke in defense of

Billy Mitchell whenever and wherever the opportunity presented itself. . . ."
He knew that his remarks "would get back to Washington." He continued:

What were we supposed to do when we went to the front in 1917?
We had to take the planes the French refused to use. Because of the
cowardice and stupidity of our own War Department and
government authorities, when the Wright brothers went to the
government with their new invention, they were refused
encouragement and had to turn to France. France saw the
possibility.

When we entered the war, we had no aircraft industry.
Hundreds of our fliers were sacrificed needlessly by defective
planes and obsolete equipment in training camps thousands of
miles from the front. This nation owes General Mitchell a debt of
gratitude for daring to speak the truth. He has learned his lesson
from the only real teacher—experience. It is pathetic to think that
military leaders, in the declining years of their lives, are in such a
position that they can, through petty selfishness and envy, destroy
a man who has done us the service Mitchell has.

It is a crime against posterity.

Reid's subsequent witness on November 19 could not claim to be one
of the pantheon of Billy Mitchell's daring young men in flying machines,
but he was a colossus among America's seafarers. Commander of the U.S.
Navy's European fleet during the war, William Snowden Sims was so
famous that *Time* magazine had put his picture on its cover with the
adjectives "Scholar, Officer, Gentleman." Among his notable achievements
was the creation of merchant ship convoys escorted by warships between
U.S. East Coast ports and England and France. A former president of the
Naval War College, sixty-four years old, with snow white hair and beard,
and retired since 1922, he had quietly been a Mitchell ally and source of

information on the navy. He also believed that the battleship was passé and strongly favored building aircraft carriers.

Asked by Reid about the navy's aircraft policy, he said, "It is going along from day to day, more or less in a higgledy-piggledy way."

"Tell the court whether or not you have encountered any officials or members of the Navy who have told you they were afraid to testify before Congress."

"If the Navy Department has a certain opinion and an officer testifies before a court in such a manner as to be markedly critical of that opinion, he endangers his promotion the next time the selection board meets."

Declaring that no "properly educated and trained officer" would have "conducted the *Shenandoah* the way it was conducted," he hastened to say that the admirals "are good men and friends of mine and honest men, but they are uneducated men."

Cross-examining Sims, Gullion pointed out that Abraham Lincoln and General Ulysses Grant had been self-taught.

"They are not parallel cases," Sims replied. "A naval officer must be educated to make his decisions immediately."

Court president General Howze inquired, "Do you believe from your experience and study that the air service of the navy should be an independent service?"

"No, sir."

Although Reid and Mitchell were disappointed that Sims was not a stronger defense witness, Rickenbacker, Chambers, Mrs. Lansdowne, and all the other defense and prosecution witnesses had proved by the solemnity and gravity of their testimony that the court-martial was certainly not a vaudeville show. But everyone who had taken the witness chair so far for both defense and prosecution had been a supporting player. Therefore, when Frank Reid let it be known that the person he intended to call on Monday, November 23, would be Mitchell, the court, both sides, spectators, the press, and the entire nation faced a weekend of suspenseful anticipation.

CHAPTER TWENTY

"WHAT'S THE DISGRACE?"

Seven years and twelve days after the end of the war and the beginning of his tireless campaign of press statements, magazines articles, books, speeches, writing official reports and memorandums that were immediately shelved or tossed away, and day upon day of testimony in Capitol Hill hearings on behalf of a credible, independent American air force, Mitchell suddenly had the greatest pulpit ever given to a serving soldier to assail the policies of the United States government. By invoking a court-martial his opponents had unwittingly handed him the golden opportunity to put them and their policies on trial in the ears, eyes, and minds of a nation that had always rooted for the underdog and lately begun to relish a bare-fisted courtroom battle in which the stakes for the accused could not be higher. Americans had intently followed the case of murder against a pair of alleged anarchists, Nicola Sacco and Bartolomeo Vanzetti in 1920, the trial of John Scopes for teaching evolution, and the prosecution of Leopold and Loeb. They listened to and absorbed legal discussions of threats from "Reds" set on overthrowing the government, the veracity of the Holy Bible, and excusing criminality on the basis of insanity.

"The whole country," said one newspaper, "and thoughtful people all over the world are following the trial with a greater interest than any since the Dreyfus Case." The periodical *Aero Digest* observed, "The defendant has become the accuser, [and] the accusers find themselves the defendants before the country whose faithful servants they pretended to be. The verdict already has been rendered, so far as public opinion is concerned, upon a court who, impatient with the weak prosecution, brazenly brushed it aside and constituted themselves a court of inquisition. Rarely in any court, civil or military, have witnesses been subjected to such brutal bulldozing from a plainly prejudiced bench."

Since the last week of October 1925 to three days before Thanksgiving, Americans had followed news accounts of the trial of their wartime hero for insubordination by making rude public remarks about superior officers, while waiting patiently, in the plain-talk of the people, to "hear it straight from the horse's mouth." Those who read the Sunday edition of the *New York Times* on November 15 found a summary of the case in an article headlined, "THE INTENSE DRAMA OF THE MITCHELL TRIAL." A subhead and drawing depicted the cast as "Beribboned Chief Actors Against Strange Setting in an Old Warehouse." Deep in the lengthy story, Mitchell was viewed as looking little older than he did "when he was of that active band who have come to be known as the pioneers of the American Air Service." An inset drawing in the shape of a cameo showed him in profile, looking somberly down at his chest.

When he entered the court on Monday, November 23, an obviously admiring reporter saw him with "head erect, shoulders thrown back, finely chiseled chin aloft, the very embodiment of defiance and the damnation of traitors." The tight quarters of the improvised courtroom, said another journalist, contained so many more very important Washington personages, press, and cameras that those in the front pressed against the backs of chairs at the counsel tables. Even General MacArthur's mother-in-law was there, seated beside Mrs. MacArthur.

When prosecutor Winship advised Mitchell of his right to remain silent and consult his lawyer, Frank Reid stated, "I've already consulted with the accused, and notwithstanding the fact we think we have proved every material fact one hundred percent, we tender the witness . . . and submit him for a full cross-examination by anybody and everyone in the world in this case."

Had Reid had any witness but Mitchell before him, he would have gone immediately to the issues at trial. But having in the chair one of the most famous military figures in the recent history of the United States, and a certified hero of the war, he invited Mitchell to summarize his twenty-seven years in the army from private in the Wisconsin Volunteers and stringing telegraph lines in Cuba, the Philippines, Alaska, and earthquake-flattened San Francisco to the skies of France, zooming above the waters off Virginia to lead intrepid airmen in sinking great airships, and then punishment for criticizing higher-ups by being demoted and exiled to Texas. This recitation and explanations of his theories on manpower and national defense lasted an hour and twenty minutes. The last question from Reid was, "How many hours have you had in the air?"

"I imagine between a thousand two thousand hours."

Turning to the prosecutors, Reid said, "Take the witness."

Rising to the invitation was Allen Gullion. In a prejudiced, but accurate, description of the combative Kentucky attorney brought in to bolster the prosecution, Ruth Mitchell wrote in her biography of her brother, "Lank, cadaverous, with thinning wisps of hair, a cavernous mouth, and given to wetting his lips with a flickering tongue, he was already noted as a master of vituperative invective. He was going to give the general staff what they wanted."

Living up to a reputation for the unexpected, Gullion asked, "Colonel Mitchell, have you any idea of the estimated wealth of the United States?"

As puzzled as everyone in the courtroom, Mitchell replied, "No."

Stating that according to the *World Almanac* the figure was $302,803,862, Gullion said, "Now I would be much obliged if you would keep that figure in solution, and the relevancy of the questions will appear later." Leaving this morsel hanging, he read from Mitchell's statement in September that in a war with the United States a "Pacific power's submarines" would mine the entrances to Pearl Harbor, Hawaii. What Pacific power, Gullion asked, had Mitchell in mind?

"Japan."

Subsequent questions established that in addition to not knowing the wealth of the United States, Mitchell had no knowledge of the number of subs and minelayers the Japanese possessed or the number of planes the U.S. Navy had in its fleet at San Francisco and how many submarines. A barrage of questions about Mitchell's grasp of statistics was met with negative replies. Therefore, Gullion asked, the report that Mitchell had presented on America's Pacific defenses contained "no statement of fact?"

"The paper," Mitchell said, "was an expression of opinion."

Having based Mitchell's defense on the truth of his allegations, rooted in facts, Reid was in the position of a skipper of a battleship hit amidships by a torpedo. But as Gullion's attack on Mitchell's credibility raged throughout the morning session, Reid remained expressionless and made few objections to the questioning. Confidence returned in the afternoon, when the queries turned to Mitchell's assertions that the flight from San Francisco to Hawaii had become a disaster because the navy planes were "good for nothing, big, lumbering" machines unsuited for such a mission. Finding an opening to explain the difference between facts and opinions in his report on Hawaiian defense, Mitchell said, "They were sufficiently worded to allow the organization which we have in the air service to take them up, look into them and solve them."

Coming out of a nosedive like a pilot in Rickenbacker's Hat-in-the-Ring Squadron, he had swung the direction of the cross-examination to his advantage. When Gullion asked if the men who ran the War and Navy Departments were traitors who ought to be locked up, Mitchell replied, "There are two definitions of treason." One was defined in the U.S. Constitution as "levying war against the United States or giving aid or comfort to its enemies." The other was betrayal of public trust by not giving "a proper place to air power" in organizing the defense of the country. "That is what I believe," he said. "It is a question of the system and not the individuals, entirely."

What about Mitchell's charge that the army and navy had been so "disgusting" in their conduct that any "self-respecting" officer was "ashamed of the cloth he wears"? Did Mitchell mean that to be taken literally?

"Yes."

"Do you think that any self-respecting person, any officer of the army, should be ashamed of his uniform?"

"No, not any officer of the army, but I think officers in the air service who are subjected to the command of people who know nothing about aviation, who come and inspect their outfits without knowing anything about them whatever and ask foolish questions . . ."

"Please answer the question."

"I think that is repugnant in every way to a man who gives up his life to his duty and is constantly exposed to danger in the air in that way," said Mitchell, forging ahead. "It is the worst example of that sort of command I have ever known in any nation in aviation."

Gullion switched to the *Shenandoah*, questioning Mitchell's expertise in air ships. Had he ever been a free balloon pilot? "No." A rigid airship pilot? "No." Had he taken much training in rigid airship operation? "No, sir." Flown in a rigid airship? "I do not think so."

It was now after four o'clock. Court president Howze decided that the cross-examination would resumed in the morning. Although the day had not gone well for Mitchell, he came out looking better in press accounts that dwelled on his repetition of criticism of the high command and downplayed Gullion's scores. Hoping to do better on Tuesday, Reid rehearsed his client after dinner by throwing at him every question he expected Gullion to raise when court resumed.

Proceeding largely as he had on Monday, Gullion scoured Mitchell's past and record on the subject of his views on the proper place of aviation in the army. He reminded Mitchell that he said in 1913 that it belonged in the Signal Corps.

"Yes, I was a member of the general staff then," said Mitchell, "and I never made a worse statement, I think, anywhere."

Mitchell and the audience laughed.

When Gullion finished questioning past three o'clock, General Howze had a few queries, beginning with, "Were there any restrictions placed on you as to the number, character, subject or contents of [your] recommendations?"

"No, general, never."

"Will you give the court specific instances of officers in the air service being bulldozed and bluffed in giving their statements before various investigating bodies?"

"You wish me to give their names?"

"You do not have to give the names, but instances."

After citing three, Mitchell concluded, "A great many other instances have occurred that could be specified." Looking toward the judges, he said, "The people have placed their trust in the government, in the War and Navy Departments, to provide proper defense for the safety of the nation. It has not been done. I consider this failure to be—the criminal offense of treason."

As he left the witness stand, the audience rose in silence.

The headline of the *New York Times* the next morning read:

MITCHELL ON STAND DEFENDS CHARGES, REINFORCING THEM

"Not a word did he retract nor did he by word or action indicate that he would, if he could, withdraw a single charge or change a word *in* the long statements which have brought him to the bar of military justice," said the article. "Colonel Mitchell faced the cross-fire of his accusers with set jaws. The flush was missing from his cheeks as he took the oath. It was evident that he realized that the hour of his supreme test at the court-martial was at hand, and every nerve was steeled to meet the onslaught that he knew was coming."

Outside the courtroom following his testimony, Mitchell said to Betty, "Suppose they do find me guilty? Guilty of what? I've committed no crime. Supposed I am dismissed? Well, I've always wanted to hunt big game in Africa. Disgrace? What's the disgrace?"

Feeling relieved that his ordeal with Gullion was over, and confident that he had made his points, he and Betty dined that evening at one of the capital city's fanciest and most prestigious restaurants, the Occidental. In some news accounts of the two-day cross-examination, the star witness was depicted as growing increasingly nervous and strained. Arthur Chamberlain in the *New York World* portrayed Mitchell as having twitching jaw muscles, somewhat sunken eyes, and chin lowered to his chest. Yet "every now and then his old-time defiance would flash forth." Ruth Mitchell said in her book that his heart began giving him trouble and that Reid became anxious when Mitchell refused to ask to be allowed to rest. "If his persecutors had expected Bill to weaken," she wrote, "to hedge on his direct charge of 'almost treasonable' mismanagement, in order to save his career, they were disappointed. On the contrary, he made it even stronger."

Court observers expected, from their experience with civilian criminal courts, that after the defendant testified, the defense would rest. But Frank Reid was not finished. Onto the Emory Building stage on Tuesday afternoon stepped the most entertaining and amusing politician in the nation's capital and the most colorful public figure in a city that had been the target of a Mitchell mock air raid. Called to the stand by Reid at the last minute, Congressman Fiorello H. La Guardia was already on record publicly and officially on Mitchell's side. The short, unruly-haired, pugnacious, squeaky-voiced, and endlessly animated representative from Manhattan Island was called "the Little Flower" because of the translation of his first name and had been the center of his own tempest since exclaiming on Armistice Day that Billy Mitchell was being unfairly tried.

Prosecution lawyer Allen Gullion felt compelled to ask La Guardia if he had really said that the case was being judged "by nine be-ribboned dog robbers of the general staff."

"I did not," La Guardia replied emphatically "say *be-ribboned*."

Amid laughter, court member Hamilton Howze interjected, "The court would like to have you explain what was meant by your characterization of the members of the court."

La Guardia chuckled and replied that if he had known General MacArthur was a juror, he would not have put him on the list. That he claimed ignorance that MacArthur was hearing the evidence was not surprising. The certified hero of the Rainbow Division in the Great War and lately commandant at West Point had asked no questions and said nothing publicly during the court-martial. Choosing to sit and listen with an expression that seemed to reporters to be inscrutable, he appeared to be distracted and even inattentive, possibly because his wife was present each day. Arriving holding a bunch of violets, she sat near the prosecutors but chatted amiably during breaks with Betty Mitchell. Running through the speculation about MacArthur was the entwined history of the MacArthur and Mitchell families, although it was not evidently known outside those circles that MacArthur had once been enamored with Mitchell's sister and had written at least one love-sick poem on the subject.

Having excluded General MacArthur as a dog robber, La Guardia expounded on the topic of lower-ranking officers kowtowing to the top brass by explaining, "From my experience as a member of Congress and from my contact with the general staff, I am convinced the training, the background, the experience and the attitude of officers of high rank of the army are all conducive to carrying out the wishes and desires of the general staff."

General William Graves was neither amused nor mollified. He snapped, "How high a rank does an officer have to get before he comes within your characterization?"

"I had one case," said the member of Congress who preferred to be addressed by his war rank of major, "where a quartermaster officer came up and testified about some patent [for a] self-greasing axle. It was about the most ridiculous thing I ever heard of, and I asked him about it afterwards, and he said, 'We had to testify to this.' I have had hundreds of such instances in my congressional life, which has been very short."

The next day's proceedings proved long and, in the words of a *Washington Post* story, "tiresome in the extreme." The defense's last shot was the reading of every word of the voluminous report of the Lassiter Board, which called for stronger aviation but had been ignored for nearly three years. When it and other documents were entered into the record, Reid rose and wearily announced, "As far as we are concerned, we are absolutely through."

What the prosecution had up its sleeve as rebuttal to the defense case and whether Billy Mitchell would be through as an Army officer were questions to be deferred until after a day off for Thanksgiving. It was a holiday that Mitchell hoped to spend visiting his infant daughter in Detroit, but the War Department had refused to let him travel anywhere outside of Washington, D.C., but his home in Middleburg, Virginia. The headline of the *Washington Post* story on Wednesday's boring session blared with what amounted to an embarrassment for the War Department and yet another Mitchell victory in the fight for the approval of a public that held no American tradition more precious than a family gathered like the Pilgrim Fathers to offer thanks to the Almighty for the year's blessings:

MITCHELL IS DENIED HOLIDAY LEAVE TO SEE HIS BABY
PERMISSION TO VISIT
DETROIT OVER THANKSGIVING REFUSED

As the next phase of the court-martial opened on Monday, the last day of November, it was overshadowed by the long-awaited report of the Morrow Board. Presented to Coolidge, it summarized two months of interviews with ninety-nine witnesses and offered suggestions for improving the air service, including renaming it "Air Corps" and giving it representation on the general staff by an equivalent of the assistant secretaries of the Army, Navy, and Commerce departments for air services. The report would become the basis for the U.S. Army Air Corps Act of 1926, but this eventual victory for Mitchell was minor. The Morrow Board found that the buildup of air power recommended by Mitchell and the Lassiter Committee would be too costly. It proposed a modest five-year program. Mitchell's prediction that the next war would be won by air power was rejected in dismissive language. "The next war may start in the air," it said, "but in all probability it will end up as the last one did, in the mud." President Coolidge pronounced that the Morrow Board's work would be "reassuring to the country, gratifying to the service, and satisfactory to the Congress."

December began with Gullion calling the leader of the ill-fated flight of the navy PN-9s. He hoped that Commander John Rodgers, great-grandson of a sea captain in the War of 1812 and the son of a serving admiral, would captivate the courtroom with the same effect as had Mrs. Lansdowne. Gullion quickly quoted Mitchell's view that the PN-9 was a big, "good for nothing, lumbering flying boat." Asked if the characterization was accurate, Rodgers answered, "Well, it is a big flying boat, but I do not think it is good for nothing."

Did Rodgers have any criticism to make of the preparations for the flight?

"No, I made them all myself."

Rodgers left the court having done damage to Mitchell's case and leaving everyone in the courtroom feeling that he resented being second-guessed by an army colonel. The next witness called by Gullion also came with a heroic background and a grudge against Mitchell. The Arctic explorer Lieutenant Commander Richard E. Byrd had felt the sting of Mitchell's tongue in a description of Byrd's expedition to the North Pole the previous June as a Navy Department publicity joy ride that "got nowhere and did nothing." Although Byrd proved an effective prosecution witness, Frank Reid got even in cross-examination.

He asked Byrd, "Did you find the [North] Pole?"

"We weren't looking for the Pole."

"What were you looking for?"

Byrd said they were "looking over unexplored regions up there."

Reid asked if Byrd had failed in his mission to reach the top of the world.

Byrd replied, "We failed in the main mission."

A trial that had been expected to end fairly quickly was now appearing to be endless. A latter highlight featured General Summerall. An object of criticism by Mitchell in his report on the defenses of Hawaii, and the challenged-for-prejudice initial president of the court-martial, he handed news-hungry reporters a good quote. "Mitchell is one of that damned kind of officer," he said, "who's wonderful in war and terrible in peace."

Friday, December 11, proved memorable, but not for what was happening officially. In an impossible hope that no one would notice, Will Rogers slipped into the courtroom and sat at the back. The resulting stir of recognition by the audience brought the proceedings to a dead stop. As Mitchell turned and gave Rogers a wink, General Howze invited Rogers to come forward. In his famous aw-shucks manner, Rogers said, "Now I know they are going to hang me."

On the morning of December 17, almost seven weeks after the trial commenced, it was time for closing arguments. As spectators waited for Reid to rise and begin talking, it was Billy Mitchell who stood up. This was not to be an impulsive, off-the-top-of-the-head summation of his defense. Copies of what he intended to say had been prepared for distribution to the press. He began the final act in the drama that he had started in Texas.

"My trial before this court-martial," he said, "is the culmination of the efforts of the general staff of the army and the general board of the navy to deprecate the value of air power and to keep it in an auxiliary position, which absolutely compromises our whole system of national defense. These efforts to keep down our air power were begun as soon as the sound of the cannon had ceased on the Western Front in 1919 [actually in 1918]." The sinking of the *Ostfriesland* in 1921, he said, "proved to the world that air power had revolutionized all schemes of national defense."

He continued, "The truth of every statement I have made has been proved by good and sufficient evidence before this court, not by men who gain their knowledge of aviation by staying on the ground and having their statements prepared by numerous staff to bolster their predetermined ideas but by actual fliers who have gained their knowledge first-hand in war and in peace." He claimed that "evidence before this court bears out" that Secretary of War Weeks and indirectly the president "were wrongfully and untruthfully informed as to the condition of our aviation and our national defense." Asserting that the court "has refrained from ruling whether the truth in this case constitutes an absolute defense or not," he said, "To proceed further with the case would serve no useful purpose. I have therefore directed my counsel to entirely close our part of the proceedings without argument."

Major Allen Gullion had no intention of forsaking a closing. Also with copies of his speech ready to give out, he rose and declared, "It is with diffidence that I now address you." Ignoring a surprising suggestion from the chief prosecutor, Colonel Moreland, that because the defense had forgone a closing argument, the prosecution could save the court time by doing the same, he went ahead reviewing evidence and testimony. As to Billy Mitchell and his defense on the basis of truth as justification, Gullion lived up to his reputation for prosecutorial tenacity:

Rarely has a cause so confidently asserted been found in the acid test to be so absolutely groundless . . . Is such a man a safe guide? Is he a constructive person or is he a loose-talking imaginative megalomaniac, cheered by the adulation of his juniors, who see promotion under his banner, and intoxicated by the ephemeral applause of the people whose fancy he has for the moment caught?

Is this man a Moses, fitted to lead the people out of the wilderness which is his own creation, only? Is he the George Washington type, as [defense] counsel would have you believe? Is he not rather of the all too familiar charlatan and demagogue type—like Alcibiades, Catiline and Aaron Burr? He is a good flier, a fair rider, a good shot, flamboyant, self-advertising, wildly imaginative, destructive, never constructive except in wild non-feasible schemes, and never overly careful as to the ethics of his method.

If Mitchell was not dismissed from the army, Gullion warned, "the good trooper will be dismayed and the malcontent and sorehead will be encouraged in his own insubordination."

At half past three, the court-martial of Billy Mitchell was over—except for a verdict.

Will Rogers left his seat in an audience grown accustomed to seeing him and threw an arm around Mitchell's shoulders. "The people are with you, Billy," he said in keeping with the "this is America, we can do it, and to heck with the big shots" personality that had brought him from Oklahoma, with a lariat, battered cowboy hat, lopsided smile, and an endless trove of down-home yarns, to the greatest success as an authentic American humorist since Mark Twain. "Keep punching. You'll rope 'em yet."

CHAPTER TWENTY-ONE

VERDICT

S ince the arrival of the freedom-seeking religious Pilgrims that the court-martial of Billy Mitchell had adjourned to honor on the last Thursday in November 1925, optimism had been a uniquely American national characteristic. It motivated immigrants from Europe to move steadily inland in quest of a better life. They also believed that claiming all the land from sea to shining sea was their manifest destiny, and that the nation they forged had been deeded to them by God to be a beacon of liberty to enlighten the world. No one in the lifetime of Billy Mitchell had stated this more ardently and forcefully than Theodore Roosevelt. In a letter to his friend John Hay, U.S. ambassador to Britain, in the centenary year of the Constitution he wrote, "The young giant of the West stands on a continent and clasps the crest of an ocean in either hand. Our nation, glorious in youth and strength, looks into the future with eager eyes and rejoices as a strong man to run a race." As president of the United States on December 2, 1902, he had declared. "This nation is seated on a continent flanked by two great oceans." It was composed of men who were "the descendants of pioneers, of, in a sense, pioneers themselves; of men winnowed out from among the nations of the Old World by the energy, boldness, and love of adventure found in their own eager hearts. Such a nation, so placed, will surely wrest success from fortune."

To show that America would not "shrink from the work of the great world powers" Roosevelt had championed fashioning a powerful navy with mighty, globe-circling battleships as defenders of the shores of the country's two oceans that since the War of 1812 had been regarded as impregnable—that is, until Billy Mitchell set out to prove that in the postwar world such a belief was a dangerous conceit. When his cries of alarm fell on deaf ears of admirals and generals, he went over their heads to appeal to the American people. Now they and he awaited the verdict of the nine generals who for seven weeks had sat as a court-martial in a dismal former government warehouse. On that December Thursday, a week before Christmas Eve, a *New York Times* reporter peered at Mitchell and later wrote that if he was nervous, he concealed it well and "appeared to be in the best of humor."

Betty was at his side, but Mitchell had persuaded her parents to return to their hotel for dinner. As in all important trials when a jury was locked away to deliberate, there was nothing the defendant, lawyers, spectators, and the press could do but remain in or close to the courtroom and debate among themselves what the verdict ought to be, and what they supposed it would be. The only indication of what as going on among the generals occurred within half an hour of their retirement to deliberate. They emerged to inquire of Colonel Moreland if Mitchell had any previous convictions. Told that he had none, they departed. This interlude was immediately interpreted by prosecutors, most of the press, and Mitchell as indicting that the generals had reached a guilty verdict and were now discussing the severity of Mitchell's punishment. They had a challenging task. If they agreed that Mitchell should be kicked out of the army, he would be able to continue his embarrassing assaults on the integrity of the general staff with all the constitutional guarantees of freedom of speech of ordinary citizens, but he would not be an ordinary citizen. If they allowed him to remain in uniform, he would be under orders to be obedient to superiors in the chain of command, but they had no confidence that he would comply. And there was the matter of public opinion.

To the vast majority, Billy Mitchell was not only a hero of the war, but a peacetime patriot who was so worried about the state of national defense that he stood up to generals and admirals regardless of the possible consequences. Most also believed that it had not been a fair fight. If anything counted as much in the American character as optimism, it was fairness and acting on the up-and-up. Americans old enough to remember Teddy Roosevelt in his heyday saw Mitchell as Roosevelt's man in the arena. In an address at the Sorbonne in Paris on April 23, 1919, the ex-president had said, "It is not the critic who counts, but the man who points out how the strong man stumbled or where the doer of deeds could have done better. The credit belongs to the man who is actually in the arena; whose face is marred by dust and sweat and blood; who errs and comes short again . . . who knows the great enthusiasms, the great devotions, and spends himself in a worthy cause; who at least knows in the end the triumph of high achievement; and who, at worst, if he fails, at least fails while going greatly; so that his place shall never be with those cold and timid souls who know neither victory nor defeat."

At 6:35 p.m., December 17, 1925, the generals were ready to judge. As they filed into the courtroom, lawyers, spectators, and reporters scrambled into chairs. In the center seat of the court-martial president, General Howze began with, "The court wishes to make an announcement that there must be no demonstration of any kind in this room."

Mitchell rose to attention. Of the eight specifications and the general charge, Howze said, the court found the accused guilty. All that remained to be revealed was the sentence.

Reading from a paper in a tense voice, Howze stated, "The court upon a secret written ballot, two-thirds of the members of the court present concurring, sentences the accused to be suspended from rank, command, and duty with the forfeiture of all pay and allowances for five years."

The Emory Building was suddenly as quiet as it had been when it was an abandoned warehouse.

"The court is thus lenient," Howze continued, "because of the military record of the accused during the World War." More loudly and probably relieved that it was all over, he said, "This court will now stand adjourned."

Mitchell patted Betty's hand. To reporters' requests for a statement he said, "Nothing now. No. Nothing to say." But one of them heard him whisper to Betty, "Why, those men are my friends." With eyes toward the general who had been his boyhood pal, he said with a slight smile, "MacArthur looks like he's been drawn through a knothole."

Because MacArthur had been aloof, silent, and enigmatic throughout the trial, and without an official record of how the generals had voted, an answer to how MacArthur decided proved to be as elusive as his demeanor on the court. Because the verdict was reached by secret written ballot, no one but MacArthur knew. None of the generals spoke about the vote, and Howze said only that the court had been split. Seventeen years later, Fiorello La Guardia, by then Mayor of New York, told a story of a crumpled slip of balloting paper being found in a wastebasket. In MacArthur's hand, it had favored Mitchell's dismissal from the service. Writing to U.S. Senator Alexander Wiley of Wisconsin in 1945, MacArthur said he had cast the lone dissenting vote, Mitchell knew this, and that Mitchell "never ceased to express his gratitude." MacArthur stated in his memoirs, "I did what I could in his behalf and I helped saved him from dismissal. That he was wrong in the violence of his language is self-evident; that he was right in his thesis is equally true and incontrovertible." MacArthur biographer William Manchester wrote in *American Caesar*, "How MacArthur voted was and is a mystery."

How Frank Reid felt about the outcome of the trial was not secret. "They may think they have silenced Mitchell, but his ideas will go marching on, and those who crucified him will be the first to put his aviation suggestions into practice. He is the 1925 John Brown."

There followed a flurry of angry denunciations of the verdict and sentence on Capitol Hill and exclamations of both outrage and approval in editorials, but everyone knew that the final official word on the court-martial must come from the commander in chief. It was spoken on January 26, 1926. Coolidge stood by his generals. Mitchell responded with perhaps the shortest letter he ever sent to the War Department. Addressed to the adjutant general, it said, "I hereby tender my resignation as an officer in the United States, to take effect February 1, 1926." The War Department and president lost no time in accepting it. A Mitchell mimeographed press release summarized his twenty-eight years in the army and stated, "I look back upon this record with the greatest pride and with the satisfaction that I have done everything possible for my country."

His words may have read as if they were written into a scene in a movie, but Mitchell was not prepared to ride off into the sunset in a country with its eyes permanently turned to the dawn. He left almost immediately on a national lecture tour, not only on behalf of his cause, but to make up for the loss of salary. His bank account was also bolstered by writing, including a book, *Skyways*, in 1930, with the subtitle *A Book on Modern Aeronautics*. He dedicated it to "my two little children, Lucy Trumbull and William, Junior, who in their lifetime will see aeronautics become the greatest and principal means of national defense and rapid transportation all over the world, and possibly into interstellar space." In remembrance and tribute to his army mentor, he wrote a biography of Adolphus Greely. Both books were favorably reviewed.

Although he believed, as he wrote to newspaperman Arthur Brisbane in 1934, that he was "the only one of prominence in aeronautics who has consistently tried to educate our people about what we should have," Americans had found other heroic figures who had dedicated themselves to the conquest of the skies. Less than two years after the court-martial captured and held public attention, Charles A. Lindbergh became adored as "Lucky Lindy" by flying across the Atlantic solo in his tiny plane, *Spirit of St. Louis*. On June 18, 1928, in an airplane piloted by Wilmer Stultz, Amelia Earhart was the first woman to cross the Atlantic. Four years later, in May 1932, flying a Lockheed Vega from Harbour Grace, Newfoundland, to Londonderry, Northern Ireland, she would make the crossing herself. Aerial achievements, record-setting flights, advances in design, and a rapidly lengthening roster of aviators, men and women, made news almost daily. Among them in 1931 was Major James H. Doolittle, setting a new world speed record for landplanes by averaging 294 miles per hour over a three-mile course at Cleveland, Ohio.

The aviation news was often mixed. On April 4, 1933, a month after Franklin D. Roosevelt took office as president of the United States, an ironic tragedy brought back the grim memories of the loss of the *Shenandoah*. One of Mitchell's enemies, Rear Admiral William A. Moffett, chief of the navy's Bureau of Aeronautics, and seventy-two others died in the crash of the dirigible *Akron* at sea off the coast of New Jersey. There was also a reminder of Commander Rodger's ill-fated San Francisco-to-Hawaii disaster, but with a happier outcome. On January 11, 1934, six navy Consolidated P2T-1's flew the route nonstop, covering 2,399 miles in twenty-four hours and fifty-six minutes. Mitchell's vision of air service to Alaska moved closer to reality on July 20, 1934, when ten Martin B-10s flew 8,290 miles in a flying time of twenty-five hours and thirty minutes from Bolling Field to Fairbanks. The flight commander, Lieutenant Colonel H. H. "Hap" Arnold, was awarded the Distinguished Flying Cross and the Mackay Trophy for aviation.

There was by this time an air racing award in Mitchell's honor. On October 17, 1934, the Mitchell Trophy was won by Captain Fred C. Nelson, of the U.S. Army Air Corps, as the U.S. Army Air Service had been renamed. At Selfridge Field in Michigan he flew an average speed of 216.832 miles per hour. Although no trophy was awarded, Jimmy Doolittle was back in the news in January 1935 for flying with two civilian passengers in an American Airlines plane nonstop from Los Angeles to New York in eleven hours and fifty-nine minutes, setting a transcontinental record for passenger planes and non-stop west-to-east flying.

Following these events from the rural comforts of Boxwood in Middleburg, Mitchell noted on March 5, 1935, that the successor to the Red Baron, Hermann Göring, whom Mitchell had met in Germany after the war, had told a correspondent of the *London Daily Mail* of the existence of a German air force, in violation of the Versailles Treaty. Mr. and Mrs. Mitchell were local celebrities and social pacesetters of a wealthy community that had not suffered effects of the Great Depression as deeply and profoundly as the rest of the country. Assigning Mitchell's removal from the limelight as the leader of aviation to the economic collapse, rather than to the rise of a younger generation of men in flying machines, Ruth Mitchell wrote, "The distracted people no longer listened."

There had been a flurry of excited speculation in the press that Roosevelt was contemplating the unification of virtually all government aviation operations. "Again the papers were full of pictures of Bill," wrote Ruth. "It was confidently expected 'that Mitchell will be put at the head of the organization.' His old, staunch supporters crowed: 'Mitchell Laughs Last.' But his enemies, more powerful than ever, again proved victorious: Roosevelt suddenly changed his mind."

Firmly, grimly, Mitchell "fought on," recalled the faithful sister, but his health began to fail. He aged swiftly. Mitchell's old friend and ally, Alfred Verville, noticed this decline. Invited by Mitchell to meet him at Washington's Metropolitan Club on January 23, 1936, he was shocked to see a pasty face, sagging cheeks, and eyes "glistening and dead-like." Over snifters of brandy, Mitchell said, "The doctors tells me that my valves are all shot. I guess my bearings are worn out, too. But you know, I've led three lives and all I wish is that I could stick around to finish up about three books I have in mind to write—and I want to be around for the next big show."

"What do you mean, general?"

"I mean the real air-power war, the real world war." Verville asked where Mitchell expected that war would start. "In the same place that it started the last time," Mitchell replied, "only this is going to be in everybody's back yard. It's going to be the air-power war, and I'd like to be around to see the color of the faces who opposed our military aircraft program when they see the real role air power plays." A week later, Betty took him to Doctor's Hospital in New York for "a rest." After a while, his sister Harriet thought he seemed more himself. They talked about her daughter, also named Harriet, and the future. On Wednesday morning, February 19, 1936, he walked around his room, then went back to bed with Betty and Harriet seated nearby. He died in his sleep.

AUTHOR'S NOTE

A fter Billy Mitchell left the army and chose to write about the life of a man who had devoted his to the service of his country as a soldier and rose from a private in the volunteers to general, it was not about himself, but his early mentor Adolphus Greely. His only autobiographical legacy is *Memories of World War I*, which began as a series of reminiscences for *Liberty*, and a short volume, *The Opening of Alaska*, in 1928. Although his books *Winged Defense* (1925) and *Skyways* (1930) contain some personal material, they were written to advance the cause of aviation. Scores of articles written between 1904 and 1936 were also devoted primarily to promoting air power and an independent U.S. Air Force. Knowing that he was in failing health and did not have much longer to live, he wrote a final article for *Liberty*. Titled "Last Message," it was published two months after his death. His first venture into print had been in the *Denver Times Friday Magazine* on June 10, 1904, followed in September of that year by "How Uncle Sam Built the Alaska Telegraph System" in the *National Geographic Magazine* and "The Signal Corps with Divisional Cavalry" for *Cavalry Magazine* in April 1906.

Except for "How to Jump a Horse" in *Country Life* in 1916, he did not publish an article until after the world war. He produced three articles in rapid succession on the role of the U.S. Air Service, covering air leadership, the air service at St.-Mihiel and at Argonne-Meuse, and "Aviation's Important Part of the War." Increasingly outspoken and prolific on the subject of the superiority of air power over naval power between 1920 and his court-martial, he broke his pattern of propagandizing on that subject to offer his ruminations on tiger hunting in India for *National Geographic* in November 1924. After his resignation he continued promoting the cause of air power and creation of a powerful air force as a separate arm of the War Department and expressing his views on aviation, from commenting on the Lindbergh flight to publishing the articles "How Europe Travels by Air," "How Russia Seeks to Dominate the Air," "How Britain Is Striding Forward in Air," "Cruising America by Air," "The Sporting Side of Aviation," "Will Japan Try to Conquer the U.S.?" and his persistent theme, "Incompetency Hampers Aeronautical Advance."

A glowing Mitchell biography, by Emile Gauvreau and Lester Cohen, *Billy Mitchell: Founder of Our Air Force and Prophet Without Honor*, was published six years after his death and in the early months of World War II, with Americans savoring the April 1942 attack of Japanese cities by the Doolittle raiders flying B-25 Mitchell bombers. Recalling that Mitchell, "like many another dauntless pioneers of human thought" had been "laughed at, flouted, disgraced and killed," the authors wrote that "his ideas are marching on, his spirit is with us, his crusade is at last coming home to the hearts and minds of his countrymen, and day by day a brighter radiance shines upon his name."

In the aftershock of the Japanese sneak attack on Pearl Harbor on December 7, 1941, newspaper and magazine articles recalled Mitchell and reminded readers that two decades earlier he had forecast that such an event would unfold early on a fine Sunday morning and that the Japanese carried out the mission almost exactly as Mitchell had predicted. Typical of these stories, a long tribute by Wayne Thomas in the *Chicago Sunday Tribune* on March 1, 1942, noted that on January 13 "he became a prophet with honor when the United States Senate, after ignoring him since 1925 when he was court-martialed for the very vision that brings him honor today, passed a bill authorizing a posthumous commission as major general," to be entered as of the date of his death.

Mitchell: Pioneer of Air Power was published in 1943. By Isaac Don Levine, it drew on his interviews with Mitchell's sisters; Betty Mitchell, who was remarried to Thomas Bolling Byrd, brother of a U.S. Senator from

West Virginia; Mitchell's army and air service comrades; allies in the drama of the court-martial; and others. Levine also consulted private files of correspondence, manuscripts, diaries, reports, clippings, and other material. Levine's access to contemporaries and his meticulous research have made the book a vital resource for Mitchell enthusiasts, students of aviation, and subsequent authors, including this one. In 1952 Roger Burlingame provided *General Billy Mitchell: Champion of Air Defense.* For younger readers there were Helen Woodward's *General Billy Mitchell* (1959) and a biography with the same title by Booth Mooney (1968). Alfred Hurley added to the Mitchell literature in 1964 with *Billy Mitchell: Crusader for Air Power.* Three years later, historian Burke Davis published *The Billy Mitchell Affair.* In 2004 Douglas C. Waller authored *A Question of Loyalty: Gen. Billy Mitchell and the Court-Martial that Gripped the Nation.*

Various attempts to exonerate Mitchell that had been made through the years had been met with fierce opposition by the War Department. A proposal to award him a posthumous Medal of Honor was formalized on October 15, 1941, when Congressman John McCormack of Massachusetts introduced a resolution citing Mitchell's World War I record and service to Congress as justification for the House and Senate to authorize it. The resolution read:

> WHEREAS the late William L. Mitchell faithfully and honorably carried out his duties as brigadier general in the Air Service of the United States Army in the World War, having served fearlessly throughout 14 major actions, and
>
> WHEREAS the march of events has proven the wisdom of many recommendations made to Congress by the said late William L. Mitchell during 1924 and 1925; and
>
> WHEREAS it is the desire of Congress to honor the memory of the said late William L. Mitchell,
>
> THEREFORE BE IT RESOLVED by the Senate and House of

Representatives of the United States of America in Congress assembled. That the Secretary of War is authorized and directed to make the records of the War Department indicate that the late William L. Mitchell's rank of brigadier general has been restored as of the effective date of his resignation from the Army; and The President of the United States is hereby authorized to issue the necessary commissions or documents incident to the restoration of such rank.

The War Department rejected the proposal on the basis that America's highest military honor should be reserved for extraordinary acts of heroism, without stating that the act would entitle the Mitchell estate to collect sixteen years of back pay. Secretary of War Henry Stimson answered that Mitchell was "adequately rewarded" for his World War I gallantry with the Distinguished Service Cross.

Congress eventually ordered the striking of a special gold medal on August 8, 1946, by way of Private Law 884. On the front of the medal is a bas-relief of Mitchell with the inscription "Brigadier General Billy Mitchell." The reverse reads, "award of the Congress, August 8, 1946 for outstanding pioneer service in the field of American military aviation."

This left Americans and the U.S. Senate Committee on Veterans' Affairs publication *Medal of Honor Recipients, 1863–1978* with the wrong impression that Mitchell had been given the Medal of Honor, which is not the case. The ultimate recognition of Billy Mitchell's vindication by the government occurred on July 26, 1947, with President Harry S. Truman's signing of the National Security Act of 1947, which brought the War and Navy Departments under a Department of Defense and created the independent and equal United States Air Force that Mitchell had fought so long to see realized.

In 1955 the Air Force Association passed a resolution calling for overturning his conviction. Two years later, Mitchell's youngest son,

William Mitchell, Jr., also petitioned the Air Force to set it aside. In a response that probably would not have surprised Billy Mitchell, Secretary of the Air Force James H. Douglas formally replied:

> It is tragic that an officer who contributed so much to this country's welfare should have terminated his military career under such circumstances. Today, however, that his services to his country and his unique foresight as to the place of air power in the defense of the country are fully recognized by his countrymen.
> The application is denied.

As this latest rebuff was being delivered, Americans who went to the movies were offered a film from director Otto Preminger that informed generations who may never had heard of General Billy Mitchell who he was and why their parents and grandparents had found him a fascinating, important, and controversial figure. Released in 1955, *The Court-Martial of Billy Mitchell*, the feature film's portrayal of Mitchell was provided by an actor who had come to symbolize American heroism in the Hollywood version of the life of World War I infantry hero Sergeant Alvin York. Gary Cooper had also given indelible screen characterizations of the wounded American on the Italian front in World war I in *A Farewell to Arms*, as Wild Bill Hickcok in *The Plainsman*, an extraordinary average man in *Meet John Doe*, Lou Gehrig in *Pride of the Yankees*, the American fighter in the Spanish Civil War in *For Whom the Bell Tolls*, and Sheriff Will Kane going it alone against a gang of revenge-minded gunmen in *High Noon* in 1952.

Believing that Cooper was wrong for the part, the Mitchell family wanted James Cagney. When William Mitchell, Jr., asked Cooper on one of the locations in Washington, D.C., what he knew of the man he was to depict. Cooper replied, "Well, son, I read the script coming in on the plane."

"Well," William asked, "do you think you can play my father?"

Cooper replied, "They pay me to play myself." He did just that in a film that took many liberties with historical fact.

Frank Reid was portrayed by Ralph Bellamy. Mrs. Lansdowne was Elizabeth Montgomery. Her doomed husband, Commander Zacahary Lansdowne, was Jack Lord, years before he became world-famous as a prosecutor on television in *Hawaii Five-0* and Montgomery created a suburban housewife who was also a witch in the TV comedy *Bewitched*. The role of the tenacious Allen Gullion was acted menacingly and sneeringly by Rod Steiger.

Two years before the movie's release, Ruth Mitchell published her biography, *My Brother Bill*. Insights into Billy Mitchell at war with Germans and later with American generals and admirals were found in Eddie Rickenbacker's World War I memoirs, *Fighting the Flying Circus* (1919) and his 1967 autobiography, *Rickenbacker*. General Patrick M. Mason's *The United States in the Air* (1928) was also instructive, as were memoirs of others who served with Billy Mitchell, learned from him, and went on to employ and prove his theories of air combat and bombing in World War II.

What might have been learned about Mitchell's domestic life with Caroline Trumbull Mitchell, alas, was thrown into an incinerator in the spring of 1964, including all their correspondence and his personal papers during their eighteen-year marriage. She kept her diaries from 1906 to 1925. She had remarried and died by her own hand in July of 1964. The second Mrs. Mitchell sold Boxwood. She died in 1963 at the age of seventy-two. Frank Reid died of a heart attack in 1945. His chief adversaries, Allen Gullion and Sherman Moreland, died in 1944 and 1951 respectively at ages sixty-five and eighty-three. Gullion had helped with legal aspects of interning Japanese Americans following Pearl Harbor and died of a heart attack while listening to the Joe Louis–Billy Conn fight on the radio. General Robert Howze died after gall-bladder surgery nine months after the court-martial. General Douglas MacArthur died in 1964.

Billy Mitchell material is dispersed in several archives, including the

Library of Congress, the National Archives, the National Air and Space Museum, and the University of Wisconsin, Madison.

Opinions of Billy Mitchell among airmen who knew and served with him were in accord. He had been a tough cookie, but brilliant and innovative. Hap Arnold remembered, "He was a hard man to make peace with. He was a fighter. The public was on his side, he was righter than hell and he knew it, and whoever wasn't with him a hundred percent was against him." Jimmy Doolittle said that Mitchell was "ahead of his time" and that his methods in fighting for air power were "so stringent that they destroyed him, and probably delayed the development of airpower for a period of time."

Billy Mitchell's name and fame have been memorialized in the ways that Americans always enshrine the heroes of their time and those of times long-since past, by naming schools, streets, a few playgrounds, sports arenas, other public spaces, halls of fame, and even airports after him. Mitchell has his share, but if you wish to find the monument that would honor and please him most, you'll find it in the skies in the planes that carry millions of Americans going about their lives and in those with white stars of the United States Air Force, Navy, Marines, Coast Guard, and National Guard on swept-back wings of jets that would lift Billy Mitchell's heart, but not surprise him.

BIBLIOGRAPHY

Arnold, H. H., and Ira C. Eaker. *Winged Warfare*. New York: Harper & Bros., 1941.

Barrett, William E. *The First War Planes*. Greenwich, Connecticut: Fawcett Publications, 1960.

Bishop, William A. *Winged Warfare*. George H. Doran Co., 1934.

Boyle, Andrew. *Trenchard*. London: Collins, 1962.

Burlingame, Roger. *General Billy Mitchell: Champion of Air Defense*. New York: McGraw-Hill Book Company, Inc., 1952.

Chandler, Charles de Forrest, and Frank P. Lahm. *How Our Army Grew Wings*. New York: Roland Press, 1943.

Davis, Burke. *The Billy Mitchel Affair*. New York: Random House, 1967.

Gauvreau, Emile Henry, and Lester Cohen. *Billy Mitchell: Founder of Our Air Force and Prophet Without Honor*. New York: E. P. Dutton and Co., 1942.

Gilbert, Martin. *The First World War: A Complete History*. New York: Henry Holt and Company, 1994.

Greer, Thomas. *Development of Air Doctrine in the Army Air Arm, 1917–1941*. Montgomery, Alabama: Air University, 1953.

Gurney, Lt. Col. Gene, U.S.A.F. *A Chronology of World Aviation*. New York: Franklin Watts, Inc., 1956.

Hudson, James J. *Hostile Skies: A Combat History of the American Air Service in World War I*. Syracuse: Syracuse University Press, 1968.

Hurley, Alfred P. *Billy Mitchell: Crusader for Air Power*. New York: Franklin Watts, Inc., 1964.

Jeffers, H. Paul. *Ace of Aces: The Life of Capt. Eddie Rickenbacker*. New York: Ballantine Books, 2003.

–––. *The Napoleon of New York: Mayor Fiorello La Guardia*. New York: John Wiley & Sons, 2002.

———. *Theodore Roosevelt, Jr.: The Life of a War Hero.* Novato, California: Presidio Press, Inc., 2002.

Kennett, Lee. *The First Air War: 1914–1918.* New York: The Free Press, 1991.

Levine, Isaac Don. *Mitchell: Pioneer of Air Power.* New York: Duell, Sloane & Pearce, 1943.

Manchester, William. *American Caesar: Douglas MacArthur, 1880–1964.* Boston: Little, Brown and Company, 1978.

Mitchell, William. *Memoirs of World War I: From Start to Finish of Our Greatest War.* New York: Random House, 1960.

———. *Skyways.* Philadelphia: J. B. Lippincott Company, 1930.

———. *Winged Defense.* New York: G. P. Putnam's Sons, 1925.

Mitchell, Ruth. *My Brother Bill: The Life of General "Billy" Mitchell.* New York: Harcourt, Brace, 1953.

Mooney, Booth. *General Billy Mitchell.* Chicago: Follett Publishing Company, 1968.

Nordhoff, Charles B., and James Norman Hall. *Falcons of France.* Boston: Little, Brown & Co., 1919.

Patrick, Mason M. *The United States in the Air.* Garden City, New York: Doubleday, Doran & Co., 1928.

Pershing, John Joseph. *My Experiences in the World War*, 2 vols. New York: Doubleday, Doran, 1928.

Rickenbacker, Edward V. *Fighting the Flying Circus.* Garden City, New York: Doubleday & Company, Inc., 1965.

———. *Rickenbacker.* Englewood Cliffs, New Jersey: Prentice-Hall, Inc., 1967.

Sweetser, Arthur. *The American Air Service.* New York: D. Appleton, 1919.

Venson, Anne Cipriano, editor. *The United States in the First World War: An Encyclopedia.* New York: Garland Publishing, Inc., 1995.

Waller, Douglas C. *A Question of Loyalty: Gen. Billy Mitchell and the Court-Martial That Gripped the Nation.* New York: HarperCollins Publishers, 2004.

Whitehouse, Arch. *Decisive Air Battles of the First World War*, New York: Duell, Sloan & Pearce, 1963.

Woodward, Helen. *General Billy Mitchell: Pioneer of the Air.* New York: Duell, Sloan and Pearce, 1959.

INDEX